CONVERSATIONS WITH COLLEAGUES

On Becoming an American Jewish Historian

NORTH AMERICAN JEWISH STUDIES

Series Editor: IRA ROBINSON (Concordia University)

ACADEMIC
STUDIES
PRESS

CONVERSATIONS WITH COLLEAGUES

ON BECOMING AN AMERICAN JEWISH HISTORIAN

Edited by Jeffrey S. Gurock

BOSTON
2018

Library of Congress Cataloging-in-Publication Data:
A catalog reference for this title is available from the Library
of Congress.

ISBN (hardback) 978-1-61811-856-1
ISBN (electronic) 978-1-61811-857-8

Cover design by Ivan Grave

Published by Academic Studies Press in 2018
28 Montfern Avenue
Brighton, MA 02135, USA
press@academicstudiespress.com
www.academicstudiespress.com

*Grateful acknowledgment and thanks
is extended to Yeshiva University
for its generous support of this book.*

TABLE OF CONTENTS

Contributions to Conversations

Joyce Antler is the Samuel Lane Professor of American Jewish History and Culture and Professor of Women's, Gender, and Sexuality Studies Emerita at Brandeis University.

Dianne Ashton is Professor of Religion Studies at Rowan University.

Mark K. Bauman is the editor of *Southern Jewish History* and Professor of History (retired) at Atlanta Metropolitan College.

Hasia Diner is the Paul and Sylvia Steinberg Professor of American Jewish History at New York University and Director of the Goldstein-Goren Center for American Jewish History also at NYU.

Jeffrey S. Gurock is Libby M. Klaperman Professor of Jewish history at Yeshiva University.

Jenna Weissman Joselit is the Charles E. Smith Professor of Judaic Studies & Professor of History at The George Washington University, where she also directs its graduate program in Jewish cultural arts.

Eli Lederhendler is the Stephen S. Wise Professor of American Jewish History and Institutions at the Hebrew University of Jerusalem.

Deborah Dash Moore is the Frederick G. L. Huetwell Professor of History and Judaic Studies at the University of Michigan.

Pamela Nadell holds the Patrick Clendenen Chair in Women's and Gender History at American University and is a past president of the Association for Jewish Studies.

Riv-Ellen Prell, an anthropologist, is Professor Emerita of American Studies at the University of Minnesota.

Jonathan D. Sarna is University Professor and Joseph H. & Belle R. Braun Professor of American Jewish History at Brandeis University, where he also chairs its Hornstein Jewish Professional Leadership Program. He is, in addition, the Chief Historian of the National Museum of American Jewish History, and Chair of the Academic Advisory and Editorial Board of the Jacob Rader Marcus Center of the American Jewish Archives.

Shuly Rubin Schwartz is the Irving Lehrman Research Associate Professor of American Jewish History and Walter and Sarah Schlesinger Dean of Graduate and Undergraduate Studies at The Jewish Theological Seminary.

Gerald Sorin is Distinguished Professor Emeritus of American and Jewish Studies at SUNY, New Paltz.

Beth S. Wenger is Moritz and Josephine Berg Professor and Chair of the History Department at the University of Pennsylvania.

Stephen J. Whitfield holds the Max Richter Chair in American Civilization at Brandeis University.

Gary Phillip Zola is the Edward M. Ackerman Family Distinguished Professor of the American Jewish Experience & Reform Jewish History at Hebrew Union College-Jewish Institute of Religion in Cincinnati, as well as the Executive Director of The Jacob Rader Marcus Center of the American Jewish Archives.

A COMMUNITY OF SCHOLARS WHO GREW A FIELD

Jeffrey S. Gurock

At the turn of the second decade of the new millennium, the study of American Jewish history is well positioned as a humanities discipline in academic conversation with scholars of American and Jewish studies. Its scholars publish regularly in the field's two foremost journals, *American Jewish History* and the *American Jewish Archives Journal*. Occasionally, a cutting-edge piece find its way in the quarterlies or annuals of the American Historical Association [AHA], the Organization of American Historians or the Association for Jewish Studies; organizations that regularly invite panels on subjects relating to Jewish life in America. Every two years, the Academic Council of the American Jewish Historical Society [AJHS], composed of more than 125 men and women who teach and write in about all aspects of that group's experience—many occupying chairs in that specific area—returns the favor. It invites to a plenary session of its Scholars Conference a senior scholar who does not work in American Jewish studies, and the guest respectfully compares council members' work to important labors in the wider arenas of American and Jewish studies. The American Academy for Jewish Research—an elite, elected association of academics of all areas and periods of Jewish studies—has its Fellows who specialize in the American Jewish experience

Occupying this perch, the field has fulfilled the dream Professor Cyrus Adler had more than a century ago. As a president of the AJHS, this first major Jewish academician to associate himself with serious examinations of American Jewish life, looked forward to the day when courses would be offered at colleges and universities and chairs might be occupied in an expansive field that include not only historians, but sociologists, demographers and other social scientists.

More directly, the discipline's present-day status represents the fulfillment of the work towards professionalization that eminent pioneers like Professors Jacob Rader Marcus, Salo W. Baron, Moshe Davis and Oscar Handlin pioneered close to 70 years ago. It was Marcus who established, in the late 1940s, the American Jewish Archives on the Cincinnati campus of the Hebrew Union College, where he taught the first college-level course in that area, even as he produced, early on, enduring works on the Colonial period of American Jewish history; a subject upon which so many ancestor-worshipping dilettantes had previously dwelled. He would ultimately write substantial books on all periods and aspects of this community's experience.

Baron, for his part, was instrumental in the 1950s, and in his own words, in "turning the AJHS around" from its own sad tradition of amateurish works. This most influential Jewish historian of the twentieth century put his prestige on the line in September 1954 when he convened, under the auspices of the AJHS, a Conference of Historians in Peekskill, New York that attracted scholars of American and Jewish history from around the nation and, indeed, the world. The many who responded favorably to his call determined to put an end to "the parochialism and fragmentation that has long held the field back." Baron also used his sterling reputation to establish an enduring relationship between the AJHS and the AHA. Another sign that the field was beginning to come of age occurred in 1957 when Professor John Higham decided to publish an important article on anti-Semitism in the AJHS's journal the same year that this preeminent scholar of nativism contributed a piece on Gilded Age anti-Semitism to the prestigious *Mississippi Valley Historical Review* (now the *Journal of American History*).

Davis may be credited not only with initiating teaching American Jewish history at his erstwhile home institution, the Jewish Theological Seminary [JTS], but also added an international academic dimension to the field when, in 1959, he convinced the doyens of Jewish history at the Hebrew University to create an institute for the study of contemporary Jewry in Jerusalem which focused extensively on the saga of Jews in the largest Diaspora, the United States. During this same era of incipient professionalization and recognition, back in America, in 1954, Oscar Handlin, the parent of U.S. immigration history, composed the first respectable one-volume study of American Jewry; quite a feat of synthesis considering the dearth of the useful primary materials and reliable secondary accounts then extant to chronicle the entire sweep of the 300-year history of this ethnic group in a land of freedom.

Perhaps as important, in ensuring a brighter future for the field, was the fact that each of these scholars either mentored directly or influenced appreciably the next generation of men and one woman who would write important works in American Jewish history as their theses and other worthy, subsequent oeuvres. The list of these distinguished contributors, who rose in the decade after Peekskill, included Baron's student, Hyman B. Grinstein, Marcus's disciple Bertram W. Korn, Naomi W. Cohen who studied with Baron and Davis, Handlin's advisee, Moses Rischin, not to mention Lloyd P. Gartner, Arthur A. Goren and Leon Jick. All of these individuals—and there were others—evidenced that Baron's lament of earlier years that he "found it difficult to persuade graduate students to choose dissertations in the field because they did not find it 'interesting enough'" no longer applied to American Jewish history.

Still, despite the approbation of leaders in the humanities, like Higham, and, of course, Baron's advocacy, the study of American Jews had a long way to go to gain full acceptance as an academic discipline. For example, as late as 1970—close to twenty years after Baron had started to "turn the society around"—the contrarian and yet respected American historian David Hackett Fischer, in delineating so much of what he saw as wrong with the study of history in America, would still characterize the work of the AJHS as "antiquarian" done by "a gentleman (or lady) of respectable origins who is utterly alienated from the present." Such people, he said, were "collector[s] of dead facts which [they] stuff full of sawdust and separately enclose in glass cases." At "the American

Jewish Historical Society," he suggested factitiously, "there may be an elderly gentleman at work on an article called 'A Jewish Tourist at the Battle of Bladensburg.'"

Indeed, for Fischer, of all "the tunnels in historiography... the narrowest and darkest are the ethnic tunnels. And of all the ethnic tunnels, none is quite as dark as that which is called [American] Jewish history... The present mode of writing is a scandal and an abomination in its profound provincialism." Evidently, Fischer was either unaware or unimpressed that his college, Brandeis University, had established in 1966—four years before Fischer's *Historians' Fallacies* was published—its Lown Graduate Center for Contemporary Jewish Studies and had appointed Jick as its professor of American Jewish history.[1]

Indeed, the paucity of courses proffered at other non-Jewish schools at that time evidences the harsh reality that many other colleagues shared Fischer's views. Into the early 1970s, the three most noteworthy schools where American Jewish history was taught, on an ongoing basis, were the Hebrew Union College in Cincinnati, the Jewish Theological Seminary and Grinstein's Yeshiva College, Jewish schools where the subject was especially relevant to rabbis and educators in training to serve communities. In stark contrast, at secular schools like Hunter College, when Cohen began teaching, she was unable for many years to convince her colleagues of the value of a course in American Jewish history. She contented herself with teaching primarily American foreign policy and U.S. Constitutional history. A portion of the Jewish story probably found its way into her courses on immigration history. Only after she had long been a full professor was she able to push successfully for teaching in the field where she had already won a number of awards for her scholarship. And notwithstanding Baron's approbation of the field's possibilities, he never taught American Jewish history at Columbia nor brought in a specialist as a visiting scholar. As it turned out, during the 1972-73 academic year, Cohen was the first to teach her research specialty on Morningside Heights.[2]

It remained for the next generation of scholars—men and women who presently range in age from their mid 50s to their 70s—to witness and contribute to the full growth potential of their field

13

within the academy. Both skilled and fortunate, these academics rode the crest of the growth of ethnic, racial and gender studies within contemporary scholarship even as they have expanded their own discipline's purview through bringing these sensitivities into American Jewish scholarly work. (One indication that at the present moment, all is well with their work—despite some naysayers who remain dismissive of what has been accomplished—was David Hackett Fischer's service in 2015 as a dissertation committee member in American Jewish history at the Lown Center that Jick's successor now heads.) For themselves, these senior scholars have deposited deep in their memory banks discouraging words about what they chose to study. All to be told, this is the success story that this volume chronicles. Here is presented a representative sample of this cohort who together have made a difference—chosen among those who have served in leadership roles in the field's national and regional academic institutions or publications, and whose works are widely cited in bibliographies, or students course reading lists, both here and abroad—in conversation about their career paths and ultimately about the past, present and future of the writing of American Jewish history.

In recruiting the men and women whose works I have read, admired, and sometimes critically reviewed, to join me in this retrospective, introspective, and, ultimately, prospective intellectual journey, I asked for essays that were more than intellectual auto-biographies or reports on the state of the field. Rather, without abandoning academic rigor, I challenged them to compose—in their own idiomatic voices—personal reflections of how and why these men and women found their ways into the field of American Jewish history, along with some of the struggles they have faced, with all due reference to their teachers and other scholarly influences that molded and directed them.

Readers of these memoirs will immediately note that my fifteen colleagues and I came to our present common labors from different places in the world of ideas and with many different academic aspirations. These peregrinations tell us as much about the evolution of our discipline as it does about how we became scholars. In other words, even if today we now share an abiding

14

interest in growing further a field that but two generations ago had only begun to be cultivated, most of us did not start our careers that way.

While as adolescents we all imbibed young adult histories of American and Jewish heroes—and not enough heroines—and as college students, most of us were intrigued with the ultimate professional goal of a life in the academy—careers as attorneys seems to have been a frequent second choice—only the fewest even conceived of becoming professors of American Jewish history. Perhaps, we might even have had to explain to the general public—much like Jenna Weisman Joselit suggests humorously and insightfully—what a historian actually does! But it is very unlikely that most would have told interlocutors that we aspired to teach American Jewish history on the college level. In due course of our education we would read the works of, and eventually, communicate with our intrepid and often frustrated predecessors, who had struggled to gain a foothold in colleges. But as graduate students, only a few of us either perceived them as role models or were privileged to have them as mentors. In so many other fields, it is a given that those eager to enter the profession would seek out the renowned senior practitioners to advise them, if only they would be admitted to their programs. Such was not the case with our generation of fledgling academics.

In fact, only Gary Phillip Zola explicitly and consistently tied himself to an eminence; in his case none other than Jacob Rader Marcus, with whom he would earn his doctorate after receiving ordination from the Cincinnati school of the Hebrew Union College-Jewish Institute of Religion. As a true disciple of his master, Zola has remained true to the principles of research that Marcus articulated. Zola's career path, of course, had led him to head up the Marcus Center that his mentor conceived and developed.

Shuly Rubin Schwartz benefitted from a close academic relationship with Naomi W. Cohen as a role model and intellectual sounding board from the time Cohen visited at Columbia University. But rather than Schwartz going over to Hunter College for her doctoral training—apart from auditing a course with Cohen at the City University Graduate Center—Schwartz earned her degree at the Jewish Theological Seminary under the mentoring of Ismar Schorsch, the distinguished professor of modern European Jewish history. While he never taught about American Jewry and rarely focused his writings on this specialty, Schorsch, a true Baronian, always saw American Jewish history as an integral part of the sweep of that people's history. While in the program, Schwartz also felt fortunate that her school invited Henry Feingold, another older and worthy historian of American Jews, to teach and advise students. Upon completing her most advanced degree, with a thesis topic that Cohen suggested, Schwartz, long a part of the JTSA family, would teach her specialty there.

For what it is worth—and it surely was meaningful to me— I did not know of Naomi Cohen's importance in the field when I approached graduate work. I became Cohen's student *after* I became somewhat aware of who's who in American Jewish studies. As fate would have it, I would succeed Grinstein at Yeshiva, the third Jewish school, where my area of academic interest was long countenanced. And while I read Grinstein's massive work on Colonial New York Jewry, as a student, I had no contact with him.

Meanwhile, just a few years after I began to find my way, Pamela S. Nadell, who also "did not set off on the road to becoming an American Jewish historian," "unexpectedly stumbled," as it were, into the field, when she came under the tutelage of Professor Marc Lee Raphael. Through his mentorship, however, she implicitly connected to Marcus and Moses Rischin, who were among Raphael's own erstwhile advisors.

While Nadell came to the Ohio State University with the objective of studying and eventually teaching the full scope of Jewish studies and ended up focusing on American Jewish history with a particular interest in women's history—her passion all along— Eli Lederhendler was fully trained as a historian of East European Jewry and was already emerging as a recognized scholar in that field before he turned his talents to the study of Jews in the United States, in particular, the East European and transnational experience of this diaspora community. Arguably, however, there is a spiritual and intellectual linkage between him and Moshe Davis whom he followed as head of the Institute of Contemporary Jewry at the

Hebrew University, even if he never studied with him. Much like his predecessor, as a migrant from the U.S. to Israel, Lederhendler has wanted to "convey to my Israeli students as much as I could" about the largest diaspora community in the Jewish world. For him, it was in his "post-doctoral phase as a young scholar" that in "Israel I really discovered America."

Of all of our colleagues, Jonathan D. Sarna was the most determined from his earliest days to spend his life in the academy and was certain that American Jewish history would be his field. Sarna came to these decisions both honestly and genealogically. Scholarship and university teaching, in his own words, was "in many ways the family business"; his father was a renowned biblical scholar. Sarna alone among contributors to this volume has proudly carried the pedigree of a second-generation scholar of Judaica. Not only that, but as a teenager, he worked in the archive of the AJHS-where his mother was a librarian—and acquainted himself with the wealth of materials in that repository. When he applied to graduate school, Sarna also had an uncommon sense of what he needed to know in order to progress in the field and with whom he wished to study. He turned to Yale University's program, reasoning that there he could integrate modern Jewish history, American history and American religious history with his specific educational pursuit. Still, even though his objectives were clear, Sarna also realized the problems a budding scholar of American Jewish history would face—even with an Ivy League degree in hand. If all failed, Sarna considered the law as an alternate career goal.

Once Deborah Dash Moore determined that American Jewish history would be her academic calling, she openly confronted another daunting reality that those in this Jewish field had to overcome. By the time Dash Moore was a graduate student in the 1970s, social history, African American history, urban and oral history and women's history were, in her own words, "reconfiguring historical studies in the United States." Dash Moore later advocated for the inclusion of the Jewish story in that narrative, but when she came to the field, she recognized the harsh truth that there was a "profound reluctance on the part of Jewish historians even to consider American Jews worthy of historical attention." For naysayers it was

17

"good journalism," nothing more, even if the renowned medieval Jewish historian Gerson D. Cohen—importantly for this account, Naomi W. Cohen's husband—encouraged her to enter this still minimally charted field. Dash Moore persevered in her scholarship and advocacy. Indeed, as late as 1995—even after a generation of forcefully pushing within Vassar College's Religious Studies Department for the integration of American and Jewish history— she still would be fighting the good fight for the "acceptance of American Jewish history—especially from Jewish historians."

Though not as outspoken as Dash Moore, Rubin Schwartz also received more than mixed messages about her academic choice. While Schorsch strongly countenanced her decision to switch, early on, from the ancient period in Jewish history, a different senior professor "good natured[ly]... cajoled" her to rethink her decision. Professor Max Kadushin would say to her: "My father was a peddler, your grandfather was a peddler. That's all there is to American Jewish history. Come study rabbinics," advised this scholar of Ethics and Rabbinic Thought.

For Jenna Weisman Joselit there was absolutely nothing amiable about comments made regarding her area of expertise when she emerged with a newly minted doctorate in American Jewish history from Columbia University. In her view as of the late 1970s, "gatekeepers of Jewish history dismissed Jewish American history out of hand" and "American historians actively doubted that close consideration of the nation's Jews might possibly bring anything to the table" even as "ethnic and immigration history were only just beginning to find their respective fields." To make matters worse for her, she chose as a dissertation topic a study of Jewish criminality in New York, which, to biased eyes, smacked of "journalism." Happily for her, Dash Moore, as an editor of a series on Modern Jewish history at Indiana University, saw the value of her study and published her first book. But Weisman Joselit remained bereft of a substantial academic post. However, as fate would have it, her worthy labors on criminality and her use of visual materials to tell an intriguing story attracted the attention of the museum world and she became a curator of an exhibit on her specialty. From there, having made much that was good out of a bad employment situation, she would rise to become an important interpreter of the history of American material culture. Most significantly, for the expansion of the purview of her initial field of expertise, she would bring her sensitivities to the study of American Jewry and to other Jewish places. Ultimately, with her feet securely planted in both American Jewish studies and the history of material culture, she would direct a "pioneering graduate program in Jewish cultural arts, the only such enterprise in the country" at George Washington University.

By the time Beth S. Wenger decided to become an American Jewish historian, many of the profound professional difficulties that had plagued Weisman Joselit and worried Sarna, Dash Moore, and her other predecessors had declined significantly. Not only that, but this youngest of our contributors—who through her work and academic leadership is a bridge between generations of professionals—could turn to senior scholars for advice and encouragement. Thus, when she matriculated at Yale—Sarna's alma mater of almost 20 years earlier—she could study with a team of a Jewish historians on staff; most importantly, with Professor Paula Hyman; a distinguished European Jewish historian who also wrote and taught American Jewish history even as she pioneered the study of Jewish women. And when Wenger thought about what she would write on as a doctoral dissertation, she could benefit from Dash Moore's advice. Of course, like all budding academicians in so many fields she could worry about the limited stock of humanities positions within the American academy. But this consideration would not stymie her choice of study area. Yet, while she secured—soon after she finished her degree—a position in the history department of the University of Pennsylvania, she still recognized that "it was more difficult for an Americanist to find a position in Jewish history, and that American historians, even those committed to ethnic history, often have little interest in the study of American Jews." However, as an optimist, she allowed that "the tide is turning, albeit slowly. As the literature has expanded and transnational history has increasingly brought American Jewish experience into broader conversation with other fields the state of American Jewish history has expanded."

Scholars like these, who have witnessed the expansion of the study area to which they have been long dedicated, have been uncommonly hospitable to academics that, after training or making marks in other disciplines—or in mid-career—have turned to American Jewish studies. Perhaps, the marginality Americanists may have felt about the status of their professional interests has contributed to the existence of a community of interest and, notably, an absence of academic snobbery. Arguably, too, the presence in our cohort of so many senior women historians—who, undeniably, had to cope with a pernicious tradition of not inviting females into what was once a men's world—also played a role in aiding this sensitivity. As a result of this cordiality, those who started out as "outsiders" have become "insiders," and their purviews have fructified the enterprise of American Jewish history.

American studies specialist Stephen J. Whitfield who "counts [himself] as among the last of the plain Americanists who have ventured into Jewish history as a sideline, and who have turned a sort of hobby into an abiding fascination" can thus, write appreciatively about a "porous" and "inclusive" discipline which "failed to police its borders with any severity and thus welcomed historians who maintained an interest in other topics." A seasoned scholar, honored in other academic realms for his work in European intellectual history, Whitfield is now known in American Jewish scholarly circles for his signal contributions to cultural history and the saga of Southern Jewry.

In a similar spirit, Mark K. Bauman could likewise relate tellingly how, in the late 1970s, he "meandered into the field that has taken primacy in my research for forty years." For him, "serendipity" rather than "design" directed his academic "journey." But once engaged, his readily appreciated contributions to exploring the complexities of Southern Jewish history—a passion that even exceeds Whitfield's devotion—has forced rethinking of not only that region's story but that of communities of varying sizes and environments.

Presently, Hasia Diner can hardly be described as other than a noteworthy interpreter of the American Jewish experience and more recently of a significant aspect of global Jewish life.

However, she too, in her own words, "entered American Jewish history through the side door." From that aperture, she believes "having come to American Jewish history from the path of studying American Jewish history made me open to the reality that Jews hardly constituted a unique element in American life." And she has challenged colleagues—who may have focused more on the idiosyncratic nature of U. S. Jews—to think likewise.

In titling her memoir "Joining Historians as an Anthropologist at the Table of American Jewish Culture," Riv-Ellen Prell underscores more strongly this endemic and characteristic openness to different perspectives. However, for her, it is not only that historians can benefit from the academic perspectives that social scientists can bring to their work, but that people in her discipline, who wish to study contemporary Jews effectively, have to be grounded in important works of historians, especially those who are concerned with the lives of so-called ordinary people. Arguably, in its own way, Prell's sense of the value of the cross-fertilization of fields fulfills a portion of Cyrus Adler's vision of a century ago that social scientists would be included among the variegated contributors to a robust academic area.

Similarly, Joyce Antler, who avers that she "became a Jewish historian by accident," came to focus her research in this area with complementary missions in mind. Here, too, an academic saw the fruitful—if not necessary—value of two fields learning from each other. As a pioneer historian of U. S. women, she embraced the "obligation to bring the Jewish women's experience to the women's table." How, in her view, could a comprehensive narrative of women's lives in this country be told without the inclusion of their Jewish sisters? At the same time, she was pleased to join American Jewish historians of long standing in integrating female accounts into the sweep of that group's saga. Though it took some convincing to have a space provided for a chair at the women's table, Antler was seated immediately at the American Jewish counter.

So much in line with Antler's experience, what is certain is that so many of our memoirists, who eventually embraced American Jewish history, have identified colleagues whose encouragement and advice assisted them along the way. There is no better example of this pervasive collegiality than Gerald Sorin's account of how after "nearly ten years " in the academy, having obtained a doctorate in American and European history, his interest in American Jewish studies changed from "an innocent flirtation" to a "passionate love affair." Early on in his graduate training, Sorin came to appreciate how American and European history were "integral parts of each other," but he "did not yet see that Jewish history would also be connective tissue in that same work, nor that Jewish studies would have such personal appeal." However, as a junior faculty member at SUNY-New Paltz, he found it worthy to introduce "Jewish materials" into a course on Western Ideas and Institutions, much like he was anxious to include African Americans, women and other otherwise overlooked groups in the narrative. Committed to learning more about American Jewish history, he turned to Dash Moore, who was teaching at that time at YIVO [The Yiddish Scientific Institute] in Manhattan. Under her tutelage, Sorin shifted the focus of his future scholarship to her field with a special interest in the exploring the influence of the Jewish left upon this country's politics and culture. Throughout this process of intellectual migration, Sorin would credit not only Dash Moore but also several of the other memoirists in this anthology for their "welcome... genuine encouragement and support."

For her first major work of scholarship, with her initial training in religious studies and other disciplines, Dianne Ashton chose to work on the life of Rebecca Gratz. Through the biography of this mid-nineteenth century Jewish woman, Ashton wanted to address, among other pressing concerns, the state of nineteenth-century American Judaism, the place of woman, organized communal and educational life, Victorian culture and gender, and American Jewish popular culture as it related to her subject, an ambitious enterprise. Her search for sources took her from Philadelphia where Gratz lived and Ashton studied at Temple University to a variety of renowned libraries and archives. But she would recall that it was at the American Jewish Archives in Cincinnati—where Marcus was still the eminence—that she found an uncommonly fruitful community of scholars; the young Sarna was particularly helpful. For her, "the place seemed a Jewish version of *Fahrenheit 451*, where people became living versions of historical figures and questions." Such is yet another example of the power of communality that has fortified the study of America's Jews as it fully matured into the contemporary period.

Notes

1 David Hackett Fischer, *Historians' Fallacies: Toward a Logic of Historical Thought* (New York and Evanston: Harper and Row, 1970), 140-41, 144.

2 For an academic biographical sketch of Cohen, see Robert Seltzer, "Naomi W. Cohen: As Teacher and Scholar," *American Jewish Archives Journal* (2009): 1-5.

Finding My Way:
Uniting American Jewish Women's History and U.S. Women's History

Joyce Antler

I became a Jewish historian by accident. Jewish history was not a part of my graduate training, which was devoted to U.S. women's history, then itself a risky and fairly suspicious undertaking. My graduate adviser reacted with more than a healthy degree of skepticism, when in a graduate course in intellectual history in the early 1970s I announced my intention to focus on a woman (Charlotte Perkins Gilman, a then unknown notable feminist theorist). History demonstrated that women were "second-rate" intellectuals, my mentor declared, implying that I might well redirect my research efforts to a worthier subject. Years later, after I had successfully completed a dissertation in women's history and written regularly on the subject, I was asked to contribute to a *festschrift* for this teacher, an innovative historian with an excellent and well-deserved reputation as an exceptional teacher. My essay for the volume debunked the myth of women's so-called inferiority as thinkers—pay-back, if you will, for my mentor's comments about women's intellectual contributions, which he later regretted, but also a reflection of the shaky status of women's history in the academy in those early days of the field.[1]

My entrance into American Jewish history in the late 1980s, about a decade or so after I completed my doctoral work, came through women's history and was grounded in the intersection between these fields. I began my teaching career at Brandeis in 1979 in the American Studies department, and the following year,

I added chairing the fledgling Women's Studies Program to my duties, a position that I held for over a decade, but without any administrative or financial support. The Women's Studies faculty numbered only a handful, but we began the process of introducing the subject of women and gender into the curriculum through much of the university. For many years, quite a number of departments remained without any faculty who taught even a single course in these subjects; these included the Department of Near Eastern and Judaic Studies and the Department of History. At the end of the 1980s, the Ford Foundation included Brandeis in a grant to formerly all-male institutions to help promote the integration of women and gender into curriculum. Brandeis had been co-educational from the start, but Ford added us to this grant, as it did MIT, because of lack of administrative support for the essential endeavor of integrating or "mainstreaming" women into the curriculum. It was in this climate that I taught a variety of women's history courses and published two books focusing on general U. S. women's history. I began doing some initial research and teaching on the history of American Jewish women.

In the course of a few months in 1988, while I was still directing the Women's Studies Program, I participated in two academic gatherings that gave me a glimpse into the gaps in the field of American Jewish women's history and solidified my research focus. The first event—the First Southern Conference on Women's History—took place in June, 1988, at Converse College, Spartanburg, South Carolina. I still remember the sticky climate and excitement of the conference, though not much about my own paper. The session that remains most embedded in my memory was one about Jewish women in the South, a marquee session at which the eminent women's historian, Ann Firor Scott, gave comments on two papers about Jewish women in the South. Scott had recently completed a term as president of the Organization of American Historians, only the second woman to hold that position, and had tremendous prestige in our profession. In addition, she was a pioneering historian of Southern women and of women's voluntary organizations, the subject of the conference papers. She did not mince words about them. While she appreciated the extensive research of the young scholars—the one I recall best focused on Gertrude Weil and Southern Jewish women's social welfare work—Scott felt that the work had been misguided. In voluntary organizations and philanthropic work, Jewish women basically followed the lead of their Protestant counterparts; studying their contributions apart from the Protestant majority seemed unnecessary.

Scott's comments provoked an immediate outcry from several audience members, who were surprised at the premise that Jews did not have a history of their own. A few speakers argued that anti-Semitism in the South distinguished organizations started and led by Jewish women from those of non-Jewish women. In the midst of this vigorous discussion, I introduced myself as chair of Brandeis's Women's Studies Program and suggested that Brandeis hold a conference on American Jewish women's history to consider Jewish women's work, family, culture, and politics as well as comparative issues like those raised by Scott's remarks. Did Jewish women have a history distinct from that of the Protestant majority? To what extent did it meld with mainstream or minority histories? How was it influenced by diverse aspects of region, education, class, religion, race, sexuality? My statement was followed by one from Clara Schiffer, a former government worker who had funded a number of conferences and archival acquisitions in women's history.[2] Clara volunteered to fund the conference. Because of skeptical comments about Jewish women's history from a leading women's historian, then, Brandeis committed itself to hold a conference and secured funding for what would become the first academic conference on American Jewish women's history.

Four months later, I took part in a gathering of scholars at the Johnson Foundation at the Wingspread Conference Center in Racine, Wisconsin, organized by Gerda Lerner, then at the University of Wisconsin, and Kathryn Kish Sklar of the State University of New York. The purpose of the conference was to examine the new arena of graduate training in U.S. women's history and assess future directions. Amid several days of passionate conversation among 63 scholar-teachers from 57 institutions, the session that generated the most energy was the one on "Questions of Difference Among Women: Specialized and Comparative Approaches." Divided into small groups, we heatedly argued the matter of which dimensions of women's experience signified critical aspects of difference and needed to be included in scholarly work and graduate training going forward. Ellen DuBois highlighted the dividing lines between black and white women. Vicki Ruiz pointed to a variety of multi-cultural differences. Alice Kessler Harris emphasized class. Elisabeth Perry noted the urban/rural divide. Such vigorous debate served as a "click" moment for me.[3] Recognizing the wide varieties of viewpoints reflected even in our small group and how each could be seen a necessary component of multicultural differences, I could not help but note the absence of Jewish women's experience in these discussions. The official conference report confirmed the fact that "Jewishness and anti-Semitism were... largely ignored as topics. Only one participant in one workshop mentioned her work and teaching on Jewish women."[4] As women's studies chair and faculty member at Brandeis, I felt that I had an obligation to bring Jewish women's experiences to the women's history table. I left Wingspread committed to researching Jewish women's historical experience and to broadening the understanding of differences among women to include Jewish lives. Since that time, my work has focused on the dual goal of integrating Jewish women into U.S. women's history and American Jewish history.

Another outcome of Wingspread was that Ellen DuBois and Vicki Ruiz determined to create a volume that would look at difference in U.S. women's history from a full spectrum of multicultural perspectives. The result was their anthology, *Unequal Sisters: A Multicultural Reader in U.S. Women's History*, published in 1990, a popular teaching text that has gone through several editions. My article on the Emma Lazarus Federation of Jewish Women appeared in the third (2000) edition of *Unequal Sisters*; the second edition included an article by Meredith Tax on the garment workers' strike of 1909.[5]

I soon began work on an historical anthology of American Jewish women writers, which was published in 1990. At the time, the notion of an entire volume of American Jewish women's writings seemed a stretch. Even Cynthia Ozick was skeptical, as were some historians of American Jewry with whom I shared my intention.

Suffice it to say that I included 23 authors in my volume and was disappointed that I could not include all those whose work I wanted to make available (including two provocative stories written by a young Gerda Lerner when she had just arrived in the U.S., escaping the Nazi onslaught.)

Gerda Lerner plays an important role in the connections I hoped to make between U.S. women's history and American Jewish women's history. A distinguished historian largely credited with initiating the field of women's history in the late 1960s and 1970s, it was Gerda Lerner who preceded Ann Firor Scott as first female president of the Organization of American Historians. Gerda broke barriers wherever she went. Yet up until this point, she had not publicly connected her social and political activism, of which she was justly proud, or her work as a historian to her experience as a Jew and a refugee.

Gerda was the first person I called as with my Brandeis colleagues Jonathan Sarna, Shulamith Firestone, and Sylvia Barak Fishman I began to plan the conference I had promised at Spartanburg. I explained to Gerda that the intention of the conference was to explore questions concerning the narrative of American Jewish women's history, then asked if she would be interested in giving the keynote, perhaps speaking about the connections between her identity as a Jew and her work as a historian, specifically as a historian of women.[6] Gerda was not happy with the question, and she unceremoniously hung up. But fifteen minutes later, she called back. She said, first, that she had "never given it a moment's thought," and second, that this was one of the most profound questions she ever had been asked. The question prompted her to reflect on a connection she had hidden even from herself; soon she would answer that "I am a historian because of my Jewish experience." This simple response revealed a multitude of deeply felt emotions and a powerful history.

At the Brandeis conference, which took place in 1993, Gerda discussed the influence of her background as Jew and refugee on her career as historian.[7] She would go on to write about these influences in several essays that grew out of the conference, including the important piece, "Why History Matters," in which she compared the experience of women and Jews. In the case of both groups, she wrote, historically based differences led to behaviors which are distinguishable from those of members of the dominant group. They demanded close historical attention. It had become painfully clear to Gerda that her own experiences as Jew, woman, and refugee were formative influences on her intellectual life. Because of the Holocaust, "history for me was no longer something outside myself, which I needed to comprehend and use to illuminate my own life and times. Those of us who survived carried a charge to keep memory alive in order to resist the total destruction of our people. History had become an obligation." Lerner believed that her Jewish background and experience with fascism disposed her toward "thinking historically," while additionally, her experience of being defined as "the Other" predisposed her toward an understanding of "outgroups." She chose race as her subspecialty within women's history, since it was the major issue in U.S. history, and since African Americans, not Jews, were the "targeted out-group"; coming out of a confrontation with Nazism, she had turned to Marxism, fearing that what she considered nationalistic solutions could only lead to war and conflict.[8]

In many conversations with Gerda about American Jewish women's history over several decades, it became clear to me how much the intellectual aspects of the field attracted her attention. She believed that questions about the multidimensional and transnational quality of Jewish women's identities, the ways in which Jewish women exhibited a "dual consciousness" as insiders/ outsiders, and the role of Jews, especially Jewish women, as prime agents of secularization and modernity, added vitality to more traditional narratives of immigration and the political and economic history of white ethnic Americans. How Jewishness overlapped, influenced, or subverted established institutions and hierarchies were emerging as questions which could illuminate the particularities of religion and ethnicity, even when Jews themselves were divided by class, race, gender and sexuality. The dialectical relations between diverse Jewish women and women of other races and ethnicities similarly called for careful probing of the gendered aspects of the American past. Although she never did specific work in the area, Gerda became increasingly involved in supporting the developing field of American Jewish women's history.

Gerda's recognition of the dilemmas of defining and histori- cally researching Jewish women's identities, and her appreciation of the importance of the field, led her to become a vigorous sup- porter of the Jewish Women's Archive, an independent organization created in 1995 to promote the collection and transmission of sources and histories about North American Jewish women. I am pleased to have been a founding board member of the Archive. Enthusiastic about the work of the JWA, directed by Gail Reimer, Gerda became a member of its Academic Advisory Council, which I chaired from its origin in 1995 through the next two decades. As a public historian and activist as well as academic scholar, Gerda loved the fact that JWA existed independently from the academy and that it targeted a popular, general audience as well as an academic one, another of her aspirations for women's history.

Gerda Lerner's stance as a supporter of Jewish women's history was not generally known. At a symposium at the Radcliffe Institute in December 2013 to celebrate the 70th anniversary of the Schlesinger Library and to honor Gerda Lerner after her death earlier that year, a panel of historians spoke of Gerda's broad influence on the field of women's history.[9] My talk highlighted Gerda's Jewish identity and its connection to her work as a historian, especially her documentation of the history of women and African Americans (Lerner compiled the first documentary anthology of African American women's history). These connections surprised the other panelists, of whom five of the six, including myself, were Jewish. Although they were aware of the vigor of Gerda Lerner's anti-religious sentiments, the panelists did not know of her deep interest in Jewish peoplehood, arts, culture, and history. The invisibility of Gerda's beliefs to leading women's historians is also seen in book and film treatments of her. Given Gerda Lerner's place in the historiography of women's history, this is perhaps an ironic emblem of the separation of Jewish history from American women's history. As gender studies have adapted successive, often overlapping frameworks in efforts to understand difference, moving from identity politics to multiculturalism to intersectionality, Jewish women's history frequently remains an outlier to main narratives rather than an essential ingredient in the mix.[10]

My scholarship has endeavored to frame the intersections between women's history, U.S. cultural and political history, and American Jewish history. In *The Journey Home: How Jewish Women Shaped Modern America* (1997) and *You Never Call; You Never Write! A History of the Jewish Mother* (2007), I take a broad chronological focus, spanning close to a century or more, in the effort to fill in the outlines of American Jewish women's roles in relation to the main currents of general U.S. and American Jewish history. Challenges remain, but with the contributions of newer generations of American Jewish historians, considerable gaps in the historical record of Jewish women are rapidly being addressed.

Like the architects of women's history who created an entirely new field of inquiry, my own generation largely had to invent the outlines of the history of American Jewish women as we went along. Of course, just as U. S. women's history did not emerge full-blown in the 1960s and 1970s, but had been shaped by perspectives derived from earlier generations, so American Jewish women's history did not originate in the late twentieth century; important precursors in previous generations showed the way. [11] Yet with some exceptions, my own generation of historians did not have mentors within either in U.S. women's history or American Jewish history. We had the sense of participating in an exciting collective endeavor to frame new currents in the field.

Among the giants of the field who pioneered the new American Jewish women's history was Paula Hyman, whose 1976 book on the Jewish woman, co-authored with Charlotte Baum and Sonya Michel, presented an early, suggestive history of U. S. Jewish women that influenced a cohort who would later work intensely by the subject. Hyman's University of Washington lectures almost two decades later, published under the title *Gender and Assimilation in Modern Jewish History*, provided a comparative framework for understanding the interactive processes of modernization, assimilation, and gender relations in Europe and the U.S, and was widely influential as well.[12] In 1997, she and Deborah Dash Moore produced a two-volume encyclopedia of women in American Jewish history that put the subject of American Jewish women's history on the scholarly map, becoming an essential reference tool and the to new suggesting new paths of inquiry that had developed over a very short period. In the preface to the encyclopedia, Hyman and Moore provided one explanation for the fact that Jewish women's history had lagged behind general histories of women and gender. "Jewish women are not constructed as a category of knowledge," they wrote. They were "invisible as Jews," because their Jewishness is not considered relevant to their achievements. "To make Jewish women visible would require exhuming their roles in culture and politics and interrogating the very nature of Jewish identity in an increasingly post-ethnic, culturally porous, society."[13] For a growing body of historians of American Jewish women, these tasks are now ongoing. In addition to Hyman and Moore, I found inspiration and guidance from the work of many scholars, including my colleagues on the early Jewish Women's Archive Academic Council, among them Dianne Ashton, Hasia Diner, Karla Goldman, Barbara Kirschenblatt-Gimblett, Pamela Nadell, Riv-Ellen Prell, Jonathan Sarna, Shuly Rubin Schwartz, Ellen Umansky, and Beth Wenger. Numerous others contributed innovative work in American Jewish women's history in these years.

My current work continues the effort to join American Jewish women's history and U.S. women's history. *Jewish Radical Feminism: Voices from the Women's Liberation Generation* (New York University Press, 2018) focuses on two distinct components of Jewish women's liberation: general feminists who were Jewish but not identified as such, who played a large role in sparking the radical wing of second-wave feminism, and more self-consciously Jewish-identified women's liberationists, who attempted to address gender inequities in Jewish religious and secular life. Both groups participated in the movement that fostered gender equality in the 1960s through 1980s, the time frame of my study.

The place of Jewish women in women's liberation is highly significant, but despite historians' acknowledgment of the salience of Jewish women in earlier social movements, their prominence within radical feminism failed to attract much attention. By making the Jewish component of the radical feminist movement visible,

I hope to offer a deeper understanding of the complexities of feminist activism and the multiple political issues in which feminists inevitably became involved as the movement developed and feminist consciousness expanded. To recover this history, my book documents and assesses the depth and diversity of Jewish women's participation in a wide range of feminist activities and actions within the second wave of the women's liberation movement broadly defined.[14]

The tendency to separate histories of these two groups, women's liberation feminists who are Jewish and Jewish-identified feminists, parallels the divisions between U. S. women's history and American Jewish women's history, which I find unhelpful. In an attempt to unify and integrate these perspectives, I invited 20 women from each group to a conference I held at New York University in 2011 that explored Jewish women's participation in second-wave feminism. By and large, women from the two groups had not met each other or directly interacted before. Most of the women's liberationists had not been involved in activities within the Jewish community, nor had most of the Jewish feminists participated in broader movement activities. Even though, at first glance, the objectives, politics, and profiles of these two groups may seem divergent, their stories are interrelated. Each group is closely related to the other in terms of background, influences, values, and associations. Each forms part of an essential whole.

I believe that integration of the stories of these two groups of Jewish feminists can provide a fuller picture of second-wave feminism and an enhanced understanding of the relationship of Jewish women's liberationists and Jewish feminists to their non-Jewish counterparts. Interrogating the connections between these branches of feminist endeavor will help to revise what Sara Evans has criticized as the "homogenized" narrative of the second wave and create what Stephanie Gilmore describes as a "more capacious definition of feminism."[15]

Connecting American Jewish women's lives to the complex dimensions of U.S. social and political change has been the continuing goal of my research. In this effort and the work of my many colleagues in American Jewish women's history, I believe that we have made great strides in realizing the ambitious visions of women's history articulated by Gerda Lerner, Paula Hyman, and other pioneers. There is much more work to be done.

Notes

1 Joyce Antler, "'The Making of a New Mind': American Women and Intellectual Life in the 1920s," in *The Mythmaking Frame of Mind: Social Imagination & American Culture*, ed. James Gilbert, Amy Gilman, Donald M. Scott and Joan W. Scott (Belmont, Ca.: Wadsworth Publishing Co., 1993), 239-269.

2 See Lois Schiffer, "Clara Schiffer, Federal Worker and Activist, 1909-2011," https://jwa.org/weremember/schiffer-clara.

3 Ellen Carol DuBois and Vicki L. Ruiz, *Unequal Sisters: A Multicultural Reader in U .S. Women's History* (New York: Routledge, 1990).

4 Gerda Lerner and Kathryn Kish Sklar, "Graduate Training in U.S. Women's History: A Conference Report," sponsored by the National Endowment for the Humanities and the Johnson Foundation (Johnson Foundation Wingspread Conference Center, Racine, Wisconsin, 1989), 18.

5 Joyce Antler, "Between Culture and Politics: The Emma Lazarus Federation of Jewish Women's Clubs and the Promulgation of Women's History," in Vicki L. Ruiz and Ellen Carol DuBois, *Unequal Sisters: A Multicultural Reader in U. S. Women's History*, third edition (New York: Routledge, 2000), 519-541, originally published in Linda K. Kerber, Alice Kessler-Harris, and Kathryn Kish Sklar, ed., *U. S. History as Women's History: New Feminist Essays* (Chapel Hill: University of North Carolina Press, 1995), 267-295. Also see Meredith Tax, "The Uprising of the Thirty Thousand," in Ruiz and Dubois, *Unequal Sisters* (1994), 203-227.

6 This account and the quotes that follow are adapted from Joyce Antler, "'History and Gender'" *Frontiers: A Journal of Women's Studies* 36:1 (2015): 16-21.

7 For essays based on conference presentations, see Joyce Antler, ed., *Talking Back: Images of Jewish Women in American Popular Culture* (Hanover, N.H.: University of New England Press, 1998).

8 See Gerda Lerner, "A Weave of Connections," in Lerner, *Why History Matters: Life and Thought* (New York: Oxford University Press, 1997), 12-16.

9 "Why History Matters: A symposium to celebrate the 70th anniversary of the library and to honor Gerda Lerner," Radcliffe Institute of Advanced Study, Harvard University, Cambridge, Ma., Dec. 5, 2013. The panel consisted of Thavolia Glymph, Linda Gordon, Linda K. Kerber, Alice Kessler Harris, and Joyce Antler, and was moderated by Nancy F. Cott. See the historians' discussion of Lerner in *Frontiers: A Journal of Women Studies* 36:1 (2015): 1-32.

10 See, for example, Eric L. Goldstein, *The Price of Whiteness: Jews, Race, and American Identity* (Princeton, N.J.: Princeton University Press, 2006), 212-239; Cheryl Greenberg, "'I'm Not White—I'm Jewish': The Racial Politics of American Jews," in *Race, Color, Identity: Rethinking Discourses about "Jews" in the Twenty-First Century*, ed. Efraim Sicher (New York: Berghahn Books, 2013), 5–55; and Marla Brettschneider, "Critical Attention to Race: Race Segregation and Jewish Feminism," *Bridges* 15:2 (Autumn 2010): 20–33; Brettschneider, ed., *The Narrow Bridge: Jewish Views on Multiculturalism* (New Brunswick: Rutgers University Press, 1996); and Brettschneider, *Jewish Feminism and Intersectionality* (Albany: State University of New York, 2016), 8.

11 See, for example, Kathy Peiss, "Women's Past and the Currents of U. S. History," in *Making Women's Histories: Beyond National Perspectives*, ed. Pamela S. Nadell and Kate Haulman (New York: New York University Press, 2013), 17-37.

12 Charlotte Baum, Paula Hyman, and Sonya Michel, *The Jewish Woman in America* (New York: Dial Press, 1976); Paula E. Hyman, *Gender and Assimilation in Modern Jewish History: The Roles and Representation of Women* (Seattle: University of Washington Press, 1995).

13 Paula E. Hyman and Deborah Dash Moore, "Editors' Preface," in *Jewish Women in America: An Historical Encyclopedia* (New York: Routledge, 1997), vol. 1, xxi.

14 See Joyce Antler, *Jewish Radical Feminism: Voices from the Women's Liberation Movement* (New York: New York University Press, 2018).

15 Sara M. Evans, "Foreword," in *Feminist Coalitions: Historical Perspectives on Second-Wave Feminism in the United States*, ed. Stephanie Gilmore (Urbana: University of Illinois Press, 2008), viii, and Gilmore, 5.

RECONSTRUCTING
AMERICAN JEWISH HISTORICAL STUDIES

Dianne Ashton

My decision to shape a career from the study of American Jews began in the verdant countryside of western Massachusetts in the mid-1970s. There I lived among other former hippies who had escaped various urban locales for the area's rural small towns. Called the Pioneer Valley, the place was dominated by five institutions of higher learning: Smith, Mt. Holyoke, Amherst, Hampshire, and the University of Massachusetts in Amherst. Although they were very different kinds of schools, they populated the area with students, faculty, and other university types. Bookstores thrived and a restaurant that served breakfast all night hummed. My home was in Wendell, a town with six hundred people and a state forest about midway between Amherst and Athol.

Athol, famed for once being an answer in the New York Sunday Times Crossword puzzle, was a very different sort of place from Amherst. Dominated by the Starretts Tool and Dye factory, it boasted several liquor stores but no entertainment venue – not even a movie theater. In Athol, I ran a women's center and obtained its funding from the Massachusetts Department of Mental Health. My BA degree in Sociology and enthusiasm for the job were enough for me to get and keep the position. One other woman, a VISTA (Volunteers In Service To America) worker who provided health education and offered free pregnancy testing, joined me in running the Center. It was a great opportunity for me to test myself and see what I could do. Looking back on that formative experience for me, I realize that those two worlds made it obvious that academia could be a good life.

Most of my friends were, like me, figuring out the next steps our lives would take. As I reflected upon my own interests, my love for reading and writing were uppermost. Second, unlike nearly all of my childhood peers, I had enjoyed religious school. I developed no firm conclusions about the nature of the divine, but I loved imagining what life might have been like for Jews in the past. My synagogue in Buffalo, New York was one of the earliest Reconstructionist congregations and Mordecai M. Kaplan himself had chosen our rabbi, so I was told. That may have contributed to the school's conceptual fuzziness about holiness, but there was an intellectual excitement to the place that I could sense, even as a child. I had no idea that Judaism treated males and females differently because my synagogue trained all its thirteen-year-olds in exactly the same way, and our bar/bat mitzvah ceremonies were identical. I thought it strange that my grandmother never thought it important to attend synagogue—but I figured that was just her own idiosyncrasy. I would not fully grasp Judaism's gender distinctions until I was much older and out of Buffalo.

I continued on through confirmation. In those classes, Rabbi Nathan Gaynor led a group of teens to question everything we had just learned in previous years of religious education, while teaching us to consider a much broader view of Judaism as it had been experienced by Jews in its long history. We did not read Kaplan's *Judaism as a Civilization*—I would do that much later—though we heard about it and its key points. As I thought about those early simple forays into the study of the Jewish past, I considered the possibility that I might find other intellectually exciting adventures if I traveled further down that road.

Clearly, religion was powerful. That Jews continued to exist seemed to me remarkable. In 1970, I had spent six months living on a kibbutz, mostly folding laundry and studying Hebrew, but also being impressed with the sense of renewal of Jewish life that I saw in Israel. Seeing Jews from many parts of the world building their lives in that little, arid country also impressed me. Modernity did not appear to be dampening religion's force despite so many theories asserting that it did. On the contrary. The Civil Rights movement made plain the power of religion to instill courage and determination among the country's African Americans, while providing a system of symbols able to convince the country's whites (especially its Christians) of its high moral purpose. Moreover, although different generations of my family practiced Judaism in different ways, our common identities as Jews were unquestioned and a handful of beliefs and practices was always shared. While some theorists argued that secularism was inevitable, I saw little evidence that religion would disappear. And, if it was disappearing, wouldn't that also be fascinating to study?

I was unsure about which route toward my goal would yield the best result. I had majored in sociology in college (Adelphi University) because in those years (1967-1970) sociology departments were exciting places to be. Although I had initially declared psychology as my major, Adelphi's undergraduate program was entirely devoted to what was then called behavioral psychology. Despite the chairman's best effort to convince me to stay in psychology by promising me that I would have my own rat, I moved on. Sociology departments saw their enrollments grow in those turbulent years because they provided tools for analyzing society. The capacious analyses of George Herbert Mead, the probing theories of the field called sociology of knowledge (then largely studied by reading *The Social Construction of Reality* by Peter L. Berger and Thomas Luckmann), and the provocative challenges to standard psychological analyses offered by R.D. Lang and Gregory Bateson dominated my undergraduate work. Sociology's more recent fascination with statistics, charts, and graphs was entirely absent from my undergraduate years, and I am sure that if they had been required of me I would not have enjoyed college so much. Cheap calculators had not yet been invented.

I knew, as I pondered my best route forward, that sociologists studied religion. And with all the confidence of a young person holding a BA degree, I felt sure that a PhD in sociology would be an easy way to academic success because I already understood what sociology could do. So I didn't do that. I feared boredom much more than I did hard work, and I was hoping for intellectual training that would provide a lifetime of interesting things to think about. I ultimately decided that instead of focusing my graduate work solely on the Jewish experience through a single discipline, I would take a route that would allow me more flexibility. By obtaining graduate training in Religion Studies, I believed, I would be trained in more than one methodology. I could study literary, historical, sociological, and anthropological analyses of religion. Studying the Jewish past through those approaches could provide a lifetime of interesting work. I entered Temple University's graduate program in Religion, the largest such in the country.

TU's Religion program was like a United Nations of religions and their associated methodologies. The diversity in scholarly approaches to religion had emerged through studies of diverse religions, and all methods were not equally useful for my purpose. My first published article developed in a small seminar that read Martin Heidegger's *Being and Time*, which aimed to do for ontology what $E=mc^2$ did for physics. Heidegger's famed antisemitism was mentioned in that seminar, but then put aside. My article suggested that anthropologists approach their subjects with a Heideggerian view of knowledge rather than one drawn from Decartes. In other words, subjects under study—whether interviewees or documents—are probably far more complex than they might claim or appear, especially when dealing with religion.

Despite that publication, it quickly became clear that philosophy was not for me. First, I was not interested in spending my life arguing. But there were also academic reasons for me to avoid philosophy. Philosophy of religion had developed largely through the rigors of Christian theology, and my philosophy of religion classes convinced me that philosophy could be used most successfully when assessing Christian and other such systems of thought. Although philosophy of religion could help me to understand medieval Jewish philosophers like Maimonides and Gersonides, I found it little use in analyzing the experience of being Jewish. I moved on to other methods.

Literary studies of religion could bring new insights to analyzing Judaism's literature, and I seriously considered focusing my career upon that but I found myself always asking more questions about the historical context of the literary piece I was studying. Temple professor, Franklin Littell, taught about the distinct way religion worked in America—which gave me a broad background for understanding the religious energy of the nineteenth century—before he specialized in Holocaust Studies with his book *The Crucifixion of the Jews*. I was fortunate to study both of his specialties with him. Zalman Schachter (before he added Shalomi to his name) demonstrated how a vibrant Jewish religious commitment could thrive in the U.S. I studied the work of Paul Ricoeur on understanding mythology and Thomas Kuhn on intellectual revolutions. Books by Sir Edward Evan Evans-Pritchard and Franz Boaz on religion in village life (whose work is most like what we would today call "lived religion") provided fascinating ways of considering how religion worked. Clifford Geertz excited everyone with his challenge to anthropologists to study their human subjects so well that they could tell "real winks from pretend ones." If I had been in an anthropology department, I would have undoubtedly studied the critiques of Claude Levi-Strauss's structuralist analyses of societies, but, as I was in a religion department, his exploration of cultural codes and symbols in *The Savage Mind* garnered more attention. Max Weber's ideas about the close relationship between religion, culture, politics, and reason stimulated many discussions. I was equally interested in Emile Durkheim's thoughts on religion's dependence upon the experience of community—described in another way by Victor Turner's idea of *communitas*. I learned a great deal about the development of modern scholarship, its links to different religions, and the variations in religious practices around the globe.

That work provided me with a way to understand how Judaism and Jewish life compared to many other ways humans live their religions. Although TU did not provide a path to studying the Jewish past, it shaped my approach to studying religious lives. I look for the ways people construct them out of ideas, objects, and relationships that are "ready-to-hand" (Heidegger), much like *bricoleurs* (Levi-Strauss). The quest to understand that fascinating process led me to history. My graduate school friend Colleen McDannell (now publishing her tenth book on Christianity) and I grew close discussing the strengths and shortcomings of those grad school ideas and the questions they raised. Our conversations and the friendship that they forged continues to enrich our lives.

Fortunately, Temple University is in Philadelphia. While I was a graduate student I met several people who had come there to do graduate work in any number of fields, but switched to either history or architecture under the city's spell. Philadelphia was not a wealthy city, but the historic old section of the town was kept in good shape because it attracted so many tourists each summer. The duty of one man on the city's payroll was to dress as Ben Franklin and walk around the old section, talk to tourists, pose for pictures, walk in the Independence Day parade, and appear at nearly every city-sponsored festival. One woman dressed as Betsy Ross. Several others, likely paid by the National Park Service, similarly wore period costumes and spoke at Independence Hall and other sites, to delight tourists. In Philadelphia, history pays. The city's oldest synagogue, Kahal Kadosh Mickve Israel, is the second oldest continuously functioning US Jewish congregation—but it's not large. For the bicentennial of the Declaration of Independence in 1976, from which Philly hoped to gain a boon in tourist dollars, Mickve Israel obtained a grant and organized what it called the National Museum of American Jewish History in a wing of its building. One summer after earning my MA in Religion Studies, I secured an internship there. I loved it.

Rebecca Gratz

I don't recall when I first heard the name, Rebecca Gratz (1781-1869), but surely it was while I was a graduate student living in Philadelphia. As I learned more about her, I realized five important things. First, that her life provided a key to understanding much more about nineteenth-century American Judaism and the ways it shaped the American Jewish future than was then understood. It got us beyond the then standard focus upon the formation of synagogues, the economics of migration, and rabbis and their debates over Reform. Second, her life showed us exactly how women entered and influenced both organized Jewish life and Jewish education in America while shining a bright light upon women's spirituality. Third, it offered a lens through which to understand the implications of Victorian culture's gender constructions that linked women with religion and gave rise to a common domestic religious culture. Fourth, her life and the legends that were later told about her could reveal the changes in American Jewish popular culture and its gender ideals. Finally, I realized that this topic was perfect for me. Moreover, research into Gratz's life would give me the opportunity to read the women's studies works then rocking the academic world, many of which assessed Victorian life in America. Caroll Smith-Rosenberg on the *Female World of Love and Ritual*, Barbara Welter on the hugely influential concepts of True Womanhood and the feminization of American religion (the ways women influenced Christian pulpits by dominating church pews), Ann Douglas on the impact of women writers on American culture, and more. My work on Rebecca Gratz became my doctoral dissertation.

Although Gratz was a Philadelphia figure, to study her I needed to work at the American Jewish Archives in Cincinnati, Ohio. I contacted Jonathan D. Sarna, then professor at HUC in Cincinnati and told him of my interest, and I was extremely fortunate to obtain a fellowship to fund my time there. Arriving at AJA I felt as if I had found the center of the American Jewish history universe. In those days (the early 1980s) the Cincinnati campus of Hebrew Union College buzzed with activity—its dorm filled with rabbinic students, graduate students, and visiting scholars. Lunchtime brought the entire campus to the cafeteria and conversations about various aspects of the Jewish experience bubbled. I recall talking with Jonathan over lunch about what evidence I might have stumbled upon that could shed light on a romance that might have existed between Isaac Leeser and Simha Peixotto, and with Lance Sussman about what book I had purchased in the campus bookstore (*The Memoirs of Gluckl of Hameln*). Abe Peck, then second in command at the Archives, had introduced me to Lance by saying, "Rebecca Gratz, meet Isaac Leeser." The place seemed a Jewish history version of *Farenheit 451*, where people became living versions of historical figures and questions. Jonathan's enthusiasm and concern for my research, and his genuine friendliness, convinced me that I had found a worthwhile topic and a doable one. His encyclopedic knowledge of the field was so impressive, my goal was to try to find something new to say to him that he did not already know.

The fellowship required me to give a talk to the campus, and I chose the topic of the lessons of the Hebrew Sunday School—the school founded and run by Gratz. I based it upon research I had conducted at the then miniscule Philadelphia Jewish Archives Center in hopes of having something new to say to the collected masters of the academic field I was just entering. Dr. Jacob Rader Marcus, who had founded the AJA & was the undisputed dean of the field, sat immediately to my right as I spoke. The fellowship gave me six weeks living on campus and immersing myself in archival work, the cache of relevant books in the HUC library, and the richly rewarding conversations with Sarna and Marcus. I was enthralled.

I became devoted to the field of American Jewish history during that fellowship. I knew I had to make good use of every minute of my time there, and often, while I waited for archivists to bring me materials I had ordered, I read the card catalog. Nothing could tell me more about the range of items that seemed valuable to the field to than did the AJA catalog. I did the same at the HUC library. No on line web inventory existed—on line meant clothes lines—and I hungrily read every card I could in those few minutes before my particular documents arrived. The Archive closed for business by 5 p.m. and I would be forced to leave. Perhaps, that contributed to my feeling that American Jewish history was tantalizing.

My time in Cincinnati helped me to understand how to use the resources in Philly when I returned home. AJA housed documents deemed valuable in understanding American Jewry, but Philly housed documents and objects—entire buildings and neighborhoods—that explained its citizens' experience. I used the Library Company (founded by Ben Franklin), whose enormous collection held documents created by the city's organizations along with newspapers, books, manuals, advertising, city directories, statuary and public art. Its archivists and librarians kindly kept a jar of candy on their desk that made conversations (quiet ones) with visitors congenial.

I began to understand how the city grew during Gratz's lifetime, its profusion of voluntary associations (an idea promoted by Ben Franklin), and its physical experience. In warm weather, the clack of horses' hooves on cobblestones as carts carried tourists around the historic area (and the aroma of horse manure!) helped me to imagine her world.

In Cincinnati I had discovered that I found archives exciting. Stumbling upon a significant old document took my breath away. I obtained funding from the Hadassah-Brandeis Institute for more research. Back in Philly, I sought every archive I could find. In addition to the Library Company I used the Historical Society of Pennsylvania for its trove of letters. While the AJA held thousands of letters written by Gratz family members, at the HSP I found letters written TO Gratz and her siblings from her Philly friends (the city supported two mail deliveries six days / week during her life) by their many non-Jewish friends and family. These sources clarified the close and significant relationships that Gratz enjoyed with the Christian women who were her co-workers in organizations, along with her dear friends and relations by marriage. I contacted Mickve Israel for permission to use its archive, but met with a suspicious refusal—I had no credential and the congregation had seen items stolen from its cabinets (yes, documents were kept in metal filing cabinets!) sold by Sotheby's. This circumstance considerably enhanced the importance of the AJA.

While I was at the Library Company, I encountered a fellow researcher who spent all his time reading old newspapers. He seemed happy in his work, but cautioned me against using newspapers too much. They were so rich in historical detail that a person could get lost in them and never complete the project that originally led him / her to open its pages. I used Philly newspapers sparingly. I would recall his warning many years later on a very different project when I tried to understand the many permutations of Hanukkah in America.

I explained my planned project at every archive, and each time I was asked when I expected to complete it. I recalled the admonition that the most important thing about a doctoral dissertation was that it be finished. I finally stayed home and wrote, my cat often purring on my lap as I sat typing at the computer—whose black screen and green glowing letters surely injured my eyesight. But I earned my doctorate with distinction.

A decade later, when I prepared the dissertation for publication as a full biography, I used the American Philosophical Society (founded by Ben Franklin). An article in a Philly newspaper explained that a local historian had arranged for Gratz family letters still owned by their descendants living in Montreal to be given to the APS. My dissertation had been a cultural analysis of Gratz and her work, but publishers wanted a biography. The Montreal letters included items written while Rebecca was still a young teen, and I quickly contacted the APS. To my great astonishment and everlasting gratitude, they handed me bundles of letters right out of the suitcases in which they had been shipped. I sat untying their ribbons and wondering who had tied them up. By then, Mickve Israel's archives were under new leadership and I was granted access to them. They were enormously helpful, of course. But it was primarily because of the APS's great generosity and trust that I was able to publish *Rebecca Gratz: Women and Judaism in Antebellum America* (1997).

Four Centuries of Jewish Women's Spirituality

Because no one in Temple's Religion department specialized in Jewish women or gender issues, Ellen Umansky very kindly agreed to serve as an outside reader on my dissertation. We had fabulous conversations along the way, and as soon as I had the PhD in hand Ellen proposed that we do a book together—a source book of four centuries of Jewish women's spiritual writings. Once again, I was able to obtain a fellowship to the AJA and happily returned to Cincinnati for a month of digging for items written by Jewish women that expressed their religious voices. This time I used both the archives and the HUC Klau library extensively. My conversations with HUC faculty proved particularly helpful. From the time that Ellen and I began this project, we heard the same response from the scholars and rabbis with whom we spoke—it can't be done. Women did not document their religious perspectives, they said. Yet nearly every man we spoke with (the vast majority of rabbis, even liberal ones, were men) knew of one woman whose writings he had encountered. Ultimately, our greatest challenge was culling the enormous collection of writings we found to a size suitable for one volume! Perhaps because the idea of Jewish women documenting their spiritual lives was so unexpected, the book was a success. It appeared in 1992 and spurred women's study classes in synagogues across the country. By 1998, when I met the rabbi of my brother's synagogue during a visit to Buffalo, he said, "Oh, you're THAT Dianne Ashton!"

Ten years after it appeared, however, Amazon's marketplace made used copies of *Four Centuries* available for $1.25 and our publisher, Beacon Press, quit printing it. Ellen and I knew that we had a good deal more data to bring out and we also had a decade of feedback on how people had used the book. Our revised edition included much new material. University Press of New England published it for Brandeis University Press in 2005. We made sure to use a new image on the cover so that people buying it on line would immediately see that it was a different volume from the first one.

Hanukkah In America

I had embarked upon the study of Jewish life seeking a lifetime of interesting things to think about. When I began my career as a college professor, I learned that undergraduate religion studies was a different world—textbooks rarely gave my young students any sense of what it was like to live Judaism. My gentile colleagues, who had been teaching from these books for years, were plainly perplexed. They could not understand how Talmud worked, why it worked, or how it offered anything like what they understood to be spiritual experience. They could not see that the structure of textbook presentations began with the elements that were important in Christianity, and then bent other religions to that mold by presenting parallel elements. The books looked coherent (and I'm sure the publishers were pleased) but they misled students about Judaism. None gave a historical explanation for why the rabbinic movement emerged and took the shape that it did. None explained the boundaries set upon Jews by the Christian or Muslim societies in which they lived. Very little was presented about holidays or food. Textbooks heavy with illustrations were particularly troublesome because they featured images that were most distinctive—Jews kissing the Western Wall in Jerusalem, ultraorthodox men dressed in black with sidecurls and beards, the ornate interior of a centuries-old synagogue in Eastern Europe or Italy—and which made Judaism seem even more foreign and mysterious than the students already thought it was. I found myself translating textbooks that were written in English as if they had been written in a foreign language. After years of reading student exams and answering student questions, I was pretty thoroughly frustrated.

But I was also frustrated by my fellow Jews. No matter how religiously observant or secular they were, the Jews I encountered would, at some point, explain in all seriousness that they were sure that some practice which their grandparents did was the way Judaism was *supposed* to be done. Grandmothers seemed to be the ultimate authorities. That attitude led them to be particularly offended by the efforts of synagogues, Jewish clubs, shops, marketers, and advertisers to enhance Hanukkah. Hanukkah is *supposed* to be unimportant, they told me. Children are the only people who are supposed to receive a gift on Hanukkah and that gift is supposed to be *gelt*—a few coins or gold-foil-wrapped chocolate coins. Nothing more. Radio and TV shows about Hanukkah should not exist—even though my friends often liked them. The huge Hanukkah menorahs erected by the Lubavitcher Hasidim, and the community menorah lightings to which they invited local dignitaries and the general public, were especially offensive to these people. Over and over I was told that Hanukkah is unimportant. But each year, without any coercion, Jews in the US created Hanukkah celebrations in homes, synagogues, and classrooms. They watched those Hanukkah shows on TV, listened to Hanukkah music, played *dreidle* games, held parties in their homes, brought menorahs to schools to tell their children's gentile classmates about the holiday, attended Hanukkah

47

events at synagogues and social clubs, ate *latkes* and *sufganiot*, talked about the Maccabees, lighted candles, joked about the Jews' miraculous rescues, bought gifts and cards for their children and for each other, and even attended the public menorah lightings. I found this fascinating.

I had encountered a small handful of scholarly books examining American celebrations, so I designed a research seminar on holidays. I wanted to think about this phenomenon and I wanted to hear from students about what went on in their own celebrations. I assigned two histories–Elizabeth Pleck's *Celebrating the Family* and Matthew Dennis' *Red, White, and Blue Letter Days*—along with Catherine Bell's brilliant anthropological text, *Ritual: Perspectives and Dimensions*. It became clear to me that a holiday is a cultural nexus point, and that perspective gave me a way to begin my research into the ways American Jews created Hanukkah each year.

I began collecting data. Lots of it. I returned to the AJA for a third fellowship and also obtained a stipend from the National Endowment for the Humanities. I read Yiddish newspapers, went to the American Jewish Historical Society for Hadassah and other organizational records, and I scoured Gratz College's impressive music department. The research became part of my life. I used synagogue archives in San Diego and Buffalo when I visited family there. I read Jewish newspapers in Chicago, New Jersey, Philadelphia and New York City along with holiday manuals and every relevant secondary source I could find. I was sure that only by showing the many permutations of Hanukkah over the broad sweep of Jewish life in the U. S. could I show its value to Jews beyond being a way to give gifts to Jewish kids in December.

I began pulling my thoughts together and delivering lectures on Hanukkah in America. I remembered the wise caution against the pitfalls of newspapers and discovered for myself the truth of it. How was I to shape a book out of the mass of data I had collected? What audience did I really want to reach? I could have a lot of fun bringing highly theoretical ideas to Hanukkah, but that would not allow me to present the many historical permutations the holiday took over the history of the Jews' lives in the U. S. I realized I wanted a book my students and non-scholarly friends could read and understand, yet one which rested upon firm scholarship. It finally appeared in 2013.

Serendipity

Just as I delivered my completed manuscript to its publisher (New York University Press), I received a phone call asking me if I would become the next editor of the premier journal in my field, *American Jewish History*. I agreed. I contacted my Dean to arrange sufficient time off from teaching (Rowan University has a 4-4 teaching load base line) to do the job, and the complex contract we agreed to required me to also claim an ongoing research project. I quickly remembered a diary I had stumbled upon many years ago on a visit to Cincinnati and I knew that it had not been published or examined. I had used a bit of it in an article I had written a few years previously. It seemed perfect for this situation and the deal was made. I edited the journal for the next five years (the first woman to do so in its 120-year history) and continued to claim that I was working on bringing out this obscure diary.

I handed the reins of the journal to its new editorial team in January 2017, and am now hard at work on the very project I described to my Dean a few years ago. It's a perfect antidote to the broad sweep of American Jewish history that consumed me during my work on Hanukkah. This, in contrast, is a very close analysis of the diary kept by Emma Mordecai during the final year of the American Civil War, a time that she spent living with her sister-in-law on a small farm outside Richmond. I'm happily reading works as disparate as theories about rhetorical analysis and histories of the American Civil War. As I look back on the many years since I lived in Wendell, I am very glad that I decided to obtain my PhD in religion studies as a way to explore American Jewish history—it has given me a lifetime of interesting things to think about.

A Meandering and Surprising Career

Mark K. Bauman

When I was about ten, I received an illustrated book on archeology. Although I did not pursue that first desired career path, this marks my first memory of devotion to studying history. My family belonged to Conservative synagogues in Elmont, then North Bellmore, Long Island, where I grew up. I received the typical for the era (1950s-1960s) instruction in Sunday and Hebrew school through bar mitzvah and confirmation which left me with the rudiments of holiday-oriented Jewish history but totally unaware of American Jewish history.

I graduated from reading Classics Illustrated comic books (that I still have) to contemporary fiction. Thus, when I met Professor William Bliss, my history advisory at Wilkes College (now University), he counseled that I could read and pursue history as a college history professor. My career path was thus set, although numerous obstacles lay along the way.

Wilkes provided an outstanding liberal arts background. Courses in sociology, cultural anthropology, psychology, American and world literature, and even art history captivated me and offered tools for my future study of history. Professor Harold Cox exerted the greatest influence. A specialist on Philadelphia transportation, he taught English history and American social and intellectual history. At Lehigh University I followed Cox's interests toward a masters degree with classes in American urban, immigration, and social and intellectual history with a minor in English history.

At the University of Chicago, John Hope Franklin, then chair of the history department, offered me and one other doctoral student a directed reading course on black history using several of his books. Richard C. Wade gave classes on urban history based on his research. Courses by Arthur Mann on social and intellectual history and Martin Marty on comparative religion turned into major books. Daniel Boorstin and William McNeill debated historical writing as accessible literature versus academic scholarship based on primary sources. Obviously, the two positions were far from a dichotomy; fine scholarship can and should also be well written and accessible. Nonetheless, I came away convinced of the importance of mining and analyzing the primary sources and placing them within the historical literature—and writing and organizing the information under logical themes. Through my career, many people have noted a second dichotomy between teaching and research institutions. My experiences at Lehigh, Chicago, and Emory and then teaching at two-year institutions belied this assertion. My best teachers immersed themselves in research and writing and brought their insights and enthusiasm into the classroom.

When my wife Sandy and I first moved to Chicago in summer 1968, Mayor Richard Daley's police busied themselves arresting demonstrators at the Democratic National Convention. During the year, student protestors occupied the university's administration building as the civil rights and anti-war movements intertwined. Students who had not completed the second year of grad school became eligible for the draft. When I received my notice, I considered moving to Canada or joining the National Guard (the local unit was filled). I enlisted for three years as a clerk hoping that would preclude a visit to Southeast Asia. Uncle Sam prescribed a different agenda. After basic training and a year as a clerk at Fort Dix, New Jersey, the dreaded list came down specifically designating me for assignment to Long Binh, Vietnam.

The Army actually used me well. For the first six month I served as the head clerk for the education headquarter of the country. I visited many of the 28 education centers throughout South Vietnam, taught GI's to read, evaluated applications to attend college under military auspices, and taught my first college classes for the University of Maryland extension program. My second six months I spent as a military historian at the headquarters in Long Binh making sure records were maintained and forwarded to the

Office of Military History in Washington, D.C. and conducting interviews. I visited fire support bases where the soldiers slept underground and the last two commanding officers failed to make it out alive. Long Binh had been partially overrun during the Tet offensive, but President Richard Nixon had ordered the bombing of the Ho Chi Minh trail through Cambodia. His decision exasperated anti-war protest, and the National Guard shooting of Kent State student demonstrators occurred within the month I flew to Cam Rahn Bay. However, the destruction of the supply line contributed to a relatively peaceful year for me. Happily, students do not have to contend with the fear of the draft and military service in harm's way hovering over their heads, but the all-volunteer army has also stifled campus anti-war sentiments against military incursions ever since.

Vietnam and three years in the army exerted a dramatic impact. When I began work toward a doctorate in 1967, the history profession remained wide open for faculty positions. By the time the military discharged me early as the Vietnam War worn down, the job market had evaporated, and, unlike today when people can denounce America's incursions overseas while still honoring soldiers, Vietnam veterans—to put it mildly—did not receive warm welcomes home. The history department at Chicago made it clear that they were obligated to allow me to return, but preferred that I go elsewhere.

My meandering continued at Emory University where I took a third year of graduate coursework. The GI Bill served as our major source of income, so I needed a dissertation topic that would not require substantial travel. In his social and intellectual history class, Charles Strickland mentioned Methodist Episcopal Church, South Bishop Warren A. Candler. Candler, brother of the developer of Coca-Cola as a major business, had been president of Emory College when it was located in Oxford, Georgia, and then first chancellor of Emory University when it moved to Atlanta. I had written essays at Lehigh and Chicago on the First and Second Great Awakenings. When I found 84 boxes of Candler papers at the Woodruff Library's Special Collection, I also found my topic. I geared papers undertaken for my remaining coursework—including auditing a course under

Brooks Holifield, a noted Methodist historian—to the topic and finished my dissertation three years after entering Emory.

I also served as Bell Wiley's last teaching assistant. Students loved Wiley, an expert on the common soldier during the Civil War, but I came away questioning his popular story telling and preferential grading. As with my first stint as a TA at Lehigh, I learned how not to teach. Following my part time worked in the special collections department where I helped catalog the papers of Ralph McGill, renowned editor of the *Atlanta Constitution*, I later undertook research on the first of two books that never reached fruition. "Pappy" McGill served as the spirited leader of white editors in the South who supported the civil rights movement. Like Hodding Carter, Harry Ashmore, and others, Jewish friends had exerted substantial cosmopolitan influence on his development.

My dissertation advisor James Harvey Young, an expert on patent medicines, later became the first president of the Southern Historical Association who did not specialize in southern history, but he never used his network to help me obtain an academic position. After receiving my doctorate in 1975, the only position I found was as a temporary instructor at Clayton Junior College (now State College and University). I received praise from my students and began publishing articles and giving presentations on Candler.

Candler outspokenly opposed women's rights and inter-collegiate athletics (he instituted the "athletic-for-all" program at Emory). A conservative/paternalist, he consistently believed in separate but equal. Thus, he opposed lynching and fostered Paine College with an integrated board of trustees and faculty in Augusta, Georgia, to train African Americans as teachers, ministers, doctors, and lawyers for their own people during the 1880s. He advocated the use of black ministers and bishops over black churches but his opposition to integration helped halt the unification of the southern and northern Methodist churches until his death in 1941. How did a Bobby Kennedy-liberal Democrat Jew from New York ever pick such a subject?! Peer reviewers from several academic presses complained that my portrait was too sympathetic or not sufficiently sympathetic. I had to win the Jesse Lee Book Prize from the Methodist Commission on Archives and History to achieve publication. The positive reviews and a talk with Oklahoma University Professor Theodore Agnew who asked me to served on the Methodist Commission (the discussion ended when I asked if he knew I was Jewish) informed my later attempts as peer reviewer for journals, university presses, and as an editor to be as fair as possible to authors even when disagreeing with their interpretations.

When I became assistant professor at Atlanta Junior College (now Atlanta Metropolitan College), I felt extremely grateful to remain in academia but never expected to remain at a two-year school for the remainder of my teaching career. I went from a white suburban student body to a year-old institution with an integrated faculty and administration and predominantly first generation, working class, African American students with large groups first of Vietnam veterans, then Iranians after the fall of the Shah, and finally students from Africa and the Caribbean. I taught American and world history, American and Georgia government, minorities in American history, and a social science field experience where I placed students as interns with state legislators including Julian Bond. Adjunct work at DeKalb College (later Georgia Perimeter College) during my first years and two classes during summers supplemented my meager salary for teaching three classes per quarter. Two decades later, after the University System of Georgia switched to the semester system and a five class per semester teaching load, I finally burnt out—still giving essay exams and term papers to 150-175 students—and retired at 56.

And I followed the model of my graduate professors. By teaching night and odd-hour classes, I maintained blocks of time two or three days a week and used weekends to research and publish on a regular basis. My articles appeared on Candler's take on race relations, academic freedom, and education, the modern Ku Klux Klan's crusade against Catholics, and evangelist Billy Sunday's Atlanta campaign of 1917, among other issues. As I informed my students, I was really a psychologist and sociologist; history served as my tool to understand people's behavior and the interaction between and within groups. The president of my college informed me that he was happy that I published but hoped that other faculty would not do so. I swam like a fish in a scholarly desert, yet was not accepted professionally. "Independent scholars" experienced far more success appearing on the programs of the Southern Historical Association or Organization of American Historians than me, as a professor at a two-year school. Marginality expanded further when students led by the student body president demonstrated outside one graduation ceremony against the "Zionist professors." They assumed that the two known Jews on the faculty—I and one other historian—were Zionists and thus, in line with the U. N. resolution, racists. I found a home in the Georgia Association of Historians, chairing numerous committees, serving as president, and gaining my first experience as an editor.

Almost half way through this essay, readers are likely pondering my association (or lack thereof) with American Jewish history. I never took a class in it and only taught it once after retirement when Marc Lee Raphael offered me a Bangel Fellowship for one semester at the College of William and Mary. The quality of those students and the scholarly camaraderie in the department of religion demonstrated what I had missed.

Nonetheless, I meandered into the field that has taken primacy in my research for forty years. In 1978 Ann Woodall, editor of the *Atlanta History Bulletin*, gathered a special issue on Jews in Georgia. Ann, aware of my interest in the history of religion and that I was Jewish, assumed my knowledge of southern Jewish history and asked me to participate. Intrigued, I began reading everything available on Atlanta Jewish history. This included Steven Hertzberg's dissertation on Atlanta Jewry, Janice Rothschild's article in the *American Jewish Historical Quarterly* (1973) and her history of the Hebrew Benevolent Congregation ("The Temple;" 1967), and Ronald Bayor's article in the *Georgia Historical Quarterly* (1979) on patterns of ethnic residential clustering among blacks and Jews in the city. Hertzberg had ended in 1915 with the lynching of Leo Frank, so my time frame would be from 1915 to the eve of the Great Depression. Delving into the primary sources, I found a complex community immersed in "centripetal and centrifugal forces." Reform Jews originating in central Europe, East European Orthodox, and Sephardic traditionalists from the crumbling Ottoman Empire worked together and apart. Although the patterns and forces were replicated throughout the country in similar communities, I, lacking a background in American Jewish history, assumed the uniqueness of the Atlanta experience. The works by Harry Golden, Eli Evans, Leonard Dinnerstein, Carolyn Lipson-Walker, Stephen Whitfield, two anthologies published by the Southern Jewish Historical Society (SJHS), and an anthology edited by Abraham Lavender reinforced this distinctiveness theme for southern Jewry.

Two editors forced me to question these assumptions. I investigated the early development and nature of Jewish social service agencies in Atlanta and, collaborating with Arnold Shankman,[1] researched and wrote about Rabbi Dr. David Marx who served Atlanta's Temple for half a century. The articles complemented each other since Marx led in the creation of the Federation of Jewish Charities and constituent agencies. The first article went to Aubry Land, editor of the *Georgia Historical Quarterly*, and the second to Ronald Bayor, editor of the fledgling *Journal of American Ethnic History.* Both editors questioned the uniqueness of my findings and urged me to read about other American Jewish communities. Thus, three editors dramatically impacted my research and career and, consequently, the study of southern Jewish history.

My reading of urban Jewish histories opened my eyes to American Jewish history and the place of Southern Jewish history within it. The comparative approach disclosed the broad themes that Boorstin had advocated, while my primary research challenged prevailing paradigms and opened new avenues for research demonstrating the correctness of McNeill's position.

Jewish social service agencies in Atlanta followed and led national patterns, and interface with national organizations negated regional isolation. Marx served as an ethnic broker between diverse Jewish sub-communities and between Jews and secular society. Marx's behavior exemplified that of numerous classical Reform rabbis of his generation in similar communities. Jewish lay leaders illustrated many of the same characteristics. To understand the reasons behind such national behavioral patterns, I read sociological and psychological studies concerning role theory. The social science background provided by Wilkes served me well.

Several historians agreed to submit articles using role theory to understand American Jewish history for an anthology I would edit. During the mid-1960s I could not locate a university press willing to publish such a work. Jonathan Sarna, then at Hebrew Union College-Jewish Institute of Religion, and I had correspondence irregularly. He had included the Marx article on his reading list. When I informed him about my predicament, Jonathan suggested that the anthology could be turned into a special issue of *American Jewish History,* and he graciously provided entrée with then editor Marc Raphael about the possibility. Marc readily agreed, and most of the articles appeared as a special issue in 1989. A few historians of American Jewry have utilized the concept of ethnic broker since then, but I regret that the broader concepts of role theory have not been more widely explored.

My second observation emanating from this early comparative reading was that beyond several obvious (the Civil War, slavery, and Lost Cause mythology among others) and some not so obvious differences, the history of Jews and Judaism in the South looked very much like that history elsewhere in the country with several significant provisos. New York Jewry—especially the experiences of East European Orthodox, socialist, and union immigrants—appeared as the template for American Jewry. Nonetheless, in its very size and nature, Gotham Jewry was almost *sui generis.* Juxtaposing the story of nineteenth-century small-town Reform Jews of central European origin with this simplistic picture was nonsensical. The more apt comparison was between Jewish communities of similar sizes and in similar environments—colonial port cities, small towns, and commercial *versus* industrial cities. From this and other vantage points, there was not one, but many Jewish Souths: the small town experiences differed from those in the cities; Charleston and Savannah, New Orleans, Memphis, Knoxville, and Atlanta also illustrated diversity; the identities and behaviors of scions of long time southern families diverged from relative newcomers to the region. Jewish history in virtually every location could be viewed as distinctive. Yet tracing economic, social, cultural, civic and political, social service and religious history, and urban identity, numerous common threads surfaced. The historian should be cognizant of the similarities and differences without exaggerating the latter, as had been and too often continues to be the case.

After the American Jewish Archives published my *The Southern as American/Jewish Style* (1996), I realized that Lee Shai Weissbach had drawn similar conclusions from the vantage point of small-town ("triple-digit") Jewish community history. Nonetheless, to my regret, my reputation has been largely defined and challenged as the arbiter of this interpretation. Why regret? First, I sense that my articles on role theory and American Jewish history, southern Jewish women, the evolution of Jewish social service agencies, southern Jews and politics, and other publications are overshadowed. Second, acting as the target for those who continue to support the distinctiveness school and dealing with the issue *ad nauseum* just does not sit well.

I must dial backward. With Arnold Shankman's encouragement, in 1979 I began attending and giving presentations irregularly at Southern Jewish Historical Society conferences. At least since the inception of the American Jewish Historical Society in the early 1890s, laypeople had explored the history of Jews in the South. Jacob Rader Marcus and his early students, Stanley Chyet, Bertram W. Korn, and Malcolm Stern, at Hebrew Union College-Jewish Institute of Religion substantially advanced the work in the field. A short-lived Southern Jewish Historical Society begun in the 1950s ended in the early 1960s. An upsurge of scholarly production during the 1970s contributed to the reestablishment of the society in 1976 with support from the American Jewish Historical Society. Early society leaders included Eli Evans, Saul Rubin, Louis Schmier, Malcolm Stern, Saul Veiner, Bernie Wax, Stephen Whitfield, and Melvin Urofsky. Nonetheless, with the exception of Schmier who specialized in small town and peddler life in south Georgia, the leadership and presenters at the society conferences tended to view southern Jewish history as a sideline to their major research interests.[2] The society published two anthologies derived from the first and early conferences but lacked a core of committed scholars. Arguably, although dating back over eight decades, southern Jewish history was not widely viewed as a viable, academic subfield of American Jewish history. It did not attract many graduate students, and few presses sought manuscripts in the area. Steven Hertzberg, whose outstanding University of Chicago dissertation appeared as *Strangers Within the Gate City: The Jews of Atlanta, 1845-1915* (1978), failed to obtain an academic position. The situation shifted dramatically over the next fifteen years, so much so since then that a person has to be a senior citizen—as I am—today to recognize the stark contrast.

My early allegiance remained with the Georgia Association of Historians, as I published more on Protestant than on Jewish history. Yet, by the mid-1980s, my commitment to southern Jewish history prevailed. I regularly participated in SJHS conferences and published one or two articles per year in scholarly journals and anthologies. The Atlanta Jewish Federation sponsored special exhibits commemorating 250 years of Georgia Jewish History (1983) and 150 years of Atlanta Jewish History (1996), both of which I served as an historian. In conjunction with the latter, I reviewed the papers of Rabbi Harry H. Epstein and extensively interviewed Epstein. Born in Europe into an important Orthodox rabbinic family, Epstein had moved with his family to Chicago as a child but attended his uncle's seminary first in Slobodka, Lithuania, then in Hebron, Palestine. After a short stint in Tulsa, Oklahoma, Epstein filled the pulpit of Atlanta's Congregation Ahavath Achim from 1928 until his retirement. Epstein saw his mission as satisfying the older East European Orthodox generation with the study of Talmud while keeping their children within Judaism through the practice of modern Orthodoxy and the fostering of activities with the shul as social center. He provided leadership locally, state-wide, and regionally in behalf of Zionism and moved his congregation into Conservative ranks in 1952 when he became convinced that Orthodoxy lacked a future in the United States. In my biography of Epstein, I depicted him as a "conduit for change" and partially used my biography of Bishop Candler as a model emphasizing their changing worldviews as major themes. Once again, indentifying a university press willing to publish proved difficult.

My coming of age as an historian coincided with the growth of southern Jewish history as a more widely accepted field. At an SJHS conference, the number of presentations on southern rabbis and civil rights startled me. The literature harked back to P. Allen Krause's rabbinic thesis at HUC-JIR for which he had interviewed several Reform rabbis on the subject in 1966. In an article he had published from his findings and in the work of others, a picture had been drawn of very few—perhaps a dozen—rabbis in the South who had spoken out. The literature stressed that southern Jews remained silent out of fear of violent attack, economic boycott, and/or the loss of place in a region that demanded conformity concerning racist mores. Yet the presentations at the conference suggested more widespread advocacy of civil rights. Consequently, I collaborated with Berkley Kalin in editing a revisionist anthology, *The Quiet Voices: Southern Rabbis and Civil Rights* (1997). A SJHS conference in Memphis launched the volume.

The same year that *The Quiet Voices* appeared, I co-edited two special issues of *American Jewish History* (AJH) on the topic of southern Jewish history with Bobbie Malone. Bobbie, whom I had met as a contributor to the anthology, had written a dissertation on Rabbi Max Heller of New Orleans. Her dissertation and those of Marc Cowitt on Rabbi Morris Newfield of Birmingham and Gary P. Zola on Isaac Harby of Charleston's Reformed Society of Israelites, all published by the University of Alabama Press under the Judaic Studies Series edited by Leon J. Weinberger, marked a breakthrough in graduate student involvement in the field and a milestone in an academic publisher's willingness to support such research. Yet, Bobbie ultimately concentrated on Wisconsin history as historian for the Wisconsin Historical Society and Marc taught at the Newman School in New Orleans and failed to pursue southern Jewish history. Gary went on to a distinguished career as the director of the American Jewish Archives, professor at HUC-JIR, and editor of *American Jewish Archives Journal* (AJAJ) that largely diverted him from the study of the Jewish South. Still, Gary has published some outstanding articles on the subject, teaches a course on it, and supports the field through hosting SJHS conferences, providing research fellowships at the archives (two of which have supported my research), overseeing the extensive archive holdings in the field, publishing in the AJAJ, and in other ways. Since these three, a stream of graduate students has produced excellent honors theses and dissertations, many of which have been published. Several of these individuals have left the field but many more actively participate. They have found positions in academia, in museums and archives, and with the Institute of Southern Jewish Life. Academics regularly teach classes in southern Jewish history. The College of Charleston now boasts a center for southern Jewish history and excellent archives. Museum exhibits and archives concentrating on the field are now widespread.

The Quiet Voices and the special issues of AJH encouraged collaboration between numerous historians. As the next step, in 1996 the SJHS decided to publish a scholarly journal and asked me to serve as editor. The first issue of *Southern Jewish History* (SJH) appeared two years hence and included a justification of the field by Gary Zola, and articles by an octogenarian layperson, a graduate student in American studies (Bryan E. Stone, now the managing editor), a piece on divisions in New Orleans Jewry by Bobbie Malone, a congregational history of North Carolina by Leonard Rogoff, and an article on two Jewish nurses. The annual conferences of the SJHS, the society's project completion grant program, and its short-lived graduate student essay competition further fostered a network in which those interested in southern Jewish history would interact regularly. A community of scholars and interested laypeople gradually matured.

One of my missions has been to mentor individuals and the field. When Lee Shai Weissbach and I had discussed the creation of the journal, he observed that a separate journal should not be necessary since southern Jewish history was part and parcel of American Jewish history. I readily agreed. Yet the journal was needed to encourage scholars and their research. Besides junior and senior historians, many contributors are graduate students and even undergraduates, lay people or from disciplines outside of history. Thus, it is not unusual for me to work with potential authors with several revisions even before their manuscripts are ready to send to peer reviewers. Soliciting manuscripts, working with diverse peer reviewers who are encouraged to give specific suggestions for revision, rotating editorial board positions, and bringing together a volunteer staff of associate editors for primary source articles, and reviews of books, exhibits, websites, and movie reviews—all of these and other activities associated with the journal have been designed to encourage the field and people to contribute and remain within it. I have also helped historians obtain publishers, nurtured networking, read and commented on numerous manuscripts as a friend and press and journal peer reviewer, and co-edit with Adam Mendelsohn the University of Alabama Press series, "Jews and Judaism: History and Culture." I remain loyal to this press because, as previously indicated, it published books in southern Jewish history when few other university presses did so. Yet the subfield is so accepted today that manuscripts are welcomed in presses throughout the country and even in Europe. I enjoy a friendly and cordial competition with the editors of *American Jewish History* and *American Jewish Archives Journal* for fine quality manuscripts.

Another serendipitous meandering: in 1999 Gary Laderman asked me to speak on a panel, "Beyond the Bible Belt," for a Journal of Southern Religion Conference at Emory University. Other panelists discussed Muslim and Hindu history in the South, while I focused on Jewish history in the region. My background in Southern Methodist and Protestant history served me well in demonstrating the pitfalls of over-emphasizing a fundamentalist/evangelical paradigm and explaining how integrating the history of other groups could illustrate diversity. In the enthusiastic exchanges that followed, audience members asked for readings in southern Jewish history that could inform their courses in southern religion. I was unable to provide readily available and up-to-date secondary works. Thus, in response, I published "The Flowering of Interest in Southern Jewish History and its Integration into Mainstream History," (in *Religion in the Contemporary South* ed by Carrie E. Norman and Don S. Armentrout [2005]), *Dixie Diaspora: An Anthology of Southern Jewish History* (2006), and "A Century of Southern Jewish Historiography," (*American Jewish Archives Journal* [2007]). When solicited by ABC-CLIO/Greenwood Press I also integrated the histories of the South and West and small towns into American Jewish history with *American Jewish Chronology* (2011) although the latter is, to me, so over-priced as to preclude widespread sales.

Extensive readings on numerous individuals and communities in the South and West disclosed additional patterns. Migration within the United States and the roles of center in relation to peripheral or satellite communities are factors standing beside immigration from overseas. The Baltimore and Charleston Jewish communities served as vanguards as Jews moved to Alabama, Louisiana, Texas, California, and into the northwest. These and other connections linked Jews and Jewish institutions together and thwarted provincialism. Jews throughout the South and southern history also provided national leadership and remained in the vanguard of national trends. They were urban minded and cosmopolitan. Leonard Rogoff explores these themes for North Carolina Jewry as I expanded on them in *The Columbia History of Jews & Judaism in America* edited by Marc Lee Raphael (2008) and *New Essays in American Jewish History* edited by Pamela S. Nadell, Jonathan D. Sarna, and Lance J. Sussman (2010).

A final meander: as Allen Krause retired from a distinguished rabbinic career, he gave presentations at SJHS conferences and I edited two of his articles for SJH on two controversial rabbis and their roles during the civil rights era. We discussed how he could transform the transcripts his 1966 interviews into a book. He undertook the work but asked me to complete it if he was unable to do so. After he sadly and tragically succumbed to cancer, I edited the manuscript with the assistance of his son, Stephen, and wrote introductions. The University of Alabama Press published *To Stand Aside or Stand Alone: Southern Reform Rabbis and the Civil Rights Movement* in 2016.

I journeyed into American Jewish history with emphasis on the south totally by accident, and my research path within it was directed more by serendipity than design. Nonetheless, my background turned out to be perfectly suitable. My courses in the social sciences and American history with emphases on the South, social movements, African American, church, urban, ethnic, and immigration history as well as my early publications provide theoretical frameworks and comparative perspectives to better understand the history of American Jews and Judaism. Coming to a South where racism continued to raise its ugly head and teaching at a predominantly African American college informed my research on Jewish-black interaction and inter-group relationships. Highly capable editors and distinguished historians greatly impacted my work. The hardships and marginality I faced further informed my desire to nurture others and a subfield I entered, to a great degree, in its infancy and by chance.

NOTES

I thank Stephen Whitfield for a careful reading of this essay.

1   A professor of history at Winthrop College, Shankman was a highly prolific author and a dear friend who wrote about Native American, African American, and American Jewish history. He published works on the 1958 bombing of Atlanta's Temple, the utopian Jewish community "Happyville" in Aiken, South Carolina, antisemitism during the 1970s at Agnes Scott College, a historiography article on southern Jewish history, and African American views of other minorities including Jews, the latter as a Harvard Fellow under Oscar Handlin. Had Arnold not passed away from cancer in 1983 at age 36, our continued collaboration would likely have resulted in far more publication then my ensuing singular efforts.

2   Stephen Whitfield's work almost belies my analysis. He started to give presentations at the first meeting of the SJHS in 1976 and has published outstanding articles in southern Jewish history continuously since then. He remains deeply devoted to the SJHS, serves as book review editor of SJH, and has published more articles in it than any other author. Nonetheless, only part of one of his many fine books— *Voices of Jacob, Hands of Esau* - treats southern Jewish history. Eli Evans deserves credit for popularizing southern Jewish history more than anyone else. Yet, *The Provincials*, as he readily acknowledges in its pages, was a journalistic effort, as was *Lonely Days Were Sundays*, and his outstanding work directing a foundation was outside of academia. Early in his career, Leonard Dinnerstein wrote an outstanding study of the Leo Frank case, co-edited an anthology with a strong section on southern Jewry and integrated southern Jewish history into his many works on antisemitism. Nonetheless, most of his publications are in the areas of nation-wide antisemitism and ethnic/immigration history.

How I Became an American Jewish Historian and What That Meant for My Professional Life

Hasia Diner

I feel at this point in my career comfortable, and indeed eager to share a bit about my professional journey and how I became an American Jewish historian. I have been at this long enough to be able to look back and see consistencies and inconsistencies, moments of change and abiding commitments to a particular way of doing history.

I take this exercise, while overly personal and potentially narcissistic, to be an exploration of how and why I became both an American historian who considers the experience of the Jews central to that national narrative. And equally, I wish to explore how I decided to become a Jewish historian who sees America as a crucial setting for the unfolding of that global history, one which played itself out across a very wide geographic canvass.

Before moving forward, I want to state the obvious. I approach these, the "Jewish" and the "American," as both an outsider and insider. I stand as an outsider to them, despite having been born in America and living here all my life and despite my sense of belonging to something I comfortably call the Jewish people. I consider myself an outsider to them because I believe that the historian must always assume the role of the somewhat removed critic who positions herself aloof and apart from any kind of stake in the outcome of events and developments in the past. It does not matter to me as a Jewish historian if my subject, Jews in the past, sided with slavery and the Confederacy or if some of them joined the ranks of the abolitionists to fight against human bondage.

I have no reason to cheer on Reform as it struggled against over traditionalism, or conversely, if the traditionalists gained the upper hand over the innovators. Did women get the right to be ordained as rabbis and cantors? In the great labor struggles of the late nineteenth and early twentieth centuries in America ought Jews be seen as contributing to worker militancy or employer exploitation? It does not matter, nor do I have particular case to make for Zionism, anti-Zionism, socialism or conventional American party politics as the political forces which won over the masses of the Jews in America.

I could say the same about the broad contours of American history. As an historian concerned with studying the past I do not go in to a project wanting to prove that Americans were or were not more open, tolerant, or charitable than others. Did a more or less expansive form of democracy, free expression, or religious pluralism hold sway in the United States as opposed to elsewhere?

What matters to me as an historian involves posing the most engaging questions I can about these issues, identifying the deepest and richest cache of sources to help answer them, conceptualizing the project in the most cogent and complex manner and then providing a narrative that engages the largest number of readers. I want to explain, not advocate, analyze and not either praise or condemn. After all, as I see it, the historian has to ask good question, provide gripping stories and get people to care about the past. What happened happened, and we, historians, do what we do in order to make sense of those developments. We have neither the right to wish for different outcomes or to impose our values on people who lived in worlds we did not, and who made choices about the problems that they faced that we have not. That is, as an historian I strive to not be a partisan at the same time that I have an extensive personal political life which I act upon as much as I can.

That, as I see it, makes me as an historian into a perpetual critic. On the other hand, I chose as an historian to study matters close to my life and my experiences, phenomena near enough to give me an insider's eye. Having been raised in a particular time and place, by particular people who themselves had been shaped by a set of experiences which they shared with me, made me attune to concerns, themes, and stimuli that I might not have had I grown up elsewhere, or under other circumstances.

Let me offer one example. I grew up in a home with a father, an immigrant from Ukraine, a Hebraist, Labor Zionist, and despite the poverty attendant upon trying to make a living and support a family as a Hebrew teacher, an activist in his community. So, too, I grew up with a stepmother Holocaust survivor. Not only did talk of one kind of another about the Holocaust permeate our home, but every year my father, with a few of his friends and colleagues from the Labor Zionist Organization of America as well as several of the other Jewish educators, organized a Warsaw Ghetto memorial program. I believe they worked with the local survivor group as well, the New Americans Club, and at the yearly ceremonies, survivors spoke to the audience about their ordeals under Nazi domination. Yearly, the mayor of our city, Milwaukee, Frank Zeidler, sat on the dais, as did the two congressional representatives, Henry Reuss and Clement Zablocki.

I knew this, and remembered it distinctly, because I was the child orator asked, or maybe forced, to render a reading in Yiddish, Hebrew, and English. So, imagine my surprise then in the early 2000s, when an editor from Hougton-Mifflin asked me to write the blurb for Peter Novick's forthcoming book, *The Holocaust in American Life*, which purported that until the late 1960s, the Holocaust not only did not function in the communal world of American Jewry but that it served no political purpose and that when Jews talked about it, they did so furtively among themselves. Survivors, he declared in the manuscript, had no opportunities to talk about what had happened to them as their words made other Jews uncomfortable.

I did not write the blurb because my insider status, my position as bearer of a particular set of memories here made me question the basic assertion upon which the book pivoted, thinking of it as flawed, as based on shoddy scholarship. On the other hand, my training as an historian, my outsider status, caused me to ask myself not only if I perhaps carried false memories (I did not. I eventually found myself in the archives, although the program notes for those events referred to me as "a little girl."), but I, the historian, had to ask if my experiences strayed from the norm. After all, I could not know in fact what American Jews said, did, and performed about the brutal deaths of millions of Jews at the hands of the Nazis and where, when, and to whom they directed their attention, without a deep immersion in the primary sources. My accurate recollections might have been utterly local, specific to a particular place and not at all reflective of a broad phenomenon. Novick might have been right about everyplace other than Milwaukee. He might have been on the mark about the other days of the year other than the one night designated for the Warsaw Ghetto Memorial program.

I did not care if my recollection of the past, once I could prove its accuracy to myself, represented an idiosyncratically atypical one or if such programs took place around the country in the post-war years in other cities, with metaphorically other little girls declaiming something about the Holocaust to other audiences including their public officials. Whether American Jews did or not do this, whether they acted as rememberers or if, as Novick saw it, they chose to be silent, I as the historian wanted to get to the bottom of what happened and then try to explain it one way or the other. Either way, as I saw it, would have made for a compelling historical story. (My memories as I demonstrated in *We Remember With Reverence and Love* conformed quite closely to a national experience, and talk and action based on the Holocaust reverberated throughout the American Jewish world.)

So as insider I had access to the sights and sounds, the languages, and the sentiments of the lived experience but the outsider in me, by virtue of my training, demanded that I step back and not hope for a particular outcome. My subjects in this project as in all the others did what they did, said what they said. I could not change that and what I wanted to know besides documenting their words and deeds involved excavating the contexts which pushed them in one direction or another. I had no interest in validating or deprecating either Jews or America.

But why did I choose American Jewish history? In a way, I did not. I took no classes as an undergraduate at the University of Wisconsin-Madison in Jewish history. I did take Hebrew language classes, and in some of them we read works that might be considered historical scholarship, but mostly we focused on literature, occasionally including some non-fiction that offered some observations about the past. In one American history course we did read Abraham Cahan's novel, *The Rise of David Levinsky*, and one European history course on the origins and background of World War II took us into what constituted Holocaust scholarship of the late 1960s.

So, too, in graduate school at the University of Chicago and the University of Illinois-Chicago where I studied American history, Jews seemingly had no place at the table and frankly, at that point, it did not dawn on me that they ought to have been there. I basically had no exposure to the existence of a scholarly community which attended to the history of the Jews.

I went to graduate school in the passion of the late 1960s and 1970s smitten with the new social history and committed to, as we said then, studying history from the "bottom up" (or even worse, I, like others at the time, probably used the phrase which got bandied about, the history of the inarticulate). I definitely wanted to study workers, slaves, the dispossessed, the poor, and ultimately those who rose up against oppression.

Despite my intense, deep Jewish upbringing, my years in a socialist Zionist youth movement, I did not make any intellectual connections between those and the program I set for myself as I trained to become an historian. I certainly had no obligation to make that analytic linkage. I did not have to study the Jews. Not studying them did not constitute a desire on my part to distance myself from them or to prove my universalistic credentials. A large part of the reason came from the reality that none of my professors made much of the Jews either as historical actors or as subjects that illuminated any of the themes or developments we considered. As they assigned books, structured syllabi, and encouraged independent research projects, the words "Jewish" or "Jews" never came across their lips to my ears.

But in an early seminar, "Race and Ethnicity in American History," the professor, after having asked everyone to go around and say something about the paper they might write for the course, did say, perhaps casually, something that made a world of difference in the long run. He said that if you know an immigrant language you might consider using it for your seminar research. Halfway around the table as I sat there both listening to the others and frantically trying to formulate what I would say, it dawned on me that I did know an immigrant language.

I grew up in a Yiddish-speaking family. I had always shifted in my brain and in my speech within our apartment between English and Yiddish, doing so with ease, with a kind of automatic, unselfconscious back-and-forth. When I happened to be home and looked for something to read, I oftentimes picked up, randomly and without design, the day's edition of the Yiddish paper my parents got, *Der Tog-Morgen Zhurnal*, copies of which just happened to be lying around. So, too, Yiddish and Hebrew books, much to my mother's chagrin, lined the shelves, the floors, the table tops, and the cushions of the chairs, just waiting for someone to grab for them. These books and magazines like *Der Yiddisher Kempfer* and *Ha-Doar* provided elements of the material landscape of growing up.

So, when my turn came during that seminar, which ultimately became a life-changing, or career-shaping experience, I announced that I knew Yiddish, clearly an immigrant language, and because I wanted to participate in the field of black history, I thought, I said, that I might research something about how Yiddish-speaking east European Jewish immigrants engaged with the issues surrounding race and the conditions of black Americans in the early twentieth century. The paper, as I saw it, which emerged from that announcement—not very thought through at all—would be one that assumed that not all people defined by law as white thought and acted the same way when facing America's racial realities. They brought something idiosyncratic or particular to it and particularly relatively new immigrants, had to learn some American lessons about race and color. Decades before the emergence of a scholarship defined as "whiteness" studies, I stumbled upon the fact that Jews, as white people, experienced a set of possibilities in America, but that despite enjoying those possibilities their engagement with African Americans reflected much about the fact of their Jewishness.

Out of that paper came my dissertation and my first book, *In the Almost Promised Land: American Jews and Blacks, 1915-1935*. To write it, I had to master the literature in African American history. That, from a logistical perspective, proved to be no problem in as much as I had taken courses on the subject, had attended lectures, had professors to guide me, and in fact did a doctoral level examination in it. But to write that dissertation, I also had to know something about Jewish history in America, something for which I had no preparation. I clearly had to come to terms with the extant literature in what I learned quickly was a field. That field in the early 1970s barely resembles what exists now as it has grown exponentially since then, but it still at that date boasted shelf-loads of journals and books that I had to master before I could write the dissertation.

Despite taking those books off the library shelves, one by one, in all honesty, I did not know at that point in time that the history of the Jews in America constituted a field, nor did I realize that in some places, Columbia University in particular, one could do a doctorate in Jewish history. I understood fields or the world of historical scholarship to be neatly cut up into nation state chunks and Jewish, whether American or otherwise, did not fit the lay of the scholarly land.

In that context I would call myself, *vis-à-vis* American Jewish history, an autodidact. I taught it to myself although one never does. I learned from the people I met as I began to go to conferences, as I sat in archives and libraries, and as I made friends with scholars also writing something about the Jews in American history. I remain grateful to them for having ushered me into a new way of thinking about history and one which allowed me to become an American Jewish historian.

But at the same time, I am grateful for having entered American Jewish history through a side door. I obviously came to it, as this overly long personal narrative suggests, from an interest in American history. Before sharing why I see that as an asset in my own intellectual journey, I do want to say that I became fascinated with American history, even as a child, because in some ways America represented a foreign country to me.

Although born in the USA, with a nod there to Bruce Springsteen, the fact of my parents' foreignness, my mother's total lack of English, their immersion in Jewish issues, concerns, and texts, and their questions about America, posed to my sister and me, made me immensely curious about this place where we lived but to which I was something of a stranger.

I first discovered American history in the library, particularly lured by a series of books, the childhood biographies of famous Americans, with their distinctive orange covers and adorned with silhouette drawings. I read about presidents, explorers, baseball players, generals, scientists, whoever's story appeared next on the shelf of my neighborhood public library. (It is amazing in retrospect to recall my favorite volume in the series, one which moved me more deeply than any other, was *Jane Addams: Little Lame Girl.* After reading it, I insisted that my aunt and uncle in Chicago take me to see what remained of Hull House. My recently published biography of Julius Rosenwald, which is part of the Yale University Press Jewish Lives Series, has much to say about Addams and even now writing about her I am transported to that book with that hideous title.)

I brought to my encounter with America a particular vision and passion, which pointed me to particular topics once I entered graduate school and embarked on my scholarly career. Before becoming a scholar who sought to take a cool, analytic stance towards the material I studied, I had been a high school civil rights activist. Through my membership in the socialist Zionist youth group, Habonim, I got involved with the struggle in Milwaukee. I, with my Habonim friends, my comrades, I guess, went to picket George Wallace when he came to speak. We joined in, and were suspended for a day from high school for our participation in the civil rights boycott of the Milwaukee Public Schools. We formed a high school civil rights organization, created jointly with the NAACP Youth Council, which we named "Youth For Integration." Short-lived, I am sure it left no paper trail. Y for I influenced me profoundly and made me feel, as a seventeen-year-old might, that some deep connection linked my socialist Zionist activism, my Jewishness, with my commitment to making America a more humane place.

Looking back over the course of many decades on that youthful activism, none of which I regret and only wish I had done more, I see how it led me to wanting to know more about America and its history, one which jarred greatly with the heroic jingoistic narrative which I learned in school. When the teachers talked about manifest destiny, freedom, democracy, and material abundance I heard the strains of slavery, racial oppression, the extirpation of the native peoples, and as befit the daughter of a socialist, the triumph of exploitative capitalism. Becoming a history major at the University of Wisconsin in the hey-day of the student movement seemed natural and exploring the discord between America's self-image and the realities of its more checkered path seemed like a perfect project for me.

Yet for all the passion of my political life, something which continues unabated, I came early on in graduate school to believe that scholarship demanded something other than moral outrage. That whatever the topic one chooses, the evidence has to dictate the analytic framework. Moral judgements about the people in the past, their goodness or wickedness, teach us little. Rather, when I sit down to write history, I am more interested in how my subjects decided what to do, how to do it, and what contradictory forces pushed them in one direction or another.

But for the purposes of this piece here, it seems to me that having come to American Jewish history from the path of studying American history made me open to the reality that Jews hardly constituted a unique element in American life. Where they experienced exclusion, for example, so did others. When certain policies or legal changes worked to the advantage of the Jews, I want to know who else benefitted and how. Thinking about American Jewish history from a broader perspective which de-centers the Jews indeed teaches us much about the Jews.

Having defined myself as much as an American historian as an American Jewish historian has rendered me responsive and sensitive to thinking about the experiences of other immigrants who arrived, metaphorically, as partners in steerage with the Jews. Jews alone did not go through the many processes which we, scholars of American Jewish history, study. They alone did not learn to navigate the space between inherited pasts and American possibilities. Others also had to figure out what it meant to them to become American, and others argued these issues among themselves, struggling about matters of language, authority, politics, and the relationship with a broader world community. Other immigrants and their progeny, like the Jews, underwent the many chores involved in creating new vernacular and elite cultures in America, and like all other immigrants, they pondered and argued among themselves over the fates of their families, foodways, languages, assumed communal hierarchies, and deepest beliefs which perchance had to undergo change because of the altered circumstances in which they now lived.

I decided that I would, as I could, carve out for myself research projects and professional activities which kept me engaged with this historical reality. I did so because it interested me and also, in large measure, to shake the foundations of our field which in some ways asserts Jewish distinctiveness. I played and continue to do so an active role in the Immigration and Ethnic History Society and having served as president for a three-year term taught me much about the many histories around which we need to think about that of the Jews in America. My first tenure track academic position had me in a department of American Studies and that too pushed me to thinking widely, comparatively, and multi-ethnically, with the Jews present but not at the center of my teaching and advising.

My second book, *Erin's Daughters in America: Irish Immigrant Women in the Nineteenth Century*, focused on a different immigrant population and explored the impact of a particular gender dynamic in their migration. It had nothing to do with Jewish immigration, but in actuality, I believed that studying Irish women's migration history, as well as attending scholarly and community gatherings of people interested in Irish American history, made me a much better American Jewish historian. Likewise, my book *Hungering For America: Italian, Irish, and Jewish Foodways in the Age of Migration* allowed me to see the experience of Jewish immigrants, hungry people who migrated with particular encounters with food before migration, more sharply because I studied it in tandem with others. They, too, migrated from places of scarcity to a place of food abundance, but their experiences with hunger before migration had been shaped in very different kinds of settings. Only, I asserted, by placing these three in conversation with each other can we understand both the commonalities and the distinctions. By studying Jews in isolation or by studying Irish or Italian immigrants in isolation, one learns less about them, and less about America, and, as such, less about the process of migration itself than if we consider their histories under a single analytic umbrella. (I am now under contract with Yale University Press to write an immigration history undergraduate-level textbook, and when I tell my American Jewish historian friends that I am doing that, they immediately assume that I am writing about Jewish immigration rather than about the overarching phenomenon of immigration to America. Jews will play a relatively small part in this book.)

I would not say that the way I have tackled the history of the Jews in America represents the only way or even the best way. It just happens to be the way I moved on my intellectual journey. Seeing however that other equally rich and productive ways exist, challenged me to think about other approaches and made me receptive to the idea of slicing the historical pie, as it were, differently.

My recent book, *Roads Taken: The Great Jewish Migration to the New World and the Peddlers Who Forged the Way*, provides a case in point. A transnational subject, the book explores peddling as the engine which drove modern Jewish migrations I however realized that no such thing as the "Jews alone" exists as an historic construct. The peddlers went to places where customers, non-Jews, bought goods from them. Had those customers not bought the mirrors and eyeglasses, watches and picture frames, the Jewish peddlers could not have embarked on their migrations. The stories of those customers, and why they wanted sheets and towels, blankets and tablecloths of a particular kind at a moment in historic time, proved as central to this narrative as did the Jews themselves who set out on their many roads which provided me with the dominant image for the book.

In the case of this book, I sought to interrogate the meaning of the concept of American exceptionalism. While I long ago –even sitting in Miss Schmidt's U. S. history class in Washington High School in Milwaukee—rejected it as patriotic rhetoric, American history had always seemed in a class of its own, as *sui generic*. Yet *Roads Taken* took me to Ireland and South Africa, Australia and Cuba, Canada, Mexico, and multiple other Jewish migration destinations. In all those places Jewish peddlers took to their roads and I wanted to see if the roads of America somehow differed. Had they proved to be more hospitable or less? Did American women treat the peddlers with greater welcome and warmth than their counterparts in Scotland, Sweden, or up and down the Amazon River? Not really, but what made a difference in the American part of the Jewish peddlers' road trip involved the economic reality that those in America had more disposable income with which to buy the stuff, stimulating, as such, even more and more Jewish migration.

Doing American Jewish history the way I have appealed to me, and I write that not to deprecate the work of others, from whom I have learned so much. I would like to think that it not only gave me a broad forum from which to present my ideas, a wide perspective from which to experiment with what ultimately fascinated me and made me an historian: the question of how women and men in the past decided what to do and under what circumstances. How, I have been fascinated by, did they confront the changes in the world around them, whether economic, social, or cultural, and how among the usually limited choices available, did they respond? What forces weighed down upon them and constricted them, and what opportunities gave them the possibilities of acting and asserting their individual and collective agency?

A Scholar-Athlete's Discovery
of American Jewish History

Jeffrey S. Gurock

Walter Cronkite, Chet Huntley and David Brinkley were my first history teachers. Growing up within Parkchester in the East Bronx, every Sunday evening my family watched, "You Are There," "Air Power," and "The Twentieth Century," classic news documentaries on the CBS network that starred Cronkite, that most iconic communicator. From Monday through Friday, we sat down to dinner with the Huntley-Brinkley Report and ritually said "Good Night" to Chet and David when they signed off from NBC at 7 p.m. Back then, in the late 1950s and early 1960s, the ABC network was a minor news outlet except for 1961 when Jim Bishop anchored films of the Eichmann Trial that were flown in from Jerusalem and shown on a daily basis.

From then on, I have been a "news junkie." I watch all Sunday morning news shows religiously for three hours with my handy remote control that enables me to switch back and forth among the shows that feature the politicians who make their rounds.

Given this extensive early exposure to contemporary history, it is not surprising that my brother became a television news producer and won several New York Emmys for his outstanding work. My other early introduction into history was my consumption of "Landmark" and "Signature," books that depicted major personalities and events of the past. To this day, when on vacation, I read military histories on the beach and rarely dip into the novels that my wife enjoys.

But the Gurocks were not a family of rarified intellectuals with university educations in their backgrounds. My father, a college night-school drop-out during the Depression, was first a firefighter and later on worked for a trade organization as what we today call a "facilitator." He modestly described himself as a "clerk," who adroitly moved permits through the bureaucracies of Gotham's several buildings departments. My mother was a bookkeeper, who had an uncanny ability to add a column of numbers rapidly and efficiently without the help of an adding machine. Neither my brother nor I envisioned following in their occupational footsteps. If I ever lay awake at night pondering what I might do when I grew up, there was, however, one part of my parents' background that I hoped to emulate. Both were terrific athletes. As a girl, my mother had played handball with the future famous Jewish baseball star Hank Greenberg at the blue-collar Castle Hill Swim Club in the Bronx. My father had wrestled for the 92nd Street YMHA in the 1930s. His greatest keepsake from those days was a purloined towel that he helped himself to when the Jewish Y fought against the New York Athletic Club. That contest was the only way his kind could get through the opponents' door. That WASP preserve did not have any Jewish members.

As an adult—and into his 70s, until Alzheimer's brought him down—he was a softball player and legendary manager at the Connecticut bungalow colony that the Ner Tarmid Society, the Jewish fraternal organization of the FDNY, established. Known around the lake for his athletic acumen, his leadership on our field accorded him recognition that was not obtainable in other walks of life. Meanwhile, for boys of my generation, our community's puberty right took place when we were admitted to the Sunday morning "Men's League." The games were so important that my brother found a part time job writing about the contests for the local newspaper. In 1967, as a precocious sixteen year old player-manager, I led my fellows against my father's squad of "AKs." [figuratively, "old timers."] In the first inning of the first league game, my guys scored 9 runs against our flat-footed fathers. We did not talk to one another much that season. [1]

Clearly, sports permeated our home. When we not watching the news, athletic events were always on our flickering small television set. That is, unless my mother, in a valiant effort to "culture" us, pushed her boys and man to change the channel away from the "Game of the Week," to watch Leonard Bernstein's Young People's Concerts from Carnegie Hall. But ultimately, sports even trumped our interest in current events within my youthful consciousness. My evidence: the first major political event that I can recall was the Kennedy-Nixon Debates of 1960, when I was eleven years old. My earliest sports memory is Yankee Don Larson's "Perfect Game" against the Brooklyn Dodgers in the 1956 World Series. I was six years old.

Though my parents, like all good mothers and fathers, wanted their children to do well in school, my mother was even more determined for us to possess a quality Jewish education. She has been raised in a strictly Orthodox Jewish home and had attended Hebrew High School in Brooklyn, a rarity for girls of her generation. She spoke Hebrew beautifully, albeit with a distinct Ashkenazi accent, not the Sephardic tongue that is today favored among speakers of modern Hebrew. Her brother had been a student at the early Yeshiva Rabbi Isaac Elchanan—today, the rabbinical school attached to Yeshiva University. He had been a schoolmate of Joseph H. Lookstein, the rabbi who, in 1937, founded the Ramaz School, the elite day school in the Yorkville section of Manhattan. In response to my mother's request, Uncle Louis with his hat in hand and yarmulke on his head, personally petitioned Lookstein to admit his nephews on scholarships. We could not afford the school's high tuition. Years later, I would muse that I was admitted on an "athletic scholarship."

At Ramaz, the religious studies curriculum provided us with extensive exposure to the Bible, as well as a modicum of training in the arcane world of the Talmud, and emphasized the importance of observing the laws and customs of Orthodox Jewish faith. The faculty also worked hard for students to acquire a fluency in speaking modern Hebrew. However, remarkably, Jewish history was but a minor part of our education. We studied our people's past only as far as the expulsion from Spain in 1492. There were no courses on modern Jewish history. While we read in Hebrew the writings of Zionist ideologues, most notably, Ahad Ha'Am, the father of cultural Zionism, there was no systematic examination of the Jewish national movement's story. As far as the American Jewish experience was concerned—within which we were being trained to take leadership roles—our only exposure was a one hour a week course for seniors. Most notably, there was no study or even formal commemoration of the Holocaust. Perhaps, since so many of my classmates were children of refugees and survivors, the school did not want to bring up to youngsters horrible family memories. Later on in the school's history, Ramaz developed an innovative integrated Jewish and general history curriculum that brought the Jewish story of catastrophe and triumph up to the contemporary day. The school always had a fine general studies social studies faculty that it turned to in this initiative. When this important change in the educational approach was in the offing, I was brought in to assist the secondary school teachers in their creative labors. I was now a distinguished alumnus, a professor of history. It was nice to be characterized as a distinguished alumnus since I had not graduated from the school with that sort of designation.

In high school, I spent more time in the gymnasium than in the library and the only faculty member with whom I had a close relationship was the basketball coach. I was not his best player but, unquestionably, I was a boy who was uncommonly committed to games and sports. Back in the classroom, I shined brightly only in history courses. However, I did well enough generally to gain admission to CCNY, that great tuition-free university. When I enrolled on campus in the fall of 1967, I thought long and hard about whether I should make a vocation out of my athletic inclinations through training as a physical education major with the hope that eventually I could become a coach, much like my mentor. Alternatively, I wondered whether I should try to major in history, the one subject where I had excelled at Ramaz. Figuring that I could always fall back towards career-training as a gym teacher, I challenged myself, took, and did exceedingly well in a wide range of modern European and American history courses with CCNY's outstanding faculty members. Without pausing to measure my growth, I was becoming a late intellectual bloomer. Most notably, when Professor Bernard Bellush, who taught the history of Progressivism, encouraged me to expand my scholarly horizons, I saw him as a role model and became enamored of his academic life-style. My goal was then to become a scholar/educator of American history.

At that point, I gave no thought towards integrating American and Jewish history through applying my strong background in Judaic studies towards this discipline. And my college's curriculum did nothing to foster this idea. While CCNY's student body was still predominantly Jewish, there was no Jewish studies department. For generations, the one course in Jewish history that surveyed our people's history from Abraham to the twentieth century—all in fourteen weeks—was tucked away in what was called the "Classical Languages and Hebrew Department." Only when I was a senior, in 1971, did the college grow the Hebrew Department a tad through the addition of a second history course—on Zionism—taught by a professor of Hebrew literature.

This minimal expansion of the Jewish studies "program" rode the coattails of the efflorescence of Black studies at CCNY. I took both the Jewish history survey and the Zionism elective. Some of my contemporaries at CCNY took evening courses in Jewish history at the Jewish Theological Seminary of America to fulfill this Jewish intellectual lacuna. But that regimen was not for me, especially since I still was sports-driven and wanted be a varsity athlete. Practices were in the evenings. I found my athletic niche as a four-year letterman on the lacrosse team. Though I excelled more in my devotion to the game and my teammates than on the scoreboard, there—ironically, in a sports venue—I received my first academic recognition. As a senior, I earned the Abraham Kalman Scholar-Athlete award. When I applied to graduate school at NYU and Columbia, I was sure to note that achievement on my application along with my cum laude transcript. NYU accepted me and offered me a $2,500 fellowship. Columbia offered to take me in if I was willing to pay the $3,000 tuition. I told my parents that Columbia had the better American history program and we somehow found funds for me to move from the St. Nicholas Heights college to the Morningside Heights university.

Over the summer before entering graduate school, I made a naïve but ultimately crucial pivot in my career plans. I decided to focus my attention at Columbia on American Jewish history, guilelessly believing that there might be college positions in the offing in this area. As just previously noted, as an undergraduate I had seen my school countenance Black studies, and there was talk of doing likewise on behalf of Latino studies and for other ethnic groups. Why not a full-fledged program in Jewish Studies that would include the U. S. experience? I made my presumptive choice of area of concentration, oblivious to the fact that my specific field of interest occupied, at most, a marginal spot within the academy. I also was not certain whether I should define myself as an Americanist with interests in this particular immigrant and ethnic group or as a student of Jewish history. Knowing so little of the complex parameters of these fields, I decided that an American Jewish historian had to be rooted in Jewish history. Not only that, but I assumed that such a scholar-in-training had to be not only conversant about the modern period, but had also to be knowledgeable of earlier epochs. I made that intellectual turn towards the Jewish history program at Columbia not only guilelessly but also guidelessly, weeks before I showed up at Fayerweather Hall to register for classes. Not asking for approval, I simply told the secretary who held my registration card that she should designate me as a Jewish history concentrator. I was now in the program.

Given my desire to immerse myself in the long sweep of Jewish history, I was not perturbed that during my first year at Columbia, Professor Zvi Ankori, a distinguished scholar of medieval Byzantine Jewry who occupied the Miller Chair in Jewish history once held by the eminent Professor Salo W. Baron, offered his specialty in his seminar. Also during my inaugural year, Professor Ismar Schorsch taught the school's first Holocaust-related courses. Linking my first graduate exposure to modern Jewish history to the American experience, I analyzed the diary of Breckenridge Long, one of the State Department officials who undermined rescue efforts during the Holocaust. I also did some reading connecting the American

Jewish story to world Jewish life in the twentieth century as part of Professor Arthur Hertzberg's course on the history of Zionism. I did not write for him. Mostly, my colleagues and I listened to his brilliant lectures and his Jewish communal war stories as he was the outspoken president of the American Jewish Congress. Still, I had yet to study American Jewish history systematically and with a mentor.

Ironically, that first year at Columbia, I did most of my reading in American Jewish history in Kenneth T. Jackson's course on American Urban history. I enrolled because I intuited that the Jewish immigrant experience and the story of the growth of cities were inexorably intertwined. And though now I was officially a Jewish history major, it also was important to bolster my Americanist credentials. The kindly Jackson helped me out through allowing me to review some of the few important works on early-twentieth century Jewish life in Gotham. I focused on Moses Rischin's *The Promised City* that had appeared in 1963 and compared his approach in narrating the downtown Jewish immigrant experience with that of Arthur A. Goren who had recently published his own classic work *New York Jews and the Quest for Community*.

At the end of the first year, still feeling that the university was not meeting my academic needs, I turned to Ankori and naively inquired why Columbia did not offer courses in American Jewish history. At that point, I did not know how little most American historians and Judaic scholars thought of the field that I wished to explore. And what was true of attitudes at Columbia was also the case at NYU—my other graduate school of choice—and, for that matter, almost all colleges and universities in the United States. In fact, in the early 1970s, the three most noteworthy schools where American Jewish history was taught were the Hebrew Union College [HUC] in Cincinnati, and the Jewish Theological Seminary [JTS] and Yeshiva College [YC] in New York. Though Professor Jacob Rader Marcus at HUC was the renowned first parent of American Jewish historiography and Professor Moshe Davis at JTS and Professor Hyman Grinstein at YC likewise did important spade work that still informs our discipline, arguably, the common goal of their pedagogy was less the raising of scholars and more the education of American rabbis who would be knowledgeable about the communities they would serve.[2]

In any event, just a few weeks after I approached Ankori, my classmates and I were informed that during the forthcoming academic year of 1972-73, he would be on sabbatical and that Professor Naomi W. Cohen would be visiting the program to offer two courses in American Jewish history. Although Ankori did not announce the proffering of these courses as a novelty, it was the first time American Jewish history was part of Columbia's curriculum.

Ankori never explained why he acceded to this request. But I think that his acquiescence was connected to his own admiration for the man whom he repeatedly called "my teacher and master," Professor Baron. Back in the late 1940s, this most influential of twentieth-century Jewish historians had approved the idea that American Jewish history could be a respected academic discipline. This community's history fit well into his "anti-lachrymose theory" of Jewish history. He would remark that since the American Jewish saga was devoid of a "succession of riots and discriminatory laws" and bereft of great rabbis and scholars, it "hardly fit traditional patterns" of Jewish historical writing. However, the struggle of Jews and Judaism to survive under the unique conditions of American freedom was important for historians' attention. Baron made these sentiments known when he served in 1949-1951 as president of the American Jewish Historical Society and helped, in his own words, "to turn the Society around" from its long-held emphases on apologetics and filiopietism. It was precisely that sort of amateurish writing that long littered the field's path towards academic respectability.[3] However, notwithstanding his approbation of the field's possibilities, he never taught American Jewish history at Columbia nor brought in a specialist as a visiting scholar.

Now, under Ankori's watch, "Baronial approval" was taken a dramatic step further when Naomi Cohen visited. She had studied Jewish history with Baron at Columbia, took courses in American Jewish history with Moshe Davis at JTS, and earned her doctorate under the guidance of Professor William Leuchtenburg, writing a biography of Oscar S. Straus, an American Jewish community leader of the nineteenth and the early twentieth centuries.

Effectively, she had carved out a curriculum for herself—much like I was doing—as an American Jewish historian rooted in Jewish history.

Given the standards of academe in her day, after Cohen was appointed to the history department at Hunter College, she was unable—for many years—to convince her colleagues of the value of a course in American Jewish history. She contented herself with teaching primarily American foreign policy and U.S. Constitutional history. A portion of the Jewish story probably found its way into her courses on immigration and ethnic history. Only after she had long been a full professor, around the time that she visited at Columbia, was she able to push successfully for teaching in the field where she had already won a number of awards for her scholarship. Thus, when she came to Morningside Heights, Cohen would once again trail blaze. [4]

I was unaware of her travails at Hunter College and I was not yet sensitive to the special burdens she bore as a woman in a male-dominated profession. All I knew was that American Jewish history had arrived at Columbia and that I might have found my mentor. I thrived under her guidance and my seminar paper on a public accommodations bill that Jews fought for in New York State in the early twentieth century was published in the first number of the *AJS Review*. The editor back then told the association that not only had "Cokhavim" (stars) contributed to that volume, but young scholars as well. I was one of the neophytes. The achievement also caused one green-eyed classmate to remark that outside of the classroom "all he ever talks about is his sports and yet he wrote a solid paper." In a distant replay of my experience at CCNY, I was acquiring at Columbia a cachet as a "scholar-athlete." [5]

In the fall of 1973, Ankori returned and Cohen went back to Hunter College. No courses in American Jewish history would be offered at the university for another decade and a half until members of Baron's own family established the Knapp chair in American Jewish history. Ankori's successor in the Miller chair, Professor Yosef Hayim Yerushalmi was no fan of American Jewish history. He, reportedly, believed that this field studied "breweries in Brooklyn", a very dismissive description of the social and economic history of

Jews in New York. But Baron also had been Yerushalmi's "teacher and master." Arthur Goren was selected as the initial occupant of that position.

In the meantime, with Cohen back at Hunter, while preparing for my doctoral qualifying "orals," I contemplated a future dissertation topic and wondered who might advise me. All of my classmates harbored similar worries since only one of my eight contemporaries defined himself as a medievalist. He was interested in the Jews of Iberia, not Byzantium. The rest of us wanted to focus on Jewish life in Great Britain, France, Germany, Austria, Eastern Europe and the United States.

Putting the "advisor" question aside, at least temporarily, I began to think about studying the complex history of Jewish-African American relations. As a New Yorker, I had witnessed how a long era of alliance and cooperation between the minority groups that had continued in the mid-1960s had turned into a time of suspicion and sometimes of hatred separating Jews and blacks. Indeed, I had seen this change in attitudes in my own life. Growing up, my family had sat in front of that omnipresent TV set and watched with great empathy black protesters down south. We were outraged when three civil rights workers—two Jews and one African American—were murdered in Philadelphia, Mississippi, during the Freedom Summer of 1964. And we were heartened when, a year later, Rabbi Abraham Joshua Heschel marched with Dr. Martin Luther King Jr. in Selma. But our feelings on the issue of race were never tested. Parkchester was segregated until the mid-1960. And as a day school student, I again had no contact with blacks, except when I passed them on the subways that went quickly through the South Bronx and Harlem, destination Yorkville. When I entered CCNY, there were very few African Americans on campus, and most of them were in the remedial SEEK program, not in the credit-bearing classes that I took. But in the spring of 1969, black students took over the campus and demanded the implementation of an Open Admissions policy that would permit graduates of the city's high schools to enter the City University, regardless of their grade point average or SAT scores. Collaterally, they called for the institution of a Black Studies program. Most importantly for me, for much of the multi-week protest, I and most other white students were barred from the campus and our classes. We were now the outsiders. At that point, both racist and anti-Semitic statements from students and faculty soiled the air at CCNY.

Seared by this event, I began to think seriously about my own feelings towards race. These contemplations led me to express myself for the first time in a semi-scholarly manner when I wrote a paper for that one Jewish history course then at CCNY. I compared the position of the Jews in seventeenth-century Poland before and during the infamous Chmielnicki revolts with the contemporary scene in America. Though my argument was half-baked, I described Jews in both historical cases as "the visual image of oppression." I contended that in Poland, Jews were victimized because they were seen as allies of the Polish nobility who oppressed peasants until the Cossack leader violently rallied them. I hypothesized that in America, Jews were problematically situated between the underclass of blacks and the WASP-dominated government.

Realizing that I wished to study this topic with greater sophistication, during my third year at Columbia, I took two semesters of African American history with the historian of the Harlem Renaissance, Professor Nathan I. Huggins. While grounding myself in black history, I tentatively approached Ankori with the idea of writing on "Jews and Blacks in the Age of Jim Crow, 1896-1954." Far from rejecting this idea out of hand, Ankori suggested that to do the job right, I should focus not so much on the pronouncements of leaders, but to look at how Jews and blacks lived in urban neighborhood settings. He suggested that I study four cities. I do not remember all four venues, but I do know that had I followed his advice exactly, I might be still working on the dissertation. But what about Harlem located below Morningside Heights? I knew that Harlem held the potential for a fine case study of race relations. I also recognized that it possessed an interesting Jewish story as a place where immigrant Jews moved to after leaving the Lower East Side. I had my topic, but could Ankori advise me?

As fate would have it, only weeks after passing my "orals" as a Jewish historian with a minor in American history, Ankori announced that he was leaving Columbia to assume a position at

Ben Gurion University in Israel. With now close to a dozen students adrift without an advisor, the History Department allowed us to turn to its faculty in related fields or to recruit outside scholars. I was privileged that Professor Cohen agreed to return to Columbia. She, along with Kenneth T. Jackson and social historian David J. Rothman became my committee. As a Jewish historian who wanted to study the American experience with sensitivity to the urban and social dimensions of immigrant Jewish life in the U. S., I had the team that guided me in writing *When Harlem Was Jewish*.

While the African American-Jewish encounter brought me to Harlem, ultimately, my work on this uptown neighborhood focused more on its Jewish communal experience. The conceit of my work was that a complex set of forces, rooted in the dynamism of Gotham, motivated Jewish relocation from one area of the city to the next and that Harlem was home to both poor and affluent Jews, to the religiously identifying, to radicals and to those disinterested in continuing their group connections as they advanced in America.

Forty years after writing my first book, as I began to rewrite that community history and bring it up to date,[6] I became increasingly aware that most of my subsequent scholarship, from my work on American Orthodoxy to studies of Jewish neighborhoods in Gotham from 1920 to the present, was connected to Harlem. Jewish communal initiatives uptown in the 1910s also informed a portion of the book that I always wanted to write, but was not ready to compose until I was well-established in the field. I had feared that a tenure committee might look at the sort of unconventional social history that I had in mind as nothing more than a study of "ballparks in the Bronx." However, after twenty-five years in the field, in 2005, I published *Judaism's Encounter with American Sports*, which examines how a foreign cultural phenomenon called athleticism entered the lives of immigrant Jews and their children and identifies the conflicts that have ensued in being a Jew, an American, and a sports person. Who was more qualified to write on that topic than a scholar-athlete American Jewish historian?

Notes

1 For a profile of my sports background, see Larry Rutman's oral history, *American Jews and America's Game; Voices of a Growing Legacy in Baseball* (Lincoln and London: University of Nebraska Press, 2013), 429-238.

2 In 1966, Brandeis University, destined to be a major center for the study of American Jewish history, established its Lown Graduate Center for Contemporary Jewish Studies and appointed Leon A. Jick as its professor of American Jewish history. See Jonathan D. Sarna, "In Memoriam: Leon A. Jick (1924-2005)," *American Jewish History* vol. 92, no. 2 (2004): 225-27.

3 On Baron's Appreciation of American Jewish History, see Jeffrey S. Gurock, "From *Publications to American Jewish History*: The Journal of the American Jewish Historical Society and the Writing of American Jewish History," *American Jewish History* (Winter, 1993-1994): 212-214.

4 For a biographical sketch of Cohen, see Robert Seltzer, "Naomi W. Cohen: As Teacher and Scholar," *American Jewish Archives Journal* (2009): 1-5.

5 Gurock, "The 1913 New York State Civil Rights Act," *Association for Jewish Studies Review* 1 (1976): 93-120.

6 Gurock, *Jews of Harlem: The Rise, Decline and Revival of a Jewish Community* (New York: NYU Press, 2016).

Object Lessons

Jenna Weissman Joselit

"You're a whaaat?" peevishly asks the receptionist, scanning the detailed biographical form she insists I must attend to before seeing the doctor. "You're a whaaat?" At first I thought she could not make out my handwriting—and for good reason. Over the years, it has gone steadily downhill, gotten murkier. But no, that wasn't it. Penmanship was not the problem; the word "h-i-s-t-o-r-i-a-n" was the culprit, gumming up the works. The receptionist did not understand what I had written: "historian" simply did not register. In her line of work, she hadn't encountered too many of that ilk.

I suppose I could have made the receptionist's life—and my own—a bit easier by writing "professor" or "author" in the little box reserved for "occupation." But something—perhaps pride—stayed my hand. It had taken me a very long time to live up to the title of historian and I was not about to surrender it simply because a receptionist did not know what it meant, let alone what it entailed. Wearing the mantle of historian was precious and hard-won. And therein lies a story. My story.

Chronicler and critic, sleuth and storyteller rolled into one, a would-be historian spends an inordinate amount of time in school. I certainly did, first as an undergraduate history major at Barnard College and then as a graduate student across the street, at Columbia University. Even now, many decades after having received my PhD in history, I am still not entirely sure why I pursued that trajectory rather than some other, like becoming a lawyer. Virtually everyone I knew at college was destined for law school. What's more, my father was a practicing attorney, and a satisfied, flourishing one, at that. But never once did I consider the law an option. Instead,

I was drawn to the study of history, the play of personality, incident and plot, the telling of stories, the process of research and the joy of discovery. I liked being in school, too.

In hindsight, I have come to see that being a graduate student furnished me with the luxury of freedom. Those who came of age and attended graduate school, any graduate school, in the 1980s, when misogyny ruled the roost; when competition rather than collegiality was the coin of the realm and the relationship between professor and student took the form of modern-day peonage (Mentoring? Professional development? Ha!) might scoff at that notion. I don't mean to minimize these structural inequities, which were all too real and profoundly destructive. Even so, the years I spent in school enabled me to let my imagination roam freely, to explore new ideas, to take up a new language (Yiddish), to travel, to write for hours on end — and I didn't have to clock in. No 9-5 for me.

No job, either. At the conclusion of my long apprenticeship, finding a position that was geographically, financially and intellectually viable was just not in the cards. For one thing, there weren't too many academic opportunities in modern Jewish history, especially not in my neck of the woods; for another, my expertise resided in American Jewish history, which then lay at the very bottom of the academic economy. Placing a premium on antiquity and on linguistic prowess, the gatekeepers of Judaic Studies dismissed American Jewish history out of hand; some even questioned whether it constituted a field. At best, it was seen as inconsequential, an enterprise notable for its good intentions rather than its robust intellectual ideas; at worst, it was believed to be irretrievably corrupted by filiopietism. The gatekeepers of American history were none too hospitable, either. In an era when ethnic and immigration history were only just beginning to establish their respective bona fides, American historians actively doubted that close consideration of the nation's Jews might possibly bring anything of value to the table.

To compound matters there was the not-so-small matter of my dissertation: an inquiry into Jewish criminality and its impact on the American Jewish experience of the late nineteenth and early twentieth centuries. These days, my chosen topic would not even merit a raised eyebrow; back then, it was deemed either too marginal or too *outré* by half to "count" as a substantive contribution. Ouch. The point here is not to settle scores, but to underscore the passage of time and with it, the contemporary academy's thankfully expansive notion of what makes for good history. But I get ahead of myself.

In a curious twist of fate, the first of many, I left graduate school a freshly-minted PhD with no prospects but with a book contract in hand from Indiana University Press, whose brand new series, "The Modern Jewish Experience," was just being launched by Paula Hyman and Deborah Dash Moore. The inaugural volume in the series, *Our Gang: Jewish Crime and the New York Jewish Community* represented a decided turn in the conceptualization of modern Jewish history—and a vote of confidence for which I remain most grateful.

On the strength of the book's ideas as well as its use of visual materials, I was approached by New York's Municipal Archives to mount an exhibition about the history of Gotham's underworld. And with that unanticipated invitation, my career took off in an equally unanticipated direction: in one fell swoop, I became a curator of interpretive historical exhibitions. Moving from the margins to material culture, I found my voice and my métier: in things. The history of objects—their circulation, displacement, repurposing and preservation over time—captured my imagination. I relished the opportunity to present and interpret the past in a new register, to engage a broad public audience, to work in venues that ran the gamut from the Manhattan District Attorney's Office to the Strawbery Banke Museum and the Yiddish Book Center, and to draw on a varied repertoire of sources—and still do. More to the point, collaborating with an entirely new cast of characters—exhibition designers, fabricators, graphic artists, lighting experts and installers—was downright invigorating. There's nothing quite like seeing your inchoate ideas take shape. Literally.

As it happened, my budding curatorial career unfolded against the backdrop of enhanced academic interest in material culture and in a growing appreciation of museums as one of modernity's key cultural venues: witness the rise in museum studies programs across the country and in the number of universities and museums seeking actively to cultivate reciprocal ties. In part, this newfound interest compensated for a lack of opportunities within the academy. The professoriat came to see museum work as an effective solution to the widespread joblessness that prevailed among the far too many history PhDs it was sending forth into the world. At the same time, it also signaled a growing, if belated, appreciation of the museum as a site of scholarship as well as stewardship; the generator, not just the recipient, of high-level research and publication.

Judaic Studies, on the other hand, was late to that dance. Only recently has the field relaxed its longstanding hostility to material culture studies, which it widely denigrated as slight and even frivolous, and opened itself up to its demonstrated interpretive value within the classroom as well as the gallery. That museums of all sorts have increasingly taken root within the Jewish communal landscape both in the United States and abroad accounted in no small measure for that about-face, as did the rise of a new generation of scholars more comfortable with "mixing things up" than its predecessors.

A novelty act, my work as an independent curator and, in short order, as a museum consultant as well, led to one thing after another: first to a position at the YIVO Institute for Jewish Research in New York where I mounted exhibitions, implemented public programs and now and again taught a graduate course on one or another aspect of modern Jewish history and then onto a guest curator spot at the Jewish Museum on New York's Fifth Avenue. Once again, serendipity took hold of my career and gave it a big shake. A chance encounter in the marbled halls of the New York Public Library resulted in this plum assignment.

Much as I love research and the pursuit of the telling detail, I'm not a big fan of footnoting. Invariably, something goes astray or awry: a quotation that I'm absolutely, positively certain appeared on page 32 of a given text is nowhere to be seen, prompting me to doubt myself (Did I make it up?), let alone mock any pretense of scholarly rigor. This situation repeats itself every time I work on a publication, and it's precisely what happened when I was putting the finishing touches to my second book, *New York's Jewish*

Jews. There I was, chasing down one citation after another when I decided to take a break, to clear my head by walking up one lengthy corridor and down another. As I made my rounds, I bumped into the associate director of the Jewish Museum, a casual acquaintance. After exchanging the usual pleasantries, I asked him what he was working on. An exhibition about home and homelessness, said he. And with that, I was off on a tear, unleashed, suggesting this, that and the other thing as possible themes and objects.

Several weeks later, the museum official rang me, invited me to a brain-storming session and before I knew it, he had asked me if I'd be interested in curating an exhibition that explored domesticity from an American Jewish perspective. Enticing, no? The rub: I had only twelve months from start to finish in which to conceptualize, research and assemble the contents, mount a show and produce a catalogue.

I did not have much of a life that year; even now, it remains a bit of a blur. But the exhibition that resulted, *Getting Comfortable in New York*, was a smash success—and a generative one, to boot. Lest anyone think curation represents a detour away from the life of the mind and the business of scholarship, please think again. Exhibitions beget scholarship, as did this one. In the whirlwind course of working on *Getting Comfortable*, I realized there was so much more that could be said about American Jewry's relationship to the home. I went on to spend the next couple of years working full steam ahead on what evolved into the award-winning book, *The Wonders of America: Re-inventing Jewish Culture*.

Rippling outward, the book gave rise to my becoming a journalist, or, more precisely still, a monthly columnist for the *Forward*, enabling me to inhabit the role of a public intellectual. For sixteen years, my column—"Wonders of America," it was called, just like the book—served as a bully pulpit from which to chronicle and interpret the often befuddling but always compelling array of institutions and practices, ideas and products that enliven the American Jewish experience, from the Jewish Agricultural and Industrial Aid Society to Barton's kosher-for-Passover candies. After my association with the *Forward* came to an end, a consequence of that bugaboo known as metrics, *Tablet* gave my column a reprieve, or better yet, an extended lease on life, by providing it with a new home.

At this point in the narrative, you might be wondering whether I had given up on teaching, a casualty of all that curation and column-writing. The short answer is "no." It's not only that I consider exhibitions and newspaper columns an exercise in teaching, a form of critical engagement. I have also spent many hours in the classroom, but not in a linear, straightforward fashion, year after year like most professional historians.

When the opportunity arose to teach, as it did at Princeton University, I grabbed it. Once again, serendipity intervened and worked its magic. I had been a candidate for a senior position at a major university and over dinner enjoyed a wide-ranging conversation with a faculty member who was then spending the year at Princeton's newly-established Center for the Study of American Religion. She subsequently invited me to that New Jersey campus to give a talk and while there, I met, and enjoyed a series of informal, convivial conversations, with the Center's faculty in Religion, History and Sociology. I didn't think anything of it at the time, but a few weeks later, the phone rang and at the other end was one of the academics whom I had just met. He wanted to know whether I might be interested in and available to come to Princeton in the fall to assume a year-long position as a Senior Fellow at the Center for the Study of American Religion. I believe I stopped breathing for a moment or two, but when I recovered my equilibrium, I managed to eke out a hearty "yes," without stopping for a second to consider anything else that I might have had on my plate.

Like the guest who came for dinner and stayed, I, too, stayed at Princeton on and off for nearly a decade teaching a wide variety of courses under the aegis of American Studies, Judaic Studies and History. It was also at Princeton, one of the most stimulating intellectual environments I've ever encountered, where I researched, wrote and published two books: the aforementioned *The Wonders of America* and *A Perfect Fit: Clothes, Character, and the Promise of America.*

Coming up with a new project took some doing and entailed a number of false starts along the way. For a while, I was at a loss, but one day, while watching the evening news, the sight of demonstrators outside the Supreme Court holding aloft gray cardboard versions of the Ten Commandments caught my eye — and my imagination. I got to thinking about the movement of these ancient passages, their circulation through time and space, and the seemingly outsized appeal they held for Americans, many of whom championed the planting of six foot monuments to the Decalogue in the public square. How did that come to pass, I wondered as I began to take the measure of a phenomenon that was at once celestial and earthy, text and object, Judaic and Christian.

A daunting project if ever there was one — the literature on the Ten Commandments is voluminous — I had help along the way, thanks to the John W. Kluge Center of the Library of Congress, where, for several glorious months, I was a Distinguished Visiting Scholar. The opportunity to draw on the library's cornucopia of materials as well as on the knowledge and smarts of its staff pushed the book in an entirely new direction, prompting me to think of the Ten Commandments in terms of scale, color, and, above all, of presence. It enabled me to take a series of bold interpretive leaps that in the fullness of time came together to form *Set in Stone: America's Embrace of the Ten Commandments.*

My stint at the Library of Congress had another tangible benefit: it opened my eyes to the possibility of living in Washington, D.C. By the time I arrived in the nation's capital to take up my position at the Kluge Center, I had become a dyed-in-the-wool New Yorker and couldn't imagine living any place else. But Washington during the Obama years was something else again: I could see myself calling it home. My newfound geographical pliability was put to the test when the George Washington University came a'calling.

I answered that call. At this stage of the game, I have a new title — the Charles E. Smith Professor of Judaic Studies & Professor of History — and a full teaching load. In addition, I've created and direct a pioneering graduate program in Jewish cultural arts, the only such enterprise in the country, and deepened my portfolio of responsibilities by directing GW's Program in Judaic Studies as well.

Funny how things turn out.

What, then, does this account add up to? A cautionary tale? A parable? An assemblage of bromides? A salute to serendipity? Given my druthers, I would prefer to think of it as just a good yarn, the kind that transforms a "whaaat" into an historian.

How I Learned to Call America "the States"
and
Became an American Jewish Historian

Eli Lederhendler

There are many things in life (indeed, most things) that one does not anticipate. Becoming an American Jewish historian was, for me, one of those things. I am not even sure that I can accurately say that I set out to be a professional historian at all. But given the direction that I took in graduate school, I would seem to have chosen a course toward the study and teaching of Russian and East European Jewish history. Had I remained in the United States, I believe that I would have carried on in that field. As it turned out, in order to become an American Jewish historian, I first had to become an immigrant Israeli. To be precise, in becoming an Israeli, I found that the scarce resource that I possessed and that was most sought-after was my background knowledge of American Jewish history, rather than my doctoral research on 19th-century Russia.

What accounted for the fact that so few scholars in Israel were professionally engaged with the study of American Jewry, leaving it to the American Jews to take charge of it on their own, as it were? There are various reasons why relatively few non-Americans have developed a more than superficial interest in American Jewish history and culture, some of which has to do with the overall balkanization of Jewish communal studies. As a rule, these have grown mainly as a kind of self-ethnography. For example, British, French, Italian, and Latin American Jewries have generally been the studied largely if not solely by scholars raised in those communities. The American Jewish case is not, in that sense, at all unique.

(There are incipient signs of change, in this regard: at least one Israeli-born historian and a handful of German-born historians are currently teaching American Jewish history at American universities, thus auguring a potential internationalization of the field.[1])

That having been said, the inbred specialization of Jewish regional studies remains only a partial and somewhat inadequate answer to the question of why, around the year 1980, there should have been such little development in the American Jewish field in Israel. Simply put, Israeli academia began in the 1920s with an already existing template for Jewish Studies: it was a German-Jewish, classicist, textual-oriented format overlaid by a deep intellectual commitment to exploring the Jewish past, and not so much geared to the present. When the added perspective of the social historians became part of the academic agenda, this was applied in Jewish studies mainly to the medieval world—at best, going up to the eighteenth century. The training of Israeli academic scholars was, in that sense, apt to make short shrift of anything that happened in the twentieth century. Israeli-based scholarship also shared only peripherally, if at all, in the sort of contemporary, multi-cultural paradigms which were gestating in American university literature, history, and sociology departments in the post-1960s era. Not only American Jewish history suffered underdevelopment as a result; the same was true for Soviet Jewish history, and even—until the 1960s—the Holocaust. Things had slightly changed, however, by the early 1980s, and the result was that a historian of American Jewry could actually be seen as an asset of sorts to a Jewish studies program.

At this point I should observe that American Jewish history as it exists today in the Israeli academy was trail-blazed by expats who established themselves during the decades before I arrived there in the 1980s. Moshe Davis, previously a dean of undergraduate studies at the Jewish Theological Seminary, went on *aliya* in 1959 and established the Hebrew University's Institute of Contemporary Jewry in that same year. He taught American Jewish history and trained a number of graduate students. Essentially, he put the subject on the academic map in Israel, as he did an adjunct field:

America-Holy Land studies, which he saw as the quintessential core of the American discourse of Judeo-Christian, Bible-based commonality.[2]

Arthur Aryeh Goren, another immigrant, taught American and American Jewish history in the Hebrew University's history department for many years before he began a stint of part-time teaching at his alma mater, Columbia University. Lloyd (Aryeh) P. Gartner, another immigrant from the States, held a long-term berth at Tel-Aviv University's Jewish history department. Both of these Aryeh's were experts in the field of Jewish migration history, and whereas Goren took a keen interest in the interface between Jews and American political culture, Gartner was more heavily engaged in studying the internal structure and development of Jewish community life.

It is noteworthy, I think, that this handful of American-born, immigrant scholars characteristically studied American Jewry "in its own right," so to speak. Among the generation of their students—that is, Israeli scholars of American Jewry who are not American-born—most have worked on Zionism and the Holocaust, as these were reflected in U. S. Jewish history. Although there are today a few notable exceptions to this rule,[3] I believe that both of the above-mentioned preoccupations are more "native" to the Israeli academy and they emerged more or less in tandem with similar orientations in modern Israeli historiography as a whole.

In contrast, Davis, Goren, and Gartner cultivated themes of the religious, ethnic, and social history of the Jews in America in a broader—dare I say more American?—sense. Their work shared much in common with that of their co-generational colleagues in the States. Thus, I would argue that, in a broad sense, Israelis of American background have given shape to a paradigm of studying the subject of American Jewry that is closely related to ethnic-heritage, religious, and cultural-history constructs.

(It has also been my experience in over three decades of teaching that American-born students in Israel, as well as some Israeli-born children of American immigrants, share that fascination with issues of identity and culture. They seem to prefer to write term papers and graduate theses touching upon those spheres rather than on political and ideological issues.)

As it happened, when I was facing the choice between taking a position at one Israeli university in Eastern European Jewish history and a job in American Jewish history at another, I took the road that I had anticipated the least. But having made the choice, I wanted to "own" it as a quest for knowledge, as an agenda and as a calling that made sense in my new home. In becoming a new Israeli—an *oleh hadash* fresh from "the States" (as we expats call the USA)—I wanted to convey to my Israeli students as much as I could about the history and culture of the largest Diaspora community in the Jewish world. Once I was offered the opportunity, I set out, somewhat belatedly, to master the field as best I could so as to design courses of my own and mentor my students.

I thus began my study of America and its Jews in earnest, reading widely and asking questions, only in my post-doctoral phase as a young scholar. It was, therefore, in Israel that I really discovered America—or, to repeat the more common phrase abroad—"the States." Ironically, I became an American specialist and an "Anglo-Saxon" at the same time—for, as many readers may be aware, all of us English-speaking immigrant Jews living in Israel are commonly (if incongruously) labelled "Anglo-Saxons," which is Israeli shorthand for all of the Brits, South Africans, Canadians, Aussies, New Zealanders, and Americans.

Those whom I have to thank for making this at all conceivable, at the time, included my marvelously supportive colleagues at the Hebrew University's Institute of Contemporary Jewry, who arranged a post-doctoral fellowship that allowed me to return to the States for a year and start on an American historical research track, before officially undertaking my teaching duties.

Ultimately, and more substantively, I owe a great debt to Henry Feingold, the veteran American Jewish historian who had initiated me into the field when I was still in graduate school in New York. Indeed, when I recently published my one-volume survey of American Jewish history,[4] I dedicated it to Feingold in a gesture of abiding appreciation.

Last but not least, honorable mention must go to the late Yisrael Gutman, a surviving participant in the Warsaw Ghetto revolt and an eminent historian of the Holocaust. In his later years, Gutman was head of the Institute of Contemporary Jewry when I was hired as a member of its faculty. When I returned from my retooling stint in New York, which I spent at the YIVO Institute for Jewish Research, Gutman called me into his office for a chat. He said that he hoped I would develop my own orientation to American Jewish history, in particular one that might owe something to the vantage point offered by Jerusalem.

At the time, I cringed inwardly at what I took to be a hard-core, ideological pitch. I thought I was hearing an established historian of the "Jerusalem school" (that is, a partisan of Zionist-Israeli historiography) urging a new member of the fold to adhere to the house rules. Later I came to understand that conversation rather differently, as I grew to appreciate Gutman's integrity as a historical thinker and his broad mental universe. It was, after all, only reasonable to suppose that my "gaze" *vis-à-vis* American Jewry would be colored by the fact that I was looking at it from a singular perspective, having one foot still in America but the other firmly planted in Israel. It made sense that, if my *American* background might be turned into a resource for Israeli academia, so too, in return, I might turn my outsider's angle of vision into a fresh perspective *vis-à-vis* the local point of view being cultivated by the American Jewish historical profession. In so doing, I knew that I would have to take into account some comparative notions about modern Jewish history at large and that what I wrote would partake of a trans-national outlook. That was evidently part of what Gutman had in mind. I willingly accepted that challenge. In that regard, I was fortunate in having prepared myself in the field of East European studies, for it pointed me toward the topic of the mass Jewish immigration from Eastern Europe to America. My background enabled me to deal with the history of that migration from within a discourse in which I already felt at home.

Over and above these professional considerations, I believe that as a scholar I have been shaped by my own particular experience of America, and that was ultimately of more lasting importance than the specific circumstances that led to the professional choices I made. The first two book-length studies that I researched and published, after I had made the turn to American Jewish history, seem to reflect this duality—the intellectual engagement with trans-national history and migration studies, on the one hand, and the fascination with the place where I grew up, on the other.[5] To turn the latter into a project required me to come to terms with the environment that I had known best, but had reckoned with least, and to try to understand at a more sophisticated level what had shaped the experiences of my youth.

Early Influences

As a historian, I know the seductive temptations and the pitfalls of trying to read a sequence of events backward from a known outcome. What I will say, however, is that it certainly helps to grow up in interesting times. That is, my mental world was shaped in a particularly stimulating place and time, and the later intellectual reworking of my early impressions owes something to the tenor of the times in which they were embedded. When I took up American Jewish history as a professional matter, I knew it would never bore me. It was, after all, a history that had claimed me personally.

Having been born in New York City in late 1952, my life, as I grew into a vague consciousness, was shaped by the arms race (we did regular shelter drills at school), the Cuban Missile Crisis, the Kennedy and King assassinations, the Vietnam War, the civil rights movement, and the Six-Day War in Israel. I took part in demonstrations on behalf of Soviet Jews and Israel; I protested the public hanging of Jews in Baghdad; and I spent most of the fall of 1968 in alternative classrooms while the New York City teachers' strike ground on and on. I received my draft card and draft lottery number at the U. S. consulate in East Jerusalem in the winter of 1970-71, during a gap year, and arrived at Columbia University the next fall, just a couple of years after the campus had erupted in unprecedented violence.

I lived during much of that time in a mixed, Jewish-Catholic, blue-collar and lower-white-collar Bronx neighborhood. All three synagogues in the neighborhood were Orthodox, but it didn't seem to occur to any of the faithful to walk the streets with yarmulkes on their heads or with dangling *tzitzis*. The area was post-melting-pot ethnic or else, if you will, multicultural *avant la lettre*: the dry-cleaner, the shoe repair and the barber shop were Italian-owned, the pizza was superb and unrivalled, the deli and three of the four butcher shops were kosher, the bakery sold challah on Fridays, and the Chinese restaurant was gastronomically awful but it was gaudily decked out to advertise its exoticism. As kids we were treated only by Jewish doctors and dentists in small, private practices. I attended a public school, junior high, and high school where the percentage of Jewish students and Jewish teachers reached roughly to the three-quarter mark. I suppose I lived a second-generation life during years that were somewhat past the classic second-generation New York era, which was largely played-out by the end of World War II.

My parents' friends all spoke a native Yiddish amongst themselves, and my (New York-born) mother taught Yiddish at the neighborhood's secular afternoon school—a place that boasted a Yiddish-immersion curriculum (plus Hebrew language instruction), five afternoons a week, and catered to families with secular, leftist, or Zionistic identity preferences. The Yiddish writer Chaim Grade lived about ten blocks away; the Yiddish poet H. Leyvick came to one of our graduation ceremonies. But at home we invariably spoke English, we watched the usual kids' shows on TV, and the streets near where we lived were named for the European heroes of the American Revolution (all except Lafayette, whose name is honored in other boroughs of the city). Down the main avenue in one direction was the colonial-era mansion where, as everyone knew, George Washington had stayed during one episode of the Revolutionary War, and further up the avenue in the opposite direction was Gun Hill Road, so-named because of its role in the battle for the Bronx. Right in between was Montefiore Hospital, which originated as a kind of hospice for Jewish patients with incurable diseases, funded at the time by Jacob H. Schiff. History was street lore just as much as it was book learning.

At school they encouraged us to read the *New York Times* and *Junior Scholastic*. At home, we had the (then-) liberal paper, the

New York Post and the liberal-Zionist Yiddish daily, *Der Tog-Morgen Zhurnal*. My younger sisters had music lessons near the co-op apartments built by the Amalgamated Clothing Workers' Union of America. Some of my father's relatives (second or third cousins who had immigrated decades earlier), who were working-class "reds," still singed by Stalinism, lived fifteen minutes down the road in the communist co-ops, sponsored by the *Arbeter Orden*,[6] a Yiddish-language affiliate of the Industrial Workers of the World (IWW). My father had no immediate family members, no parents or brothers and sisters, since he was the only one of them all not to have been immolated in the *khurbn* (destruction). His parents and siblings lived in the framed sepia photo on the bookshelf. As a youngster, I knew all about the tattooed numbers on the forearms of some of our close friends and relatives, I knew the words to the Partisans' Hymn by heart, and at the Pesach *seder* table we recited (in Yiddish), "In the Warsaw ghetto, the month of Nissan has arrived...."

At public school we did the presidents' birthdays, Thanksgiving, the Revolutionary and Civil Wars and all that, while at Yiddish school we entered a different universe: the walls were decked with framed portraits of I. L. Peretz, Sholem Aleichem, and (then) Israeli President Yitzhak Ben-Zvi. History was my favorite subject: it was all about the Land of Israel, the Babylonian Exile, the Maccabees, the Talmud, the Spanish Inquisition—a curriculum of epic events and great sacrifice, crafted by and for East European *maskilim*—the Jewish humanists who turned a select part of the Jewish heritage into a grand narrative for a dislocated generation, still hoping that some decency might prevail in the world. My exposure to modern history, on the other hand, was limited to what we got at public school (no Jewish content there), or else ritualized through the customs of the Jewish springtime holidays (we did Tu B'Shvat and Shavuot, more or less along an Israeli kibbutz format, with an emphasis on Jewish national rebirth, rites of fertility, and the solace of living in a blessed time of bounty).

In later years, after I'd began teaching at the Hebrew University, my senior colleague and much admired mentor, the late Ezra Mendelsohn (another New York-bred American-Israeli), described me as someone who had absorbed the world of Yiddish

New York, the Jewish labor movement, and the American Jewish ethnic experience with my mother's milk, you should pardon the *cliché*. That may be true, but upon reconsideration, I believe that what I absorbed was how to live trans-nationally, partaking of the cultures of three continents.

Languages

I trained my mind in my college years with little evident interest in my New York surroundings, other than as streets to pass through and bookshops to dawdle inside for hours. At Columbia I worked at learning Russian and lapped up the ever-intriguing narratives of Russian history—especially its political and ideological aspects. Simultaneously, up the block at the Jewish Theological Seminary, I endeavored to cope somehow with a massive curriculum that covered all of Jewish history from biblical and post-biblical times to the verge of the twentieth century.

With Yiddish as a first-hand inheritance via my immigrant father and my American-born mother, the Yiddish schoolteacher, I knew I had at my disposal a monumental, never-ever-to-be-mastered world of East European Jewish letters. Hebrew, a third language, was acquired at another immersion-type supplementary Jewish school, which I attended during my high school years and which was called *Marshalliah*, to honor the memory of Louis Marshall (whose significance I did not know at the time). I then reinforced my Hebrew during a gap year spent in Israel. Muddling through in college to intermediate and advanced Russian courses seemed at the time to be just what I needed to embark on a bulky work of research that would justify all those intensive years in the classroom. Little did I suspect that my native English would become my major occupational resource.

Becoming an American Jewish historian in Israel has made the language issue of particular relevance. Without a doubt, I have carried on publishing primarily in English, in large part because the sphere of discourse on American Jewry is so predominated by U.S.-based scholars and academic journals and because international academic conferences tend to be conducted in English. Clearly, my intended reader lives, on average, in North America more than anywhere else.

Nevertheless, teaching in Israeli classrooms—in Hebrew— prompted me to address my immediate audience in appropriate formats. I was given one such opportunity when the Open University of Israel commissioned me to write a Hebrew-language textbook about Jewish immigration from Eastern Europe to America. Other opportunities to publish in Hebrew have also presented themselves, and I appreciate the advantages of this "language mobility" in terms of reaching out to non-specialists who live here in Israel.

Over the years, I have tailored my courses at the Hebrew University with language accessibility in mind. Naturally enough, I assign my graduate students a great deal of reading and research projects involving English-language publications and documents. But a critical mass (small, but vital) of translations from English and other Hebrew-language publications now exists so that undergraduate students struggling with their unusually large course-load can be offered the relief of doing at least some reading in their native tongue. More to the point, among graduate students I have been fortunate in mentoring several whose linguistic palette not only included Hebrew and English, but also Yiddish, Spanish, or German. This linguistic dexterity, it seems to me, will increasingly be a prerequisite for future specialization in our field.

What the Future May Hold

It would not be an exaggeration to say that the most popular questions that I am asked about American Jewry have to do with its future—not its past. That is disconcerting for a historian, who is trained not to attempt too many prognoses (which are more properly the realm of the medical profession and some of the social sciences). Yet, I don't believe this exists only in Israel. On the contrary, I have found that sketching out a trajectory for the future existence of the Jews in the United States constitutes a barely concealed subtext in most writing about U. S. Jewish history, which takes place of course in America.

As far as I can make out, there are a number of different perceptions currently prevailing in Israeli public discourse in relation to American Jewry. One of these avenues of discussion at least asks some of the right questions: Do Israeli and American Jews understand one another? Is there a strong sense of mutual commitment? Is Israel as a Jewish society even conceivable without the heft that a long Diaspora heritage brings to bear on a relatively new national culture? How do we know what "they" are thinking about "us"? Are the electoral politics of American Jews and that of Israeli Jews distinctly out of accord with each other? These are the questions that I like to get from students and colleagues, and when I teach or lecture on the subject, I invariably end up addressing them.

Unfortunately, I think that these "right questions" are raised less frequently than ought to be the case. Parallel to these are some other questions, which also pop up. Are American Jews disappearing? Is antisemitism going to lead American Jews in large numbers to make *aliya*, like the French Jews are doing? Aren't Jews in America plagued with guilt feelings over the Holocaust?

I like to think that, over time, my colleagues and I will eventually reinforce the Israelis' curiosity about American Jewish history and culture in such a way as to put the worst of the clichés onto the back burner. It will take a while longer, though. In the meantime, I consider my choice to teach this subject in Israel to be a modest but positive step toward such a desirable outcome.

Notes

1   I could name, for example, Gil Ribak, and Tobias Brinkmann, author of numerous studies on Jews and German culture in nineteenth-century America.

2   See, for instance, remarks on Davis's pioneering activity in this field and contributions by some of his colleagues in *America and Zion: Essays and Papers in Memory of Moshe Davis*, edited by Eli Lederhendler and Jonathan D. Sarna (Detroit: Wayne State University Press, 2002).

3   Some "exceptions," for example, are Uzi Rebhun, a sociologist and demographer and a colleague of mine at the Hebrew University's Institute of Contemporary Jewry, whose interests lie mainly in the sphere of social identities; Gur Alroey of Haifa University, who is an alumnus of the Institute, who writes on Jewish migration history and on other non-Zionist themes related to U. S. Jewish history; and Hagit Cohen, of the Open University of Israel, a graduate of Bar-Ilan University, whose dissertation on Yiddish publishing in the social world of East European Jewish immigrants in America recently appeared in book form

4   Eli Lederhendler, *American Jewry: A New History* (New York and Cambridge: Cambridge University Press, 2017).

5   Eli Lederhendler, *New York Jews and the Decline of Urban Ethnicity, 1950-1970* (Syracuse: Syracuse University Press, 2001); idem, *Jewish Immigrants and American Capitalism, 1880-1920: From Caste to Class* (Cambridge and New York: Cambridge University Press, 2009).

6   The communist-oriented *Arbeter Orden* should not be confused with the *Arbeter Ring*, a socialist Jewish fraternal organization, known in English as the Workmen's Circle, which once had a mass membership and took up staunchly anti-Stalinist, social-democratic positions.

Sidewalk Histories,
or Uncovering the Vernacular Jewishness
of New York City

Deborah Dash Moore

In third grade, our class took a memorable field trip to do stone rubbings. I attended Downtown Community School (DCS), a parent-teacher-cooperative. A progressive and integrated elementary school, DCS typically linked art projects with social studies, in this case, the required local history curriculum on New York City. However, instead of taking our gear across the street into the cemetery of St. Marks on the Bowery where we might have done classic rubbings of early American gravestones, we walked around the school neighborhood staring at the sidewalks. When we found a manhole cover, we stopped, pulled out the paper and charcoal, and made a rubbing. How many different metal covers adorned the streets of lower Manhattan! I think we rubbed well over a dozen patterns. Each one, we learned, had been placed by a corporation and represented some type of utility underneath the city's streets. Gas, electric, water, sewage, and telephone were most popular, but we also found old covers from defunct companies—an education in 19th century urban history.[1]

Manhole covers and their lessons stuck with me. Even as I acquired a steadfast commitment to studying the city, I remain fascinated with their often-elegant designs and emblematic stories. The covers also hint at some aspects of American Jewish history, especially the ease of overlooking what is in plain sight, a willingness to take much that is unexamined for granted, and the rewards of careful excavation of mundane historical features.

I learned secrets of New York City in third grade just by examining manhole covers. So, too, did I come to realize that any effort to study American Jewish history required a similar sensitivity to appealing facades that merged seamlessly with their surroundings. Such is the power of acculturation. It naturalizes ethnic Jewish distinctiveness, seeming to reduce it to symbolic dimensions that appear on occasion as the calendar and life cycle demand.[2] Yet the reality is far more complex. There exist visible clues, like manhole covers. They suggest that what is needed is curiosity and a measure of stubbornness to explore off the beaten path.

I didn't start examining Jews with any measure of historical consciousness until high school, but I did regularly take the measure of New York as I traveled its streets. These observations implicitly linked the Jewish world of my family and childhood with New York's urban milieu. As my passion for history blossomed, so did my love for my rather Jewish city. In those postwar years New York's Jewish population still hovered around two million, a population then roughly equal to Israel's. Jews made up around 25% of the city's residents.[3] "As no other city is," a 1960 *Fortune Magazine* article put it, "New York is their home: here a Jew can be what he [sic] wants to be."[4] In short, I lived as close as possible to the center of Jewish life outside Israel.

My New York City meant Manhattan; my Manhattan meant Greenwich Village. In those days, "the city" referred only to New York, the biggest and baddest city of all, the one I grew up in, the one my parents had grown up in, the one three of my grandparents had known as children (my other grandmother grew up in New Haven). I called my neighborhood "The Village" even though I lived on the northeast corner of 16th Street and 7th Avenue, two blocks north of Greenwich Village's boundary. (My actual neighborhood, Chelsea, had no caché then.) It was a treeless world of concrete sidewalks where we played games, rode our bikes, roller-skated, jumped rope, and bounced balls. In fact, I can remember when the city planted trees on our block. I thought these skinny trees were laughable, totally inappropriate for a middle-class block. (Nowadays, when I walk the block, I marvel at how strong these 60-year-old trees are.) The urbanism of my childhood neighborhood also manifested itself in its mixed class and ethnic character. I lived in one of three middle-class twenty-story apartment buildings that dominated the corners of the intersection. Lower-middle class six-story apartments lined my block of 16th Street, surrounding a small French church that abutted the Hebrew Arts School. To the west, working-class four-story tenements housed a Catholic mix of Irish, Puerto Ricans, and Italians. The neighborhood also contained a fairly standard urban combination of industry and commerce along 7th Avenue: factories, offices, and bars, as well as candy stores, drug stores, newsstands, and a grocery. Barney's, a discount men's clothing store in those days, occupied the largest commercial space in my building.

My points on the compass also measured my father and grandfather's place of work. The family printing business, a typically Jewish industry in New York, initially stood on Greene Street in a dark building with creaking wooden stairs, then across 7th Avenue in a modern factory building on 17th Street with an elevator, later on 19th Street and 6th Avenue in what had once been an elegant department store before World War I. As children, we could gaze out our living room window into my grandfather's office that fronted 7th Avenue. Subsequently I learned that the Jewish builder who constructed our building in 1930-1931—and then lost his shirt in the Depression—intended the apartments for people working nearby. The printing industry, one of the city's largest, extended up 7th Avenue from Canal Street to 23rd Street. My parents could not have located a better apartment.

The spine of my urban knowledge stretched along 14th Street, which I traveled daily on my way to elementary school. A major crosstown artery, 14th Street contained many clothing, fabric, and hardware stores, Salvation Army headquarters and union locals, an occasional restaurant (Luchow's near Union Square), a huge Con Edison building (across from Luchow's), Klein's (a discount department store bordering Union Square), and pawnshops. These features I noticed; others passed me by. I regularly walked along 2nd Avenue across from the Café Royale, a popular Yiddish theater hangout, and ignored it—only later realizing that it was once a landmark of the Yiddish intelligentsia. Although I saw plays in what had been Maurice Schwartz's Yiddish Art Theater on the corner of 12th Street and 2nd Avenue, they were all in English. (I remember a particularly funny show, "Once Upon a Mattress," with Carol Burnett.) Aside from the dairy restaurant Ratner's further south on 2nd Avenue and the Second Avenue Deli on the corner of 10th Street, I remained oblivious to much of the area's character as a Yiddish theater center. Instead, I gravitated to Washington Square Park, initially for its playgrounds and later for its folk music, fountain, and for the coffee houses south of the square.

If I paid no attention to the lingering Yiddish theater scene, I did recognize Jewish urban religious and ethnic culture. I saw it in my neighborhood and as it flourished on the Upper West Side. I understood from my brief attendance at Hebrew school in a small, orthodox congregation on Charles Street in the Village and from classes in music and Yemenite dance at the Hebrew Arts School up the block that Jews were part of the city's religious and ethnic milieu. As were Catholics. St. Francis Xavier church and parochial school dominated a section of 16th Street east of 6th Avenue; I never failed to notice it (though I never entered) when I walked by to visit girlfriends who lived on the block. And I recognized, albeit dimly, the radical Jewish heritage of organizations clustered around Union Square, a few more blocks to the east. I also took in the rich, visible Jewish ethnic and religious culture on the Upper West Side. For Jewish holidays our family attended the Society for the Advancement of Judaism (SAJ) on West 86th Street, joining my maternal grandparents, who were supporters of Rabbi Mordecai M. Kaplan and Reconstructionism. After services, which often included sermons by Rabbi Kaplan that I struggled to understand, we occasionally went to Steinberg's dairy restaurant on Broadway, or the Tip Toe Inn at the corner of 86th Street. I did not fail to observe the many kosher bakeries, butcher shops, and small stores along Broadway. Occasional trips down to Orchard Street to buy yarn for hooked rugs added the Lower East Side to my urban Jewish geography.

Years of Hebrew school at the SAJ, including study for my Bat Mitzvah with Cantor Moshe Nathanson, followed by additional years of Hebrew high school, introduced me not only to Jewish religious life but also stimulated my intellectual interest in studying

Jews. Neither urban nor Jewish history appeared on the public high school curriculum at Music & Art [M&A], but Hebrew high school, a cooperative project supported by the SAJ, Park Avenue Synagogue, and B'nai Jeshurun, encouraged me to study both. The Jewish labor movement—an urban subject if ever there was one—formed the topic of my first serious research paper, which I wrote for Paul Ritterband, the head of the school and at the beginning of his illustrious career as a sociologist of American Jews. Ritterband had recruited a cadre of young scholars who were pursuing doctorates, many of them rabbis like himself, to teach us teenagers. Most went on to academic careers as universities gradually expanded to include Jewish studies. Some immigrated to Israel. Hebrew high school gave me the opportunity to fuse the histories of New York and American Jews, presaging my growing passions for both, and for their moral dimensions, especially struggles to provide decent living conditions for workingmen and women.

As a teenager, I never questioned my life's particular urban ethnic synthesis or the association of aspects of my identity with different institutions. I absorbed the textured dimensions of New York culture, noting how varieties of Jewishness appeared in public and private. In this way I learned urban history together with Jewish history. By then I regularly traveled the length of Manhattan up to 137th Street and Broadway. I studied modern dance at Martha Graham's school on 61st Street by the East River and Israeli dance with Fred Berk at the 92nd Street Y; I learned French at M&A and Hebrew at Hebrew high school (though I could have studied Hebrew at M&A as well); I lived downtown at the edge of the Village and attended high school uptown on the border of Harlem. Urban New York vernacular Jewishness could be found throughout the city as my travels around town for my studies and various extra-curricular activities demonstrated. At M&A many of my teachers (including a social studies teacher I developed a crush on) were Jewish, an unremarked upon identity. When I encountered strangers, they occasionally took my combination of blue eyes and pug nose for Irish. Such mistakes amused me even though I usually sized up the city's residents according to a similar ethnic calculus. The notion that we were all "white," as historians later taught, would have seemed irrelevant at the time. We were all different New Yorkers; we all picked up ethnic cues. The color line mattered on the subways and sidewalks but neither in M&A nor DCS, both integrated schools.

I left the city for college. Brandeis University seemed to me to be almost rural. It had lots of trees, a couple of ponds, and winding paths from the dormitories to the classrooms. To reach the city of Boston required a train ride. Yet like New York, Brandeis allowed for uninhibited public expressions of Jewishness. One evening during freshman orientation, a large group of us formed circles for Israeli dances outside in the quad. I found it exhilarating. Brandeis closed for the Jewish holidays, not just the High Holidays of Rosh Hashanah and Yom Kippur as the New York City public schools did, but also the holidays of Sukkot and Shemini Atzeret.[5] At Brandeis, I realized with pleasure, I could (and did) study French and Hebrew, and do both modern and Israeli dance.

Yet while Jewish studies and American history figured during my college years, they remained distinct as they had in high school. At Brandeis I gravitated to African American history (then called Negro history). Black history appealed to me. So did urban history. Both seemed to resemble my inchoate version of American Jewish history. They provided acceptable ways to explore moral questions stemming from exploitation that I had dealt with in my paper on the Jewish labor movement in New York. My experiences at M&A and DCS heightened my consciousness of black history. (I did a research project in 6th grade on Frederick Douglass. My parents had never heard of him. They thought I had been assigned Stephen Douglas.) My friendships crossed the color line and my politics impelled me to boycott Woolworth's. Although not very active in civil rights protests, I felt a deep commitment to integration and considered myself a liberal. I did a senior honors thesis, under David Hackett Fischer's supervision, on two cities during Reconstruction—Baltimore and St. Louis—paying attention to implications of their border status and the roles of free blacks. When I returned to New York as a graduate student at Columbia University, I intended to focus on black history during the era of Reconstruction, when freed slaves possessed more agency. I did manage to complete an MA thesis on Robert Smalls, a black politician from South Carolina. I even got my first job teaching African American history.

Then politics intervened. 1970 was a year of upheaval on college campuses. Students wanted the History department to hire an African American at Montclair State College, where I was teaching. My political sympathies lay with the students and their identity politics.[6] So I switched my teaching to American history, including a course on the Civil War and Reconstruction. But the experience spurred me to reflect on my identity as a Jew, a woman, a New Yorker. Simultaneously, the feminist movement was raising my consciousness, making me aware of how all my professors had been men. My cohort of graduate students in history at Columbia was 25% female, an enormous leap from previous years. Still, bias and discrimination endured, along with negative assumptions about how serious a female graduate student could be (especially a married one). As a pregnant married graduate student, I testified at hearings held at Columbia on discrimination against female students.

My experience of losing the opportunity to teach black history after only one semester prompted me to reconsider my graduate studies. Perhaps it would make sense to turn to one of my enduring intellectual interests. I had always loved studying Jews and identified Jewishness with scholarly rigor and intellectual excitement, as well as moral consciousness. My courses in Hebrew high school with such teachers as Paul Ritterband and the gifted historian Yosef Yerushalmi (when he was a graduate student) had been immensely rewarding. How Ritterband recruited such stellar graduate students remains a mystery. I assume that they needed the money in the years before full funding packages for doctoral students had become the norm. (I also taught Sunday school in New Jersey, together with Samuel Heilman.) Indeed, the Hebrew high school's faculty roster belied its modest position as a supplementary form of Jewish education, meeting only twice a week. We were taught as though we were college students, with substantial reading lists and vigorous discussion. At Columbia, I had already met Gerson D. Cohen, the senior Jewish historian. In an intimidating interview that included an impromptu Hebrew reading and translation test, Cohen nonetheless encouraged me to study American Jewish history. I suspect that his wife's career as a widely respected American Jewish historian facilitated his response to my inquiry. Now I contemplated switching fields, making my minor the major, melding American history with Jewish history. I did not realize at the time that I was embarking on a project that would take decades: American Jewish history as a field didn't exist. Yet the more I studied its components, the more determined I became to give it legitimacy. Just as African American history and Women's history acquired acceptance, so, too, could American Jewish history.

Only one book on American Jews ever crossed over into my history courses: Moses Rischin's *The Promised City*.[7] John A. Garraty assigned it as reading in his seminar on the Gilded Age. Rischin examined New York Jews from 1870 to 1914. He linked the history of Jewish immigrants with that of the city. My favorite part of the book—chapter five—presents his incredibly rich excavation of diverse residential patterns and quotidian life on the Lower East Side. It remains a fecund source of historical insight to this day. The diagrams of dumbbell tenements and maps of Jewish ethnic concentration within the east side opened my eyes to other dimensions of urban Jewish history. Rischin later explained that he had been influenced by the Annales school, trying to integrate their insights and methodology.[8] I had not read those studies, but *The Promised City* spoke to me as an exciting way to approach American Jewish history.

Before I settled on a dissertation topic, David J. Rothman gave me a dissertation to read that had just won the Bancroft prize: Arthur A. Goren's study of the New York Kehillah, subsequently published as *New York Jews and the Quest for Community*.[9] Goren picked up the story of New York City Jews in 1908 and carried it through World War I. He used communal organization as a framework to examine topics that had never been studied, such as Jewish criminal activity. Although he focused less than Rischin on neighborhood ecology, he elucidated dimensions of communal culture that tested possibilities for urban democratic community, a concern shared with Rischin. Invaluable pioneering models, both books pointed to New York

Jews as a worthy historical subject and the interwar years as a rich period.

So I decided to follow the eminent footsteps of Rischin and Goren. In truth, I entered virgin territory. Both had studied immigrants in the city, but in shifting my gaze to the period that saw the triumph of immigration restriction, I gravitated to the study of second generation Jews, the children of immigrants. I conceptualized this American Jewish story as an integral part of urban and social history, my first gesture toward establishing it as a separate field. Historians had ignored the second generation; sociologists had dismissed it as a conflicted, weak cohort eager to escape immigrant neighborhoods and forget its foreign past *en route* to becoming American. Historian Marcus Lee Hansen posited that only the third generation wanted to remember; sociologist Will Herberg popularized Hansen's "law" in his book, *Protestant Catholic Jew*.[10] The second generation lacked credibility and status, especially in the eyes of such second-generation writers as Nathan Glazer. Perhaps one of the reasons he reprinted Hansen's essay in *Commentary* magazine was to assuage worried American Jews.[11] I intended to study not the storied, rich immigrant "ghetto," but what sociologist Louis Wirth called "areas of second settlement," neighborhoods that many didn't perceive as particularly Jewish.[12] Had I not been a New York Jew myself, I probably would have accepted the conclusions of Wirth and other sociologists at face value. But I knew that my grandparents had lived in a Jewish world in Brooklyn—the world my parents had grown up in. Thus I had other authorities to whom I could turn. They were second generation Jews raising a third generation. What had been their experiences?

Of course, I didn't start there. As a good social historian, I started with numbers, specifically the 1925 New York State census. After poring over manuscript census returns I discovered what a host of Jewish neighborhood surveys had also demonstrated: Jews tended to congregate in certain sections of Brooklyn and the Bronx, as well as parts of upper Manhattan. This concentration posed linked questions: how and why did Jews go to these neighborhoods? The most straightforward answer came from urban historians who studied transportation networks and their role in dispersing populations. Sam Bass Warner Jr.'s *Streetcar Suburbs* helped me to account for the "how."[13] But why did Jews choose some neighborhoods and not others? Certainly residential discrimination prevented Jews from renting in various sections of the city. Neither Warner, nor Wirth's theories of urban migration helped much. So I turned to my family, specifically my mother's mother.

Bella Lasker Golden had grown up in Brownsville, Brooklyn, and lived there as a young married woman until her husband's printing business began to prosper. Then she moved to other neighborhoods in Brooklyn, especially Flatbush, and continued to move as the business struggled during the Depression. A final move in 1939 brought her to Emery Roth's elegant art moderne apartment building, The Normandy, located between 86th and 87th streets on Manhattan's Riverside Drive. Several brothers stayed in Brooklyn. One day she asked her older brother, Morris, who lived in Sea Gate by Coney Island, to drive the two of us around the borough. I sat in the back seat as she pointed out tenements, apartment buildings, private houses, synagogues, and community centers—the urban streetscape of Brooklyn Jewish life in all its diversity. And when I asked her why she picked one neighborhood and not another as she moved, she described informal Jewish networks that linked those who were seeking a place to live with those who were building the homes. She also introduced me to some of these builders. As I sat at their kitchen tables, they explained how they switched from manufacturing buttons or blouses to building apartments. I learned from them the ethnic calculus of the city's construction industry and how they assembled the pieces required for building an apartment house, from finance to designs, from scheduling contractors to ordering supplies. Then I located books, articles, and newspapers that provided lively prose accounts.[14]

In focusing on Jewish neighborhoods in Brooklyn and the Bronx, I drew upon Rischin's initial insights into the physical world of the Lower East Side. Instead of dumbbell tenements, I described art deco apartment buildings (and included a blueprint of a typical apartment building layout).[15] Instead of immigrant ethnic groups,

I mapped political and religious networks. The neighborhood emerged as the heart of my story, the place where Jewish and American features could get shuffled, merged, and sorted out, the space where Jews could leave their stamp upon the city. Later I argued that through their modern apartment houses on tree-lined streets these areas articulated a Jewish urban vision.[16] I knew from experience how parochial a neighborhood could be, even in the most cosmopolitan of cities. I knew, too, how one could cross invisible boundaries created by ethnic groups. I had learned to walk on the east side of 7th Avenue and not the west to gain a bit of distance from the bars, and I also regularly took a more circuitous route to the public library on 13th Street to avoid passing the technical high school on the block where the teenaged boys hung out. I had local knowledge.

Once I realized that I could talk to people and not rely exclusively on numbers and written sources, I started to conduct more interviews. Oral history was developing as a relatively new field in the 1970s. Herbert Gutman had initiated an oral history project with retired union garment workers, but most formal oral history projects targeted famous or influential people. I read a number of interviews, including one with Herbert Lehman, the Democratic Jewish governor of New York (1933-42). However, I soon realized that if I wanted to learn about Jewish State Assemblymen or local political figures, beyond what was reported in the press, then I had to speak to them or to sons who followed in their father's footsteps. Judge Nathan Sobel granted me an interview. Walking across Court Street to one of his favorite Brooklyn restaurants, we attracted looks—older man and younger mini-skirted graduate student— and a few good-natured comments. Sobel told me about the first time he tasted clam chowder and about the intricacies of running for office, even about choosing which synagogue to join. Stanley Steingut, State Assemblyman from Brooklyn (1953-78) received me in his office. Just seeing the long wooden table with him sitting at its head taught me something about expressions of political influence.

Political figures, public school teachers, and builders, responded not only to my questions but also to their own agendas. Most New York Jews knew why they moved where they did, why they took the jobs they worked at, why they pursued their politics, why they joined or refused to join a Jewish organization. My interpretations often failed to match their own understanding of their lives as New Yorkers. To start with, they thought of themselves as first generation Americans. The Jewish American story began with them, not their immigrant parents. They spun narratives of assimilation, whereas I emphasized enduring Jewishness. Some of what they perceived as American, I described as Jewish. And my account occasionally seemed to slight their achievements, though I had not intended it.

By the time I finished my dissertation, called "The Persistence of Ethnicity," a title that reflected my explicit argument with social scientists, I discovered that I had entered a field that barely existed. I couldn't follow Rischin, who held an appointment at San Francisco State University as an American historian.[17] Nor could I follow Goren, who held an appointment at the Hebrew University in American studies.[18] As scholars of Jewish immigration, both were recognized as American historians, but both had traveled a significant distance from New York. In Jerusalem and San Francisco, New York City was hardly familiar territory. I, on the other hand, intended to forge a path as an American Jewish historian, despite the field's newness and some Jewish historians' profound reluctance even to consider American Jews worthy of historical attention. Compared with the many centuries of Jewish history in Europe, North Africa, and the Middle East, the brief American Jewish past warranted good journalism, they claimed, not scholarly study. To make matters worse, most second generation American Jews didn't speak or read Yiddish (though many understood it), so their Jewishness appeared even more superficial than that of their immigrant parents.

In the 1970s, social history, urban history, oral history, black history, and women's history, were reconfiguring historical studies of the United States. As a young female graduate student, I participated in these movements to rethink American history. For several years I posted in my office a cartoon by Jules Feiffer portraying a befuddled hard-hatted man. First he describes the American history he learned as a child; then he describes what his son is learning. His conclusion: they're teaching his son some other country's history. I decided upon graduation to define myself as an American Jewish historian. When I agreed to start teaching the subject to graduate students at the Max Weinreich Center for Advanced Jewish Studies at the YIVO Institute for Jewish Research, I entered another intellectual world with deep roots in Eastern Europe and Yiddish culture. My association with the YIVO widened my perspectives on social science research and introduced me to new ways of studying Jews. YIVO had pioneered in the use of autobiography by young men and women in order to elicit narratives of self-transformation as well as detailed descriptions of everyday life.[19]

The path from "The Persistence of Ethnicity" (1975) to *At Home in America: Second Generation New York Jews, 1920-1940* (1981) involved several additional way stations that modified my understanding of New York Jews. Most importantly, I accepted a position in the Religion Department of Vassar College. It was an odd turn of events. Vassar had been my mother's dream school, the one that didn't admit her, due to quotas on Jewish students from Brooklyn. Furthermore, neither Vassar nor religious studies had been on my radar. I thought of myself as an American Jewish historian and assumed I would continue to live in New York City. Vassar, located seventy miles north of New York City on the Hudson River in Poughkeepsie, appeared even more rural than Brandeis, though like Brandeis, regular train service connected it to a major city. (I would become familiar with the vagaries of train travel when we moved to Poughkeepsie in 1976.) Indeed, hiring me involved something of a leap of faith for my colleagues in the Religion Department. During my campus visit, as I strolled in Vassar's Shakespeare Garden with a future colleague, a scholar and Christian minister, he asked if I would be happy as a historian in a religion department. I answered as a good New York Jew with my own question. Would he be happy with a historian in a religion department? Both answers turned out to be affirmative. I entered the department as its first female faculty member.

The position at Vassar took me by surprise. It introduced me to another newly emerging field: religious studies. I had studied the history of Protestantism in the United States (especially in the eighteenth and nineteenth centuries) as part of my doctoral studies. I considered Judaism integral to New York Jewish history. Influenced by Goren's emphasis on community, I devoted two chapters of my dissertation to Jewish religious life; both looked at implications of institutional innovation. One chapter explored the rise of Yeshiva University during the 1920s and another charted the creation of synagogue centers. I paid attention to religion because it was integral to the history of New York Jews. But my department colleagues at Vassar initiated me into new ways of thinking as a religious studies scholar. After my first department meeting, I immediately bought a pocket-sized dictionary of religious terms so that I could look up such words as phenomenology and ontology. By contrast, I struggled to win recognition from Vassar's history department as an American Jewish historian.

In 1978 I received a fellowship to attend a yearlong seminar in Santa Barbara, California with Walter H. Capps on the formation of religious studies as a discipline. This provided a timely introduction to the emerging field of religious studies, now being untethered from divinity schools and theology. The National Endowment for the Humanities [NEH] seminar targeted faculty members like me who were teaching in religious studies departments but had no training in the field and little comprehension of its intellectual pedigree. I was invited to enter another new arena of scholarship and contribute to its creative growth.[20] At the same time, I obtained a grant for YIVO to organize a conference on "Culture and Community among New York Jews." The conference aimed to demonstrate the potential of studying Jews in New York. I hoped to encourage YIVO to enlarge its focus from Eastern Europe to encompass the United States, especially New York City. The NEH-supported conference mobilized an amazing assortment of academics and activists, men and women who were creating New York Jewish culture and community as well as studying it. Significantly, NEH funded both seminar and conference. Both hinted at transformations to come and pointed to the importance of Federal initiatives in broadening academic discourse on religion and ethnicity in the 1970s. American Jewish history and New York Jews belonged in this mix.

When *At Home in America* appeared as the first volume of a new series on urban history in New York City, under the editorial direction of Kenneth Jackson, it seemed as if I had achieved my goal of synthesizing Jewish and American urban history. Jackson had encouraged me to publish in his Columbia History of Urban Life series because he felt that urban historians had not paid enough attention to New York, one of the world's great cities. Jackson's passion came at a particularly low point in the city's modern history. Teetering on the verge of bankruptcy, hemorrhaging population to the suburbs, plagued by wholesale abandonment of housing stock (especially in the Bronx, much of it built and owned by Jews), and rattled by a crack epidemic and dramatic rise in crime, the city looked as if it were heading for disaster. While a new publishing venture could hardly rescue New York, it could help contemporaries understand its past, both its mistakes and accomplishments. The series continues to publish impressive studies, many of them path breaking, and to influence urban history by documenting and analyzing the importance New York.[21] Jackson's prediction that my book would remain in print for many years proved true.

Yet synthesis eluded me for more than decade. In 1995 I spoke as a Professor of Religion and Director of Vassar's American Culture Program at a session on "Regional History as National History" at a conference organized by Rischin under the auspices of the American Jewish Historical Society [AJHS]. My official titles implicitly acknowledged the recognition I had received as an American Jewish historian in religious studies and American studies. Jewish studies was another matter. In opening the conference, Rischin described himself as a New York Jew displaced to San Francisco, "an inner émigré of sorts." He intended the unprecedented conference, the first time in over a century the AJHS had ever met in San Francisco, "to celebrate the coming-of-age of a new Western Jewish historical consciousness," and a transfer of people and intellectual creativity to California.[22] My recently published book, *To the Golden Cities,* had documented an aspect this transformation with respect to Los Angeles during the postwar decades.[23]

In his invitation, Rischin asked me to reflect upon the renaissance of Jewish studies from my own "personal, academic, intellectual and cultural history." From my vantage point, there was much work to be done. Coming to Vassar as the only visible Jew on campus had plunged me into an extended series of small battles. The history department refused to cross-list my courses; I had to prepare a bibliography on the Holocaust for the German historian to convince him that there were enough sources available for him to teach the Holocaust as part of the history of World War II; the staff at the bookstore consistently called me Judith Goldstein, an anthropology professor who arrived the same year I did, because she had the appropriately "Jewish" name and I did not.[24] My education in New York, at Brandeis, and then at Columbia had convinced me that Jewish and American urban histories intertwined. Vassar revealed a very different academic world. Unlike Brandeis, Vassar scheduled final exams on Saturdays until some activist students agitated to eliminate it. Even my efforts to get the YIVO interested in New York City had failed.

My paper mentioned barriers to acceptance still faced by American Jewish historians—especially from Jewish historians. "Why," I asked, is American Jewish history "still a step-child of Jewish history and not, at least in this country, one of its cornerstones?" When I remarked that only one chair existed in American Jewish history in a non-Jewish university in the United States, my audience gasped. Later several men and women questioned me. They were surprised. I acknowledged only two areas where American Jews were studied as legitimate subjects of American and of Jewish history: as immigrants and in relation to the Holocaust. I concluded: "our own history is waiting for us to claim it and give it a place in our best universities so Americans can learn it, share it, wrestle with it."[25]

My current position as Frederick G. L. Huetwell Professor of History and Judaic Studies at the University of Michigan, one of those "best universities" where I imagined teaching American Jewish history, undoubtedly influences how I interpret the past. What seemed frustratingly impossible in 1995 has actually been achieved. American Jewish history is a field with several chairs, senior and junior professors, not to mention graduate students. The opposition of Jewish historians has faded. Some American historians ignore the field and others encourage American Jewish historians to devote less attention to communal issues and more to questions that animate scholars of American history.[26] I consider the transformation remarkable.[27]

At Home in America provoked diverse responses from scholars.[28] Some rejected my claims for the centrality of New York Jews in the United States. They did not find persuasive the idea that New Yorkers set a pattern recognized by other American Jews, what the critic Robert Warshow called "the master pattern."[29] New York Jews made up 40% of the total American Jewish population and formed a critical mass in the largest Jewish city in history. How could these Jews not exert exceptional influence on other American Jews? I told a compelling history in *At Home in America*, but some argued that it described only a particular, not a representative, group. Other scholars objected to "generation" as an organizing concept for a cohort. They noted, correctly, that large numbers of Jewish immigrants began arriving in the 1880s and 90s and that a second generation emerged in the early twentieth century as well. Still others challenged my upbeat tone, my unwillingness to place anti-Semitism front and center. They questioned my optimism.[30] What I characterized as being "at home in America," Jonathan Sarna called "a parallel universe that shared many of the trappings of the larger society."[31] Not attuned to New York's rambunctious urbanism, he failed to recognize how the city was composed of multiple, intertwined ethnic worlds that together created a larger whole. Like most New Yorkers, second generation Jews found their paths into the city through their neighborhoods. Eli Lederhendler contended that the second generation's achievements collapsed after World War II under the twin impact of suburbanization and a growing African American population in the city.[32]

These critiques came later. After *At Home* appeared, it managed to cross over into courses on American urban history, following in the footsteps of *The Promised City*. It has occupied an important place in the still emerging field of American Jewish history. Reviewed widely by sociologists as well as historians, the book also attracted attention in the Jewish press. More recently, its influence registered in an impressive range of articles reconsidering the book on the 35th anniversary of its publication.[33] Its title, *At Home in America,* articulated a powerful thesis that has had sturdy legs, even when historians questioned it.[34] My title responded to Irving Howe's last chapter query, "At Ease in America?" in his history of Eastern European Jewish immigrants in New York, *World of Our Fathers.*[35] It asserted the integrated, vernacular Jewishness of New York Jews, a perspective informed not only by my understanding of New York Jews' experiences in the interwar years but also by my perceptions growing up as a Jewish city girl.

One review of *At Home* recognized its intimate dimensions. Writing in *Commentary* magazine, David Singer bemoaned the "fair number of statistical tables," but he also remarked, "these are more than made up for by the abundant photographs, some of them charmingly amateurish, that dot the volume."[36] Photographs were a rarity in works of scholarship in 1981. Although he did not explicitly comment that I had used a number of family pictures, his characterization of them as "charmingly amateurish" referred to their snapshot reality. When it came time to choose illustrations, I raided my family's albums. The cover photograph features my grandparents as a young married couple in the back yard of their Brownsville home. Behind them are flowering bushes and in the background, a six-story tenement looms. They pose for the camera; my grandfather, standing behind my grandmother, leans over his wife's shoulder. Both are well dressed in stylish clothes. My grandmother wears a white dress that she sewed; my grandfather wears a suit, white collar, and elegant tie. Two of my grandmother's brothers, her oldest brother Morris and her youngest brother Teddy, stand next to them. Morris, a big grin on his face, is dressed casually, his shirtsleeves rolled up. Teddy wears a sleeveless undershirt, a sign of his youth; a large cap shades his eyes. When the photo was taken, Morris was living with my grandparents, although I never determined whether he paid board.

The photo conveyed to me important aspects of *At Home.* It pictured a Jewish home in Brownsville (I included an interior shot in the book). To the extent that one could glean emotion from a snapshot, it portrayed what these Jews felt about living in their predominantly Jewish working-class neighborhood after World

War I. The photo had been sufficiently important to be placed in an album. As my book cover, it also hinted at insights I had gathered from family who lived as New York Jews. Finally, the photo was a gesture of my gratitude to my family members for introducing me to their world. (Teddy always appreciated that he had appeared on the cover of a book. Many years later at my younger son's bar mitzvah, he still talked about it.)

In some ways, the photographs constituted my version of manhole cover rubbings. I delighted in placing them in plain sight, properly titled and credited. They were visible markers of an infrastructure undergirding the book. My family infrastructure sustained my research, stimulated intellectual questions, and guided my commitments to become an American Jewish historian. In a third grade history lesson on New York's sidewalks, I first learned how to pay attention to ordinary dimensions of the urban world. Those lessons accompanied me on many trips around Brooklyn and the Bronx. They helped me recognize expressions of vernacular Jewishness throughout the city and encouraged me to look for critical ethnic relationships that guide and fuel the life of a city.

Notes

1 As Mimi Melnick writes, "Water, Power, Sewer, Gas, Telephone, Steam: each cover has a story to tell," in Mimi Melnick, *Manhole Covers* (Cambridge, MA: MIT Press, 1994), 1.

2 The sociologist Herbert Gans calls this "symbolic ethnicity." Herbert Gans, "Symbolic Ethnicity: The Future of Ethnic Groups and Cultures in America," *Ethnic and Racial Studies* 2:1 (January 1979): 1-20.

3 Ira Rosenwaike, *Population History of New York City* (Syracuse: Syracuse University Press, 1972), 98, 101.

4 Sam Welles, "The Jewish Elan," *Fortune Magazine* (February 1960): 134.

5 The public school system only closed for the Jewish High Holidays starting in 1960, but I didn't realize it then since I took off for holidays. Eli Lederhendler, *New York City and the Decline of Urban Ethnicity* (Syracuse: Syracuse University Press, 2001), 55.

6 Ironically, student protests led to hiring an African scholar, someone who had little understanding of what it meant to grow up in the racist United States.

7 Moses Rischin, *The Promised City: New York's Jews, 1870-1914* (Cambridge, MA: Harvard University Press, 1962).

8 This followed my discussion of that chapter, see Deborah Dash Moore, "The Ideal Slum," *American Jewish History* 73:2 (December 1983): 134-141, in this issue of *American Jewish History* devoted to Rischin's pioneering book.

9 Arthur A. Goren, *New York Jews and the Quest for Community: The Kehillah Experiment, 1908-1922* (New York: Columbia University Press, 1970).

10 Will Herberg, *Protestant Catholic Jew: An Essay in American Religious Sociology* (Garden City, NY: Doubleday, 1956).

11 Nathan Glazer, "Hansen's Hypothesis and the Historical Experience of Generations," in *American Immigrants and Their Generations*, ed. Peter Kvisto and Dag Blanck (Urbana, IL: University of Illinois Press, 1990), 170. "The reprinting of Hansen's essay in 1952 was occasioned by the concern of a second generation Jew (and a journal edited by second generation Jews) about the coming third generation," Glazer explained.

12 Louis Wirth, *The Ghetto* (Chicago: University of Chicago Press, 1928), 247-261.

13 Sam Bass Warner, *Streetcar Suburbs: The Process of Growth in Boston, 1870-1900* (Cambridge, MA: Harvard University Press, 1962).

14 For example, Leon Wexelstein, *Building Up Greater Brooklyn with Sketches of Men Instrumental in Brooklyn's Amazing Development* (New York: Brooklyn Biographical Society, 1925).

15 Deborah Dash Moore, *At Home in America: Second Generation New York Jews 1920-1940* (New York: Columbia University Press, 1981), 37.

16 Deborah Dash Moore, "The Urban Vision of East European Jewish Immigrants to New York," *Proceedings of the Eighth World Congress of Jewish Studies, Panel Sessions: Jewish History* (Jerusalem, 1984): 31-38.

17 Rischin had not anticipated where his career would lead. See Moses Rischin, "Jewish Studies in Northern California: A Symposium," *Judaism* 44:4 (Fall 1995): 417-419.

18 Arthur Aryeh Goren, "Epilogue: On Living in Two Cultures," *Divergent Jewish Cultures: Israel and America*, ed. Deborah Dash Moore and S. Ilan Troen (New Haven: Yale University Press, 2001), 333-350.

19 Jeffrey Shandler, ed., *Awakening Lives: Autobiographies of Jewish Youth in Poland before the Holocaust* (New Haven: Yale University Press, 2002).

20 Out of this seminar came "David Emile Durkheim and the Jewish Response to Modernity," *Modern Judaism* 6:3 (October 1986): 287-300.

21 Edward K. Spann's *The New Metropolis* was the second book published in the series. The next book on New York Jews in the Columbia History of Urban Life was by Andrew R. Heinze, *Adapting to Abundance: Jewish Immigrants, Mass Consumption, and the Search for American Identity* (New York: Columbia University Press, 1992).

22 Rischin, "Jewish Studies in Northern California," 417.

23 Deborah Dash Moore, *To the Golden Cities: Pursuing the American Jewish Dream in Miami and L.A.* (New York: Free Press, 1994).

24 And the staff regularly called Judith, who became a good friend, Deborah Moore.

25 Deborah Dash Moore, "I'll Take Manhattan: Reflections on Jewish Studies," *Judaism* 44:4 (Fall 1995): 420-26, quotes on 420, 425.

26 See David A. Hollinger, "Communalist and Dispersionist Approaches to American Jewish History in an Increasingly Post-Jewish Era," *American Jewish History* 95:1 (March 2009): 1-32 and responses of Hasia Diner, Paula E. Hyman, Alan M. Kraut, Tony Michels, 33-71.

27 For a brief overview see Deborah Dash Moore, "Remarks on Friedman Medal," *American Jewish History* 97:2 (April 2013): 101-104.

28 See Deborah Dash Moore, "At Home in America? Revisiting the Second Generation," *Journal of American Ethnic History* (Winter-Spring 2006): 156-168.

29 Robert S. Warshow, "Poet of the Jewish Middle Class," *Commentary* (May 1946): 17.

30 Todd M. Endelman, "The Legitimation of the Diaspora Experience," *Broadening Jewish History: Towards a Social History of Ordinary Jews* (Oxford: Littman Library, 2011), 57.

31 Jonathan D. Sarna, *American Judaism: A History* (New Haven: Yale University Press, 2004), 222. As a second generation Jew, Sarna also discounts the generational model as useful for understanding American Jewish history.

32 Lederhendler, *New York Jews and the Decline of Ethnicity*.

33 See *American Jewish History* 100:2 (April 2016), guest edited by Lila Corwin Berman and Tony Michels, with articles by Jon Butler, Eli Lederhendler, Cecile E. Kuznitz, Max D. Baumgarten, Lily Geisman, and Eva Morawska.

34 Leonard Dinnerstein, *Uneasy at Home: Anti-Semitism and the American Jewish Experience* (New York: Columbia University Press, 1987).

35 Irving Howe and Kenneth Libo, *World of Our Fathers: The Journey of the East European Jews to America and the Life They Found and Made* (New York: Harcourt, Brace, Jovanovich, 1976), 608.

36 David Singer, "Second Generation," *Commentary* (July 1981): 73.

Becoming an "All-of-a-Kind" Jewish Historian

Pamela S. Nadell

It was the mid-1950s. Thanks to the GI Bill, my parents, with two children under the age of three, escaped a one-bedroom apartment in one of New Jersey's largest cities for a modest cookie-cutter home on a brand new suburban street. It was one of tens of thousands of such homes being built to satisfy pent-up demand in postwar America. Out front lay a postage stamp of a lawn; out back, a clothesline on the patio, so that my mother would not have to haul laundry for four to dry on the roof. The down payment was nominal; my father could afford the mortgage; and the township promised that P.S. #19 would open just down the street by the time I was ready for kindergarten.

The township kept its promise, and there my life as a reader began. *Fun with Dick and Jane*, my generation's basal reader, unlocked the wondrous mystery of reading. Then I began devouring books. In my house we rarely bought them, but ten-minutes away, across a highway, was the library.

I remember it as old, but I have no idea if it was in the same building in the 1950s that it was when it opened in 1877. What I most remember is that, on one of the shelves in the children's reading room, was a series of biographies. I wish I knew whether I was reading Random House's Landmark Books on history for young readers or the Bobbs-Merrill fictionalized biographies of the Childhood of Famous Americans "Orange" series.[1] Perhaps I read from both. But what strikes me is that I only remember reading biographies of famous women: Clara Barton, Amelia Earhart, Dolly

Madison, Florence Nightingale, Molly Pitcher, Betsy Ross. In fact, I was so sure that I only read female biographies that, looking back for this reflection, I assumed that famous women had their own juvenile series. But, if one existed, I cannot find any reference to it. Nevertheless, from age seven or eight, I was already reading women's history.

P.S. #19's building was new; its curriculum was not. The notion of teaching social studies—that mishmash of history, government, economics, geography, sociology, and anthropology, all rolled into one—dates to the early twentieth century. Yet, oddly, this township had retained the old-fashioned division of history and geography as independent subjects. History came before lunch, and I loved history, its stories, its characters, its other times and places. Geography came after lunch, and I found its topographical maps and inventories of nations' natural resources insufferable.

Every day, rain or shine, we walked home for lunch. If there were any working mothers in that spanking new suburban subdivision, then their mothers must have come in to feed the kids. An hour later, on time, I was back at school.

P.S. #19 had a tiny library. By fifth grade, as one of the big kids, I, along with two friends who also loved to read, were invited to check in and re-shelve returned books just as soon as we could rush back from a quick bite at home. In return for our service, we got fabulous benefits. We did not have to wait until our class's weekly turn in the library. We could take out and return books whenever we wanted. Even better, playing librarian ladies, we had to finish putting away the waiting stack of books before heading back to class. Invariably, we three musketeers would run late and miss, without penalty, some of that day's geography lesson.

In that library I discovered another corner of the historical past, Sydney Taylor's *All-of-a-Kind Family*. In 1951, Taylor invented the memorable Brenners—papa, mama, five sisters and baby brother—a Jewish family on the Lower East Side in turn-of-the-century New York. In the years ahead the children would grow up in *More All-of-a-Kind Family* (1954), *All-of-a-Kind Family Uptown* (1958), *All-of-a-Kind Family Downtown* (1962), and *Ella of All-of-a-Kind Family* (1978.) I read the first four in the series in P.S. #19's library.

When the entire series was republished in 2014, I quipped: I became a Jewish historian because of these books.

The one that left the greatest imprint, likely because I own a 1989 reprint, was the first. The five *All-of-a-Kind Family* pinafore-clad sisters—Ella, Henny, Sarah, Charlotte, and Gertie—loved books, and I loved books. Their story opens with a calamity: Sarah has lost a library book, but a kindly lady librarian resolves the crisis. In another chapter, a peddler dumps a treasure trove of books at their father's junk shop, and the excited girls leaf through them and take some home. The novel also drew me in for its depictions of the family's religious observances—shopping for the Sabbath, reading around its table until the candles burned low, delivering Purim baskets, the Passover *seder* where there were enough Haggadahs to go around because four of the girls lay in bed with scarlet fever. My family was Jewish, but, except for the *seder* that my Berdichev-born grandfather rushed through so that we could get to the good part and eat, none of these customs was familiar.

Most of all, *All-of-a-Kind Family* wove the enchantments of reading about another place and time, the same delights that I experienced when reading those female biographies and school's history lessons. Taylor's words and the drawings of illustrator Helen John set the scene of a world so very different from the one I knew. A calendar in the parlor announced that it was 1912. The girls wore three petticoats, long underwear, and woolen stockings their mother knit. The city streets, lined with tenements, had gas lampposts. The junk shop, heated by a stove, had a pail of coal sitting nearby. A peddler, his socks soaked through his torn soles, cut cardboard to fit his shoes. The Yiddish-speaking grocer wore a yarmulke and had a long white beard.[2] He looked nothing like the grocery men at the A & P where my mom shopped. I wanted to know more about that world, about junk shops and the Rivington Street market stalls, about living up three flights of dimly lit stairs and women sitting in the back of the synagogue behind a curtain. I wanted to understand the Jews who lived in that world and find out what happened to them.

I read one more history book in these years. In my three-day-a-week Hebrew school, Sundays were for history lessons from

Deborah Pessin's three-volume series *The Jewish People*. To this day, in my mind's eye, I can see its illustration of Hillel, lying on a Jerusalem rooftop, with his ear to the grate of the schoolhouse to hear the lesson below. Each year, when I teach ancient and medieval Jewish history to my American University students, I tell them about Hillel, his poverty, love of learning, and that sketch imprinted in my memory.[3] My reading as a child drew me to Jewish history, American history, and women's history. It pointed me on the path to becoming an historian.

When I was eleven, we moved to another historic New Jersey community, one with roots in the colonial era and young republic. After World War II, its population exploded, quadrupling over the next quarter-century before leveling off at just under 30,000. In this more affluent suburb, the houses had more rooms and bathrooms; the lawns were more spacious, and the schools reputed to be excellent.

A lot of the new homeowners settling there in the 1950s and 1960s were Jews. Leaving behind the urban center of Newark, they abandoned that city's steamy streets, as its most famous alumnus Philip Roth wrote, to ascend a mountain, climbing to the suburbs of Essex County, bringing them "closer to heaven."[4]

How many Jews lived in my promised land of Livingston when I was growing up is unknown. In high school, we joked that the town was a third Protestant, a third Catholic, and a third Jewish. In the years that I lived there, the *American Jewish Year Book* lumped together the county's Jewish population. Not until 1988 did the *AJYB* disaggregate its statistics to report that Livingston's 13,000 Jews were just under half the town's population. Whatever the figure for the years that I grew up there, Livingston was and remains today an American variant of the *shtetl*.

School closed on the High Holidays. The synagogue and its Hebrew school sat on the corner opposite my junior high. I remember most of the kids in my classes as Jews; even today, I can name the few gentiles. My brother and I and our friends went to Hebrew school as a matter of course. There were holiday meals at Rosh Hashanah, candles at Chanukah, never a Christmas tree. Being Jewish was very much a matter of neighborhood, friendships, family celebrations, and gastronomy. We ate bagels and lox on Sunday mornings; one grandmother was famed for her *blintzes*; the other kept a kosher home, but we grew up eating bacon, lettuce, and tomato sandwiches.

I had a Shabbat morning bat mitzvah where I chanted the Haftarah for Parashat Tetzaveh (Ezekiel 43:10-43:27), but, as a girl, was not permitted to read from the Torah. That was just fine with me since I found it torturous having to memorize the tune for my Haftarah using a record. I had absolutely no interest in the paper that I had to write for the rabbi about Ezekiel's vision of the Temple and its destruction. I don't think I had any understanding of what I read. That rabbi would surely have been astounded to learn that in graduate school, my reading took me to the prophets and that I would write a Master's thesis on them.

This thick Jewish world influenced my reading choices. We readers keep lists, lists of books to read, lists of books that we read. I still have mimeographed pages of titles my teachers recommended. I also have lists of books that I read dating back to eighth grade, the year I learned touch-typing on the antique Underwood that led my father to his U. S. Army posting as a typist at the Nuremberg trials.

Those lists show that I never stopped reading books set in other eras and distant places: revolutionary France (*The Scarlet Pimpernel*), the eighteenth-century South Seas (*Mutiny on the Bounty*), the waning days of imperial China (*The Good Earth*). Improbably, for I am sure that I scarcely understood it, I spent part of a summer with *War and Peace*, immersed in Russia during the Napoleonic campaign. But what really leaps out are the number of Jewish-themed books. Of course, I read *The Diary of Anne Frank*. But I also read Leon Uris's *Exodus* and *Mila 18*, Meyer Levin's *Eva*, Herman Wouk's *Marjorie Morningstar*, John Hersey's *The Wall*, and Sylvia Golden's *Neighbors Needn't Know*, the fictionalized story of her Hungarian Jewish family, although the 1953 *New York Times* book review ignores the Jewish part. Holocaust themes dominate this list, likely because so many of these books were best-sellers then. I also read the classic *Ben-Hur* whose story of a Jewish prince enslaved by the Romans is subtitled *A Tale of the Christ*.

I even read James Michener's *The Source*, not once but, inexplicably, twice. This 1965 book still sells in the top one hundred on Amazon.com under Jewish historical fiction. The book uses the device of a dig at a *tel* in the young State of Israel to narrate stories set in different eras of the Jewish past. Since I was not reading history outside of whatever was the standard Advanced Placement curriculum of the day, I have to think that I turned to this 1,100-plus page book to learn Jewish history.

Not until I got to Douglass College, the women's school of Rutgers University—the latter was, for most of my undergraduate years, a men's school—did I begin taking classes in Jewish history. I graduated from the historical fiction of novelists James Michener and Leon Uris to the historians Benzion Netanyahu, Cecil Roth, Abram Sachar, Leon Simon, and Yigal Yadin; and the writers S. Y. Agnon, I. B. Singer, and Elie Wiesel. Outside of class, I also happened upon Max I. Dimont's *Jews, God, and History*. Reading it demonstrated the distinctions between scholarship and popularization. That book was justifiably criticized by scholars, like Arthur Hertzberg, who wished the author would have "read more Jewish history" to avoid so many "major howlers."[5]

What is clear from these titles is that I was not heading towards American Jewish history; I was training for Jewish studies. My interests were Jewish history and literature. As an undergraduate, I was a Hebraic Studies major; the college avoided the word "Jewish" since it threatened to breach the wall between church and this state university. That meant that I took courses in Hebrew language, Jewish history, Jewish literature, Jewish thought, and, during a junior year abroad at Hebrew University, more of the same plus Bible, archaeology, and Jewish education. My general history courses were in European civilization and Russian history. My honors thesis was about antisemitism in France. These choices made sense since most of the Judaica that I was studying was set in Europe and the Russian Empire.

As an undergraduate, I had a single course titled History of the Jews in the Americas. What I remember mostly about it was studying with the Brazilian historian Anita Novinsky, who must have been a visiting professor for a few weeks, and learning about her discovery of the vestiges of marranism in Brazil and Portugal.

I did not set off on the road to becoming an American Jewish historian until I found myself in graduate school in history at Ohio State University, which only a few years earlier had established a graduate program in Jewish history. There, meeting Professor Marc Lee Raphael, I unexpectedly stumbled into American Jewish history. Over the next eight years, I read more intensively and more deeply in history, with rare breaks for escaping into novels between quarters, than I had ever done before. I read Jewish history, ancient, medieval, and modern. Because I was a teaching assistant and kept getting assigned to the Russian historians, I read huge chunks of Russian history and enough American history, again because of TA placements, to teach my own sections of the first half of the survey course. I never did TA for the survey's second half. Once again, I am struck by my eclectic approach to reading.

But I was not the only one reading broadly. The very first course that I took with Marc Raphael was on Ancient Israel. Raphael, who was just about to publish his first book, *Jews and Judaism in a Midwestern Community: Columbus, Ohio, 1840-1975*, taught Jewish history across the ages. So, too, did Robert Chazan, the distinguished historian of medieval Jewish history, who was teaching at Ohio State then. I would TA for his undergraduate survey in modern Jewish civilization, and, as a graduate student, teach my own section of that class.

This broad training in Jewish history has shaped my teaching career for the more than three decades that I have been a professor at American University. Others contributing to this book came to American Jewish history from different paths, from American history or ethnic history. But I came to this subfield out of Jewish history, and, probably because I know no other path, I remain convinced that it was the right one. It led me to view the American Jewish experience first and foremost through the lens of the Jewish experience. Moreover, when American University could hire only one person to cover Judaica, the breadth of my training and stretch of my teaching were surely attractive. Even today, I teach Jewish history broadly. In my regular rotation of courses is ancient and medieval Jewish civilization, modern Jewish civilization, Holocaust, and, every once in a while, a survey of American Jewish history or a course on American Jewish women's history. I have also occasionally taught courses in Jewish literature.

Perhaps, then, it is not surprising that my scholarship, starting with my dissertation, "The Journey to America by Steam: The Jews of Eastern Europe in Transition, 1881-1924," while contributing to American Jewish history, nods to the world across the Atlantic. In the dissertation, I traced the passage from shtetl to Ellis Island. I wrote of the encounters with agents, scrupulous and un-, self-proclaimed experts advising emigrants how to conceal money and diseases on their journey. I traced how Russian Jews stole across the border; how, if their passage took them through Germany, their journey was controlled from the moment of that crossing until they set sail from the seaports of Bremen and Hamburg. I then peered into the discomforts of their voyages in steamship steerage, which, I have gone on to tell my students, bore little resemblance to the jolly below-decks scenes of the epic film *Titanic*.

I never published the dissertation as a book, although I published a number of peer-reviewed and popular articles out of it, two of them while I was still writing the thesis. Instead, just about the time that I settled into American University, I was invited to write *Conservative Judaism in America: A Biographical Dictionary and Sourcebook*. This was admittedly an untraditional choice for a first book, but I knew so little about publishing that I hesitated to turn down a bird in the hand to find a publisher on my own for a revised dissertation. So, I signed on for the Conservative Judaism volume in a three-part series on the institutions and leadership of the American Jewish denominations.

I like to think that I was attracted to this project not only because of the contract but also because it allowed me to continue reading broadly in the Jewish experience. I spent the next several years, sitting two or three days each week in the Library of Congress to learn not only about the men who had shaped this religious movement but also to read the books that they had written on Jewish history, thought, law, culture, and literature. I look back on this time, when I was also teaching six courses a year, as my equivalent of a postdoc and advanced Jewish studies fellowship.

That book published and with tenure in hand, I embarked on the research that had long beckoned to me, but which was not a subject widely pursued when I was a graduate student and assistant professor. Somehow, I had intuited that not until then should I dare pursue the topic that sat at the crossroads of my childhood reading, American Jewish women's history. As late as 1994, the deeply influential pioneering scholar Paula Hyman was writing that "graduate students in Judaic studies have gotten the message: if you want to succeed in this field, do not write your dissertation on a woman's topic. Wait until you have tenure."[6] I, promoted to associate professor in 1988, did just that. Tenure gave me the freedom to write what I had long hoped to write.

* * * * * *

A few years ago, preparing for a keynote at Brigham Young University, I reread the introductions to two of my edited collections, *American Jewish Women's History: A Reader* (2003) and my co-edited *Making Women's Histories: Beyond National Perspectives* (2013). Only then did I realize that, in the opening paragraph to both, I had used the very same quotation from Gerda Lerner. In her autobiographical essay in *Voices of Women Historians: The Personal, the Political, the Professional*, a volume of essays much like this one, Lerner, who fled Austria after the Anschluss and went on to found the academic study of women's history in the U.S., reflected: "My commitment to women's history came out of my life, not out of my head."[7] I keep returning to this quotation and turning it over because it also describes my own arc from my childhood reading in biographies of famous women, the *All-of-a-Kind Family* series, and Deborah Pessin's *The Jewish People* to my first book in women's history, *Women Who Would Be Rabbis: A History of Women's Ordination, 1889-1985* (1998).

I opened this book with the conceit of a reporter who proclaimed that, "with the ordination of Rabbi Sally Priesand in 1972, Judaism learned that a great religious debate over women in the pulpit had been settled before it began."[8] I then spent the next three hundred pages, proving that, in fact, this great religious debate had waxed and waned and occasionally raged for more than a century.

It had begun in 1889, on the front page of Philadelphia's *Jewish Exponent*, when the writer Mary M. Cohen asked: "Could not—our *women*—be ministers?" It had continued in the 1890s, in an era of rising expectations, partly fueled by the 1893 Congress of Jewish Women at the Chicago World's Fair and by the career of Ray Frank, the "girl rabbi of the golden west." In the 1920s and 1930s, five women spent enough time in rabbinical seminaries to force their students, faculty, boards of trustees, and Jews around the country and beyond to contemplate seriously the notion of a woman in the pulpit. One of them, Regina Jonas, in Germany, ultimately received private ordination. But, because she shared the tragic fate of her people and perished at the hands of the Nazis, her story was mostly lost for the next half-century. The others all failed to become rabbis, although each would later raise the question of the woman rabbi once again.

Changes in the 1950s and 1960s unexpectedly brought more women to attend rabbinical school. One of them, Sally Priesand, riding the crest of the new wave of American feminism, was ordained a Reform rabbi in 1972. That breakthrough and the surrounding publicity sparked a highly public and painful debate among Conservative Jews. When that movement decided, in 1983, to ordain women, the Orthodox began asking, "Will there be Orthodox women rabbis?" Today there are, but that happened after I published this book.[9]

Writing *Women Who Would Be Rabbis* connected the threads of my lifelong reading. A topic in Jewish history, mostly centered in the U.S. but partly in Europe, it harked back to those biographies of famous women that were among the earliest books that I read.

Few of the Jewish women whose lives grace my pages were well known. There are a couple of exceptions: Henrietta Szold, the iconic founder of Hadassah, the best known Jewish woman of her day and age, makes an appearance. So too do the first women ordained in their respective denominations—Reform's Sally Priesand, Reconstructionist's Sandy Eisenberg Sasso, and

Conservative Judaism's Amy Eilberg. In their movements, they are well known. But most of the women whose stories flicker to life briefly in my pages were not renowned: the proto-rabbi Ray Frank, the historian Dora Askowith, the Hadassah leader Irma Levy Lindheim, the writer and editor Trude Weiss-Rosmarin, the Reform sisterhood executive Jane Evans. Of course, I was not writing a shelf of their biographies. Instead *Women Who Would Be Rabbis* lines these women up and inserts them into the historical narrative, hinting that there is more to tell about them than their brief moment on the stage of the debate over women's ordination. Others would indeed write some of them deeper into history.[10]

The women who would have been rabbis if they could have been rabbis were, like me, readers. But, because they had no collective historical consciousness, they were unaware that, independently, they had read the same texts of Jewish law and concluded that no statement specifically prohibited a woman from becoming a rabbi. Like me, they too were interested in women's lives, and they searched in the past to discover seekers and readers who had transgressed fixed gendered boundaries to take what they learned from their reading to teach and lead. Arguing that these women had functioned just like rabbis, the women who would be rabbis sought to climb on their shoulders, to claim their places as rabbis, teachers, and preachers.

* * * * * *

A few paragraphs suffice to summarize the story and arguments of *Women Who Would Be Rabbis*. Once we writers send our books out into the world, we are curious. What do our readers think of what we wrote? We scan reviews, and are content when reviewers write positively and bristle when they take exception. We expect the academic journals we read to review what we write. We await our colleagues citing our work, and are intrigued when we find references in unexpected places.[11] Occasionally, some of our books manage to cross over the divide between town and gown, garnering reviews in the press, usually the Jewish press.

But I will confess that I had greater expectations for *Women Who Would Be Rabbis*, ambitions that some of my reviewers noticed.

They understood that my project was political, that I was crafting a usable past for those who would read this book in the future.[12]

Over the years, I have indeed heard, from time to time, that my hope that this book would propel readers on their journeys was realized. In one chapter, I had written briefly about one woman who spent time in rabbinical school before doing what most women did back then, marrying who she wanted to be and becoming a rebbetzin, not a rabbi. Decades later, after her husband died, she tried to return to that rabbinical school. When the admissions officers dismissed her application, she pointed to her few lines in my book. A door opened; the rebbetzin became a rabbi.

I have also heard from Orthodox women. I ended this book with the question, borrowed from the title of an article by the Orthodox feminist Blu Greenberg. She asked, and I echoed: "Will there be Orthodox women rabbis?" In the less than two decades since this book appeared, a sea change in the Orthodox world has occurred. At seminaries in New York and Jerusalem, Orthodox rabbis are ordaining women using a variety of honorifics. No matter the title—rabba, maharat, rabbanit, rabbi—the first generation of Orthodox women rabbis, in the U. S. and in Israel, now preach, teach, and lead. Some of them have approached me to tell me what discovering my book meant to them. One recalled, being in high school and gulping it down in a single Shabbat afternoon, enthralled to discover that she was not alone, that her dreams for her future had been shared by those who came before.

Their confidences affirm that, for some, my book charted a usable past. Gerda Lerner had argued that women needed to grasp that those before them had struggled with the same questions and ideas. Knowing women's past was indispensable for climbing onto the shoulders of their predecessors to gaze out at the whole wide world, the view no longer obstructed. In *Women Who Would Be Rabbis*, a book about American (mostly), Jewish, and women's history, I had connected the dots of a century-long debate into a single work of scholarship. My book validated for some readers what they wanted to be as they set off on their life's path. Their reading had urged them forward, just as my lifetime of reading had steered my course.

Notes

1 David Spear, "Generation Past: The Story of the Landmark Books," *American Historical Association Perspectives on History* 2016. Nancy Pate, "Publisher Gives Memorable Orange Biographies an Update," *Online Athens Banner Herald*, 21 October 2003, http://onlineathens.com/stories/102103/boo_20031021014.shtml#.WOQTPG_yvcs, accessed April 4, 2017.

2 June Cummins, "Becoming an 'All-of-a-Kind' American: Sydney Taylor and Strategies of Assimilation," *The Lion and the Unicorn* 27:3 (September 2003): 324-343; Sydney Taylor, *All-of-a-Kind Family* 1951 (rpt., New York: Dell, 1989).

3 Deborah Pessin, *The Jewish People: Book Two* (New York: United Synagogue of America, 1952), 119-120.

4 Philip Roth, *Goodbye, Columbus and Five Short Stories* (New York: Modern Library, 1959, reprint 1966), 8.

5 Arthur Hertzberg, "Review of *Jews, God, and History*: Dimont's Book Is Not History. It Is Not Even Historic Myth-Making," *Commentary*, 1 September 1963. More than half a century later, that book not only remains in print, it ranks in the top twenty-five books sold on Amazon.com under Religion and Spirituality>Judaism>History.

6 Paula E. Hyman, "Feminist Studies and Modern Jewish History," in *Feminist Perspectives on Jewish Studies*, ed. Lynn Davidman and Shelly Tenenbaum (New Haven: Yale University Press, 1994), 120-39, quotation 120.

7 Gerda Lerner, "Women among the Professors of History: The Story of a Process of Transformation," in *Voices of Women Historians: The Personal, the Political, the Professional*, ed. Eileen Boris and Nupur Chaudhuri (Bloomington: Indiana University Press, 1999), 1-10, quotation, 1.

8 Quoted in Pamela S. Nadell, *Women Who Would Be Rabbis: A History of Women's Ordination, 1889-1985* (Boston: Beacon Press, 1998), ix.

9 Pamela S. Nadell, "Rabbi, Rabba, Maharat, Rabbanit: For Orthodox Jewish Women, What's in a Title?," *Sightings* (January 28, 2016), https://divinity.uchicago.edu/sightings/rabbi-rabba-maharat-rabbanit-orthodox-jewish-women-whats-title

10 For examples, see Deborah Dash Moore, "Trude Weiss-Rosmarin and the *Jewish Spectator*," in *The "Other" New York Jewish Intellectuals*, ed. Carole S. Kessner (New York: New York University Press, 1994), 101-121; Rebecca Kobrin, "The House [of Living Judaism] That Jane Evans

and NFTS Built, 1951," in *Sisterhood: A Centennial History of Women of Reform Judaism*, ed. Carole B. Balin, Dana Herman, Jonathan D. Sarna, and Gary P. Zola (Cincinnati: Hebrew Union College Press, 2013), 86-103.

11 See, e.g., Michael Maher, "A Break with Tradition: Ordaining Women Rabbis," *Irish Theological Quarterly* 77 (2007): 32-60.

12 See, e.g., the reviews by Dianne Ashton (*American Jewish Archives Journal* 51:1 & 2 [1999]:155-159) and Diane Lichtenstein (*American Historical Review* 107:3 [June 2002]:907-908).

Joining Historians as an Anthropologist at the Table of American Jewish Culture

Riv–Ellen Prell

> People everywhere live lives that are being
> constituted out of the past. Culture is constantly
> being invented or modified without being totally
> transformed. Intention and action are turned
> into culture by history.
>
> (Bernard S. Cohen, 1980)[1]

I began my graduate studies in anthropology in 1971 at the University of Chicago at a moment in American life that was polarized, despairing, and yet filled with possibility and a sense that ordinary citizens could make great change. It was an era in which scholars wrestled with the urgent issues of the day that were shaping political and social movements devoted to inequality and war. It was a time when some activists found inspiration in historical and cultural studies that provided a foundation for understanding power, hierarchy, and change.

I came of age in this period. The dramatic transformations in society were deeply personal. They challenged the gratitude of my birthright as a middle class American Jew who was raised to feel grateful for my parents' newly won mobility. They undermined my inherited view of America as a virtuous nation that won WWII. They made me understand that racial injustice did not occur only in the South. They allowed me to question the endless rules that put tremendous limitations and rigor on being the daughter of the house rather than the son.

Education was central to negotiating the remarkably complex terrain of the world my family had offered me. History, the social sciences, and literature told a different story of the United States. If conventional courses left out my own history as a Jew, a woman, and the stories of so many others in revolt, they provided access to an unfolding world of protest and demands for change. I had the opportunity to learn what had been suppressed about race, about war, about social movements, and about the economy from a growing scholarship newly available to me. I no longer had to rely on "official" stories. I could seek out alternatives. As I saw it, education was the oxygen of life. It opened the world and it provided the path through that terrain.

As an anthropology student I had already discovered a field that offered me a powerful perspective on that moment of political and cultural crisis, transformation and polarization. Anthropologists demonstrated that the structure and organization of societies varied considerably, if not infinitely. Political structures, "religious" systems, and family relationships were dynamic, variable, and complex wherever they existed in the world. Nothing could be taken for granted as inevitable in societies. Nothing could be ignored or dismissed about them as irrelevant to social analysis. Who held power and how power was manifest also varied. If the anthropology of my young years was slowly turning to a more historical and global understanding of its traditional subject matter, the ethnographic study of communities and regions nevertheless still offered a rich vein for analysis of the comparative dimensions of how power and hierarchy were constituted in societies. Anthropology provided me the greatest freedom and liberation from what was narrow not only about the power structures of the nation, but of my family as well. Their assumptions no longer had to be mine.

My life as a graduate student in anthropology addressed the political culture of the United States in a second way. The activism in which I came of age moved from the Old Left to the New Left, and with that transformation came a new definition of who were the primary agents of change: students in universities rather than workers. In particular, while the New Left's activists certainly were concerned with class, capital, and imperialism, they took up a new mantle when they also rejected the traditional institutions of American life, particularly the family, and advocated for freedom from any form of repression.

New Left activism, however, splintered around what came to be called movements built on "identity." An ambiguous and imperfect term, "identity" was associated with a group's shared experiences of oppression based on an identity, not simply social class. Oppression was based in structural relations, of course, but it also took emotional forms grounded in experience. While many young white, hyper-verbal men of the New Left were deeply concerned with racism, their primary fight concerned the Southeast Asian war. The men of the New Left were also notoriously indifferent to the power dynamic in their own intimate relations, usually with women of the New Left. Over time, the first generation of feminist activists wondered why traditional gender roles around domesticity and leadership persisted in "liberated" relationships in the New Left?[2]

Identity movements were not cohesive. Within the Black Freedom movement, or the somewhat later Women's Movement, or any other of the late 1960s and early 1970s social movements related to oppressions there were, of course, significant internal differences among activists. Feminists could be oriented to a fight for equal rights or radical social transformation, which involved different strategies and theories of oppression. They shared little more than a capacious umbrella, but they stood apart from others— if not entirely together with one another—based on gender, though not sexuality for some in the early years.

For women, in particular, the New Left, like the Old Left, faltered because its classic texts and theoretical underpinnings largely erased gender, sexuality, and race. Their aim to provide a universal and all-encompassing understanding of oppression and power could not accommodate the powerful and pervasive identity-based movements. Nor could feminists ignore the "personal" in the "political," in their political lives. The New Left lost its generational hold before the middle of the 1970s.

The Questions I Sought Answers for in Anthropology

In the midst of this political and cultural turmoil I was especially interested in how these new identity movements shaped political activism, and in turn, how often that activism sought ritual, symbolic, and sometimes religious formulations. Examples of this dynamic included the central role of the black church in civil rights, and the place of Catholicism and indigenous Mexican beliefs and rituals in Ceasar Chavez's farm workers movement, as well as its political theater based in Aztec mythology. Another example of this fusion was Baby Boomer Jewish activists in their twenties who were creating a variety of communities that experimented not only with new religious formulations, but combining them with political activism. Feminist Jewish women, like feminists in other American religions, were also struggling with traditions rather than abandoning them, and often linked that struggle for equality to larger political movements of the period.

What set this political, religious and cultural activism apart from the New Left was a strong orientation to "identity." The New Left was allergic to religion and to what it took to be the parochialism of the particular. The Left's abiding passion for what it considered cosmopolitanism rendered ethnicity, religion, and family traditions as problematic divisions which could only prove to be stumbling blocks to political change. Their easy ridicule of women on the New Left for their claim that they suffered oppression was also a variation on that theme.

These movements clearly begged to differ. They found that change grew out of communities, that the campaign for labor rights in the Central Valley of California, or civil rights throughout the United States, could be shaped by what held "parochial" communities together. Not all activists shared these religious or communal histories or strategies, but they were remarkably compelling, not only because they succeeded but because they defied a traditional understanding of political change on the Left.

I found myself beginning to struggle with these issues in more than one way. Undoubtedly, I sought freedom from the constraints of a middle class upbringing that had accepted too much of what American seemed to offer. Education opened a world I might have thought of as parochial. On the other hand, I now could see as a scholar-in-training that cosmopolitanism carried its inherent cultural biases, and its ability to simply replicate all sorts of hierarchies, including gender.

What interested me for my research required an understanding, in part, of diversity, nation, and pluralism as they shaped and were shaped by culture and traditions undergoing change, all issues newly emerging in anthropology as it turned to the study of modern and modernizing nations. I saw a way to address some of these questions, however, in the area of symbolic anthropology that had emerged so forcefully in the 1960s. Symbolic anthropologists focused on the tangible and powerful symbols and rituals in societies throughout the world that shaped and were woven into the fabric of social relationships of power, conflict, connection and transformation. In rituals of daily life, the life cycle, and the cycle of seasons, and in formal offices of power, rituals and symbols revealed to anthropologists the dynamics of social life on a different plane. In expressive activities built on emotion, unconscious meaning, and cultural authority, matters of social life were engaged, articulated, and affected. They were understood as vehicles for issues large and small in the lives of communities and villages or towns. Nor were the symbols and rituals of these groups afterthoughts to power and economy; they were crucial media through which social groups were constituted.

For all the considerable differences among the scholars who created and shaped this field in that period—Victor Turner, Clifford Geertz, Mary Douglas, Claude Levi-Strauss, Sherry Ortner, Barbara Myerhoff and many others—their attention to the symbolic dimensions of social relationships, the social order, and what one might think of as the sacred, were all closely attuned to the ways in which symbols and rituals allowed men and women to negotiate the worlds they occupied.[3] Making sense of the world constituted making the world, and a "toolkit" of symbols and rituals was part of a process that would help me understand the terrain of cultural and political change in the United States in communities and groups that drew on their own cultural traditions to engage change.

When I decided to study American Jews, who were engaging these issues, I put myself on a path to the study of American Jewish history, though I hardly knew that at the time.

Studying Jews

My dissertation research focused on an incipient movement of Baby Boomer Jews who variously called themselves, and were called, "New Jews," "Counter culture Jews," or "Radical Jews."[4] The umbrella term covered young Jews who created a variety of communities and groups that involved political activism, radical Zionism, feminism, and alternative religious communities, which included *havurot* and *minyanim*. Many people belonged to one or more of these groups, mostly in the Northeast, but in Chicago and Los Angeles as well. The majority of these young men and women, in addition to sharing a generation as Baby Boomers, were highly educated, many still in graduate school and professional schools, and identified with the New Left, particularly in opposition to the war in Southeast Asia. Yet, many were simultaneously alienated from it because of the anti-Zionist stand taken by much of its leadership following the Six Day War.

I conducted an ethnographic study of one of these communities, a *minyan*, which I called the Kelton Minyan in my writing about the group, in Los Angeles for fifteen months beginning in 1972. I was one of a number of anthropologists who conducted a different type of ethnographic research. These scholars worked in major metropolitan areas, where "natives" had jobs, went to school, and gathered formally, often for religious services or other shared interests. Other interactions were out of public view. I certainly wished for a "town square" where people hung around, or an informal ethos, where walking into a neighbor's house was considered normal. I was not part of this group, but I was essentially indistinguishable from its members by age, religion, ethnicity, race and other factors. Nevertheless, I was still an outsider, and they were certainly conscious that they were being studied. I had sought formal permission to conduct the study. I pleaded my case and the members voted on my request in the spring before I began my fieldwork. I needed not only to win formal approval, but like all ethnographers, to create relationships, to listen, and to document what happened.

The Minyan was an ideal site for me to study the questions that had emerged as central to understand the role of community, culture, and religion in political and cultural transformation in the 1970s. How and why would traditional rituals and symbols become a medium for social transformation for members of a particular generation? How were they changing Judaism? How could Jewish life serve them as a medium for political activism and change? How were newcomers to these Jewish practices, as well as young men and women deeply steeped in them, negotiating questions of identity and culture in their communal life? How were the counter cultural norms of the period shaping their Jewish practices? What would happen as young women and men in this community were increasingly challenging the norms of gender difference in Judaism?

I not only observed their services and discussions, but also interviewed virtually all members of the Kelton Minyan. I learned about their individual lives, and how they thought about religious practice, politics, education, work, and their personal aspirations. I studied, as well, their meetings outside of Shabbat services, and how they negotiated creating an alternative community, and why they wanted to avoid membership in conventional synagogues. As other ethnographers of urban, contemporary communities usually discovered, these "natives" were often sophisticated about the issues of interest to the ethnographer.

Ultimately, my research led me to learn how the rituals and symbols of Jewish life provided a powerful frame for these young men and women as they identified with a counter culture, but understood themselves to stand apart from it. Their Jewishness was shaped by their political and cultural engagements, but they reshaped them as well. Their rejection, to some extent, of a dominant, homogenizing culture, found powerful expression in the texts, holidays and rituals of a larger Jewish people with whom they identified.

Ritual became a medium through which to express those differences. Prayer was both a medium of community life, and one challenged by their lives as cosmopolitan people. I had to understand that contesting prayer—its theology, its patriarchal language, and its demands—was also the foundation of their community. Doubt, affirmation, and challenge were all part of the prayer experience, and that approach as a community challenged not only the Minyan members, but much of the social science literature on religion of the period.

Initially, my ethnographic study of the Kelton Minyan did not take into account American Jewish history or American history. My view of a context for the study was, like a good deal of anthropology of the time, atemporal. The rich events of the present seemed to suffice to explain the complexity of Minyan members' complex practices and ideas. However, as I dug deeper into the context for this community I turned to American Jewish history. Initially, I was simply curious about how to understand their family histories, the history of synagogues and prayer, and past struggles for women's equality. What I found was far more profound. I discovered that these young Jews were part of the very fabric of American Jewish life. For centuries, American Jews had continually re-thought or even re-invented Jewish life through the lens of their generation, their aesthetics, and their relationship to the nation. These Jewish Baby Boomers participated in a strand of that history that rejected the dominant culture rather than assimilating to it. On the other hand, the American counter culture provided a strong shape for this generational rebellion.

I came to understand that Isaac Mayer Wise called his mid-nineteenth century *siddur* for the New World *Minhag America* because he imagined it would serve American Jewry indefinitely.[5] He imagined that his prayer book could provide a new synthesis, which left behind the jumble of Old World Jewish prayer practices that immigrants brought with them to the United States. Instead, his aesthetics and theology provided a new framework for Jewish life in his *siddur*. It lasted less than fifty years for the Reform movement. Similarly, the leaders of postwar Conservative Judaism found a synthesis of a traditionalist formulation of religious life with an American commitment to rational thought and aesthetics that appeared perfect for the young families that were new residents of suburbia. This movement looked forward to a continuous domination of American Jewish life as Orthodox Judaism would wither away, and Reform Judaism would be marginalized.[6] Similarly, the generational formulations of Conservative Judaism lasted about one generation, and proved to be the springboard for the revolt of the Jewish Baby Boomers who founded the Jewish countercultural movement.

The rich historical scholarship that I found grounded my research in a dynamic understanding of what Jews did over time. It guided me toward considering the complexity of American Jewish life through its practices, its aesthetics, and its generational developments. I saw how fruitful it could be to integrate historical narratives with studying the behavior and reflections of these Jews. How did these young men and women think about what they were doing, link what they did to their understanding of Jewish history and of their own families? What role did memory play, imagined or real, in finding models for Jewish life that rejected assimilation or acculturation? How did they understand their relationship to others in the New Left and the Women's Movement? Why did they insist on their differences? These questions helped to construct a story about how Jews understood their Jewishness. It was the opportunity to look at Jewishness from what anthropologist called "the native point of view." I did not draw on the survey methods of my sociology colleagues of the time who answered that question by measuring behavior quantitatively. While I began to consider historical questions, at the same time historians were only beginning to consider ordinary people as an important subject matter.

A Revolution: Gender and Judaism?

My mid-1970s research coincided not only with young women creating a cultural and political movement, but with scholars beginning an intellectual revolution. My study of the Kelton Minyan demanded that I understand I was not only looking at a Jewish point of view, but a gendered Jewish one. Because these young Jews gathered together in a minyan, even a religiously "liberal" one largely shaped by Conservative Judaism, they still had to contend with Jewish law and its practice. Their minyan was founded on a principle of egalitarianism. They did not differentiate between men and women in their practices. At the same time, they did not have a rabbi who led the community, although they counted among their members rabbis and scholars of Jewish life and Judaism.

Questions of gender and equality in Judaism were hardly settled by simply declaring that all Jews could participate fully. Inevitably, as happened in other Western traditions at that time, women members raised theological questions. What was the significance for them of the Hebrew pronouns that made God male, the symbolic language of power and war associated with much, though hardly all of Jewish conceptions of divinity? How were women to pray through and with this language and find a place for themselves not only in the tradition, but in the community?

Issues of gender were unique and alienating to many of them, but also parallel with other types of questions raised about the ways in which Jewish traditions set members apart from a larger America. Were the symbols and practices of Jewish life "broken," as some scholars of the time suggested was the impact of secularization on religious life? Were they more vital because they could withstand change? Was this community and movement to be understood as innovators, inventors, or a new form of traditionalists?

In this research, and subsequent work that I have done, it became clear that the Jewish feminism that raised these questions in communities and in Jewish life itself, not only in the United States but throughout the world, constituted a true transformation.[7] Previous efforts at egalitarianism in America had taken strikingly different formulations. Like Jewish feminism, they had been inspired by struggles for women's equality in churches and in the larger society. Jewish women immigrants were inspired by what they understood as women's higher status in the United States compared to Europe.

The Baby Boom's inspirations were certainly grounded in various waves of feminism. But this generation of women demanded, more forcefully, rights to education, to leadership, and a full equality that really had not existed before, other than in a few powerful exceptions. They embarked on a revolution whose future implications really could not be seen in that historic era that began at the very end of the 1960s. Rather than understanding Jewish feminism on the historic model of "religious" life, I argued it was better understood as part of the emergence of modern Jewish experience and the power of entering societies committed to the Enlightenment. Women, like men, sought to fully embrace the values of egalitarianism.[8]

Telling Other People's Stories

Through graduate school and the early part of my career I was accused by some advisers, though not all of them, and some colleagues as well, of engaging in a search for my own identity, seeking personal meaning and compromising "objectivity" and intellectual rigor. Few anthropologists studied their "own" groups, failed to go far from "home," or avoided disease and suffering. I had no horror stories to swap with other anthropologists at conferences. My scholarship was not primarily a personal journey; my own Jewishness was not my subject matter, and the intellectual grounding of my work applied to other people and cultures and not simply Jews. It is rewarding now to link my scholarship to a memoir project, since inevitably biography has a place in our work. It was challenging to have to fight for decades to defend my research choices.

What most likely made me an anthropologist was growing up in a world that was drenched with Jewishness at every turn, and one almost entirely lacking in Jewish culture, Zionism, or Judaism, other than in the much maligned form of the "symbolic ethnicity" of the children of immigrants. Even that symbolic ethnicity was compromised by growing up in post war Los Angeles, in a neighborhood in which Jews lived in the middle of the block sandwiched between non-Jews at either end with whom we did not socialize. That neighborhood dissolved in 1960 with the arrival of a freeway that claimed our house, which catapulted my family into an entirely Jewish world of West Los Angeles. There the ethnicity was denser, Jewish cultural life non-existent, and religious life was scattered over great distances in synagogues. That everyone on my new block and most of the other blocks around me was Jewish did not seem to count for much. That virtually all of my friends were Jews similarly seemed inevitable rather than having much content. For all the stereotypes of what a girl from Los Angeles looked like in the 1960s, I actually remember the first time I saw someone who was blonde, and I gawked.

My own family still mystifies me in late middle age, despite the convenient label of ethnicity to describe them. My father had deep ties to the Jewishness of his youth though his practice was minimal, and was shaped by a synagogue rather than his own family. My mother as an adult wanted to flee a stifling orthodoxy of her own childhood, which changed dramatically when she was wrenched from Montreal, Canada to Los Angeles. My grandmother purchased a home away from Jewish communal life, requiring my *Shomer Shabbat* grandfather to live with others on Shabbat. He lived only a few years in Los Angeles before he died, after which the family's Judaism and finances changed dramatically for the worse. No one could ever explain to me the mysteries of this accumulation of family choices that shaped my parents, and my Jewish life.

Was it my father always reminding me that the Reform synagogue we attended twice a year was completely inauthentic and not "really" Jewish that attuned me to the double experience of insider and outsider? When I learned that when my parents first married my father set down an ultimatum that my mother had to give up smoking or stop lighting Shabbos candles and she voted for smoking, did that lead me to appreciate the complexity of Jewish practice and personal choice and how it reshapes religious practice? Was it the profound presence, and silence about the Holocaust that further confused me and my friends? We lost no family members. We worshipped Franklin Delano Roosevelt, dead many years by the time I was growing up. But I was not alone in my generation of feeling the imminence of disaster from economic Depression, the antisemitism my parents experienced, or the "what if" scenario of a Nazi victory all around me. I grew up in a period in which the popular culture was not saturated with the Holocaust, and the few encounters with it in the *Diary of Ann Frank*, or photos that appeared in *Life Magazine* or elsewhere spoke volumes.

Something in this very odd mix of what was almost a racial sense of Jewishness, combined with deep emotional ties to certain practices and not others, led me to an endless fascination with cultures, with ordinary life, with stories people told, and commitments they rejected, even while they hankered for them. My parents' obsession with the dangers of my or their mixing with those who were not Jews was by turns confusing, confounding, but also compelled me to understand contradictions in ideas and behavior.

I was surrounded by stories, my parents', my aunts' and uncles', and sometimes it seemed those of every person I ever met, as well as those of their parents and grandparents' too. I always wanted to know people's stories. I did not want to "treat" them as a psychologist might. I did not want to quantify them. I wanted to understand what animated their lives, what happened to them, and how they thought about the world. I wanted to know about worlds other than my own. I was attuned to the ways that people shaped their lives before I understood what that actually meant. However, it made me very suspicious of what we might think of as normative judgements about how people lived in society, and how different norms were from what people actually did or believed.

And then there were the 1960s, which fundamentally shattered the America of my childhood by revealing anything but a virtuous vision of the nation's "norms" about justice, equality, and international benevolence. War, violence, and political struggle shaped my generation, which is where I began this essay. Family, generation, political change, and cultural transformation are my inheritance. They made it impossible for me and my friends to believe what we were told, which created a generation that was unique in its distrust of authority, hyper-critical to a fault of its parents, and deeply suspicious of inherited wisdom. It allowed women like me to demand the right to do what we were told was not allowed.

If all of this made me an anthropologist who believed that Jews could be interesting, and that the United States belonged on an ethnographer's map of possible subjects, it also drew me to history. What the anthropologist Bernard Cohn wrote in the epigraph of this chapter is profoundly illuminating. History undermined the positivism of anthropology, which suggested that what one encountered in the present was an objective reality. Rather, seeing reality unfold through the lens of a contested past reveals that meaning is made in and over time. What interested me was precisely what he captured. How did intention and action become culture, challenge culture, and transform it?

Whatever drew me to a field created by colonialism, and that took its practitioners far away to understand other worlds, allowed me to study how change was created in my own society. But it was history, as anthropologists were to learn, that allowed me to understand the depth of change and its impact on the present. In turn, as an anthropologist, I hope that I have raised new questions for historians about the experiences that created the world of ordinary people as they sought to make sense of the culture around them. In their companionable relationship, I believe that the anthropologists and historians of my generation immensely complicated questions about culture, the diversity of meanings of Jewishness and Jews, and created new models, all to be challenged by our younger colleagues, about how American Jewish cultures have shaped the experience of Jews.

Notes

1   Bernard S. Cohn, "History and Anthropology: The State of Play," *Comparative Studies in Society and History* 22:2 (April 1980):198-221.

2   The classic work on this era of feminism is Sara Evans. *Personal Politics: The Roots Women's Liberation in the Civil Rights Movement and the New Left* (New York: Vintage Books, 1979).

3   The following were the classic works that launched symbolic anthropology. Victor W. Turner, *The Forest of Symbols: Aspects of Ndembu Ritual* (Ithaca: Cornell University Press, 1967). Clifford Geertz, *The Interpretation of Cultures* (New York: Basic Books, 1973). Mary Douglas, *Purity and Danger: An Analysis of Pollution and Taboo* (London: Routledge Press, 1966). Barbara G. Myerhoff, *The Peyote Hunt: The Sacred Hunt of the Huichol Indians* (Ithaca: Cornell University Press, 1974). Sherry Ornter, *Sherpas through their Rituals* (Cambridge: Cambridge University Press, 1978). Reflections on symbolic anthropology include: Sherry

B. Ortner, "Theory in Anthropology Since the Sixties," *Comparative Studies in Society and History* 26:1 (January 1984): 126-166; Ann Swidler, "Culture in Action: Symbols and Strategies,"*American Sociological Review* 51:2 (April 1986): 273-286; Donald Weber, "From Limen to Border: A Meditation on the Legacy of Victor Turner for American Cultural Studies," *American Quarterly* 47:3 (September 1995): 525-536.

4 This study was published as Riv-Ellen Prell, *Prayer and Community: the Havurah in American Judaism* (Detroit: Wayne State University Press, 1989).

5 A facsimile is available at huc.edu/research/libraries/guides/earp/ MinhagAmerica.

6 Marshal Sklare, *Conservative Judaism* (Glencoe: Free Press, 1955) was the early statement of that synthesis, though Sklare ultimately rejected the vitality of the movement.

7 There are many critical works on feminism and American Judaism. Riv-Ellen Prell, ed., *Women Remaking American Judaism* (Detroit: Wayne State University Press, 2007) reviews this literature and includes a number of essays on the impact.

8 This point is elaborated in the introduction to the Prell volume. It was also made by Paula Hyman in "Jewish Feminism," in *Jewish Women in America: An Historical Encyclopedia*, ed. Paula Hyman and Deborah Dash Moore (New York: Routledge, 1997), 694-498.

My Life in American Jewish History

Jonathan D. Sarna

I first became interested in the field of American Jewish History in high school. The psychologist will no doubt attribute much to the influence of my parents: Jewish studies was in many ways the Sarna family business. Gary P. Zola, in the *Encyclopedia Judaica*, quotes me as theorizing that my interest in the field stems from the fact that I am the first member of my family born in the United States. "He became convinced," his article reports, "that by synthesizing American and Jewish history, he could gain a deeper understanding of his own world."[1] There is a lot of truth to that. An alternative possibility, suggested by more cynical analysts, is that I went into the only Jewish field that my father, Nahum M. Sarna (1923-2015), a world famous Jewish scholar, knew nothing about.

Whatever the case, in my senior year in high school, I produced a long paper, adorned with no fewer than 250 footnotes, entitled "Antisemitism in the United States 1778-1945." The paper introduced me to the literature of American Jewish history and whetted my appetite for more.

A new occasion soon presented itself in, of all things, a driver's education course. In Massachusetts, it had been decreed that driver's education was henceforward to be a serious subject. To pass, one needed to do more than simply learn how to drive safely; a written paper on some aspect of the automobile and its history was added to the requirements. Those were rebellious days, so I decided to write about the "antisemitism of Henry Ford." I wrote what was judged to be a very fine paper using both primary and secondary sources, and received, as I recall, the best grade in the class. Unfortunately, this had no impact whatsoever on my ability to drive a car, and my poor parents, despite my excellent grade, had to pay for extra driving lessons until I finally passed the road test. Henry Ford had the last laugh.

I studied American Jewish history formally, for the first time, at Brandeis University under Professor Leon A. Jick. He provided students with a superb reading list that served as an introduction to the entire field. I read everything on the list (Leon later admitted to me that not every student did.) I also wrote papers on Jewish related subjects for many of my American history courses, particularly with Professor Morton Keller. My senior thesis resulted in my first published scholarly paper—the first of several by me dealing with East European Jewish immigration to Canada and why it differed from parallel Jewish immigration to the United States.[2]

In addition, I had the extraordinary opportunity to work, as an undergraduate, at the American Jewish Historical Society, then on the Brandeis campus. There I learned, first hand, about archives and research and rare volumes of early Judaica Americana. I also met many visiting researchers who came to the society. I particularly remember Professor Melvin I. Urofsky who, at the time, was the most technologically proficient scholarly visitor (he dictated his notes into a little cassette recorder) and also the most sartorially extravagant. I am almost embarrassed to admit that I got paid for my apprenticeship at the AJHS. I only later realized that I received there a training that was literally priceless. I still draw upon what I learned in the early 1970s under the tutelage of Dr. Nathan Kaganoff and Bernard Wax.

At some point in my undergraduate training, I came to the conclusion that I should make my career in American Jewish history. It was, at that time, a wide open field, a kind of new frontier. I have always enjoyed writing about subjects that nobody has previously explored. To this day, American Jewish history is filled with unexplored highways and byways—*terra incognita*. That for me has always been a big part of the field's allure.

Still, two questions remained: first, it was not at all clear to me *how* one should train to be an American Jewish historian. There was, at that time, no graduate program in the field. And Harvard's well-known Professor Oscar Handlin, who had trained Moses Rischin, was retired and not taking on new students. The second question was, even if I did earn a PhD in American Jewish history, how would I ever find a job? In today's bleak academic market it is easy to forget that in the late 1970s, the market for historians was likewise very bleak. There were certainly no jobs in American Jewish history, and precious few in US history either.

Still, the second question turned out to be easy to answer: since I was only twenty when I graduated Brandeis, I vowed to finish graduate school quickly so that if no job materialized I could retrain as a lawyer and be gainfully employed by the age of thirty.

The first question, though—how to train in the field—proved far more difficult. In some ways it continues to occupy me, since I now stand on the other side of the desk and am in the business of training *future* scholars for the field. I already knew back in the 1970s that two of the most respected senior scholars in the field—Salo Baron and Jacob Rader Marcus—trained in Jewish history. Their approach to American Jewish history, especially in the case of Baron and his students, was deeply shaped by the central questions of Jewish history—questions concerning Jewish community, emancipation, antisemitism, and the like. American Jewish history, according to this view, needed to be understood within the framework of the modern Jewish experience as a whole.

The opposite view, which my Brandeis professors had impressed upon me, and which Oscar Handlin had championed, was that American Jewish history should be understood within the context of American history. The contours of American history were widening in the 1970s to embrace Black history, women's history, immigrant history, and ethnic history. Why not American Jewish history, too? Moreover, it was clear that American Jewish history was shaped by the Constitution, by debates over slavery, by American immigration law, and so forth. These obviously, I thought, needed to be understood within their American historical context.

Adding to this complexity was the fact that American religious history was coming into its own as an important field in the 1970s. Sydney Ahlstrom's *A Religious History of the American People* attracted a great deal of attention when it appeared in 1972, and the modern study of religion looked like an exciting new frontier. Perhaps, I pondered, I should study American religious history.

In the end, I applied to all those programs—four to be exact—that taught Modern Jewish history, American history, as well as American religious history. Rather than choosing among those different frameworks, I determined to study American Jewish history within all three of them. That, I continue to believe, was the right decision. Today's new emphasis on "transnational approaches" to American Jewish history underscores the value of approaching the field from as broad and multi-layered a perspective as possible. At least in my case, I think that some of my best scholarly work brings together material from American and Modern Jewish history, and draws upon the modern study of religion as well. In general, the field of American Jewish history has benefited from new tools and approaches. We need to encourage students to master new methodologies, approaches and historical frameworks, even as we properly insist that they familiarize themselves with the ever-expanding literature of the field.

I made the unusual choice, back in 1975, to pursue my graduate training in American Jewish history at Yale. It made me the best financial offer, I confess, but it also seemed open to someone who wanted to take courses across disciplines (history, Jewish Studies, American Studies and Religious Studies). It also boasted a fabulous faculty, including Professor Ahlstrom, the religious historian, and Professor David Brion Davis, the path-breaking historian of slavery and of nineteenth-century American culture, who later won the National Humanities Medal. I believe that I am the very first person who ever entered the sacred portals of Yale's Hall of Graduate Studies with a yarmulke on his head and the explicit intention of studying American Jewish history in his heart.

Yale's president, the late Ambassador Kingman Brewster, certainly found me unusual. When he greeted all the new graduate students in a formal ceremony, he took me aside, questioned me at length about my interests and background, introduced me to his wife, showed me through his mansion—all this while a long line of waiting students buzzed with astonishment. Then he spoiled everything, for when he led me outdoors for refreshments, he suddenly turned to me, pointed upward to the threatening sky, and said "Mr Sarna, do you think you might intervene with the Divine to see to it that it doesn't rain on our little gathering this afternoon?" Kingman Brewster was a deeply tolerant man who broadened Yale immensely, but I don't think he ever quite understood Jews like me.

Still, Yale turned out to be a wonderful place to study American Jewish history because it had an incredible library, tremendous resources, a capacious sense of what scholarship was about, and world class scholars who took a genuine interest in my work and my somewhat unusual (for Yale) research projects.

During my Yale years, I helped to found the New Haven Jewish Historical Society, became friends with lay Jewish historians in the city like Harvey Ladin, and made the acquaintance of Rabbi Arthur A. Chiel, an historian and the leading Conservative rabbi in New Haven, who encouraged my pursuits and wrote to Jacob Rader Marcus in Cincinnati, by then the acknowledged 'dean' of the field, to tell him about me.[3] That led to a correspondence with Dr. Marcus. He invited me to Cincinnati to pursue research at the Archives, and from our first meeting there I knew that I had found a scholarly mentor. During that summer of 1977, I also became acquainted with the American Jewish Archives, now named in Dr. Marcus's honor. Both the AJA and the AJHS, through the years, have been central to my work.

My doctorate, approved both by Yale and by Dr. Marcus (who carefully read every word), was a biography of Mordecai M. Noah (1785-1851), a Jacksonian-era journalist, politician, diplomat and playwright, and the foremost American Jew of his time. Noah interested me for two reasons: first, he confronted throughout his life the challenge of how to be a public figure in America as well as a serious Jew. How to be "both an American and a Jew" is in many ways the basic American Jewish dilemma, and I looked to Noah to shed light on its origins. Similar interplays between past and present (likewise a feature of David B. Davis's work), have characterized much of my subsequent scholarship. Second, writing about Noah posed a methodological dilemma. His era had been dubbed the "dark period" in American Jewish history, because (except for his final years) it preceded the emergence of American Jewish newspapers—that is what made the subject challenging and exciting. What I showed, and what I have also tried to show in more recent work, is that a great deal of American Jewish history lies buried in general sources (correspondence, newspapers, magazines and so forth). It is a mistake to try and write American Jewish history on the basis of Jewish source materials alone.[4]

I graduated Yale in 1979, and I didn't have a job. Neither, by the way, did most of my fellow newly minted PhDs; we were, that year, a rather somber group. Dr. Marcus and Hebrew Union College-Jewish Institute of Religion in Cincinnati, came to my rescue awarding me what was practically unknown in 1979: a postdoctoral fellowship. Apparently, they found me a good fellow, for a few months later I was invited to join the faculty in the field of American Jewish history. I was all of twenty-five at the time—younger than all of the HUC students—and everyone knew that I was not a Reform Jew. But Dr. Marcus supported me, and lots of senior faculty members befriended me. In the end, I spent eleven happy and satisfying years at HUC, where I also met and married my wife, then an HUC student, Ruth Langer. In Cincinnati and also through Ruth and her family, which boasted deep roots in Reform Judaism, I came to understand the Reform Movement and its history. This proved invaluable to me. Having grown up in Conservative and Orthodox circles, I now feel that I know all three major movements in American Judaism as an insider. If God turns out to be a Reconstructionist, which given that movement's understanding of God would be a great irony, I will have more of a problem.

During my years in Cincinnati, I published in five major areas that have continued to characterize much of my work: immigration studies, religious studies (American Judaism), Jewish-Christian relations, the history of American Jewish culture and scholarship, and community history.[5] Serendipity determined some of this. In the amazing Klau Library at Hebrew Union College, I found a copy of Moses Weinberger's rare Hebrew volume on *Jews and Judaism in New York*. Weinberger's portrait was so different from Irving Howe's *World of Our Fathers* that I decided to translate the book so that it might become better known. I had once taken a course on translation with the Hebrew poet and critic Eisig Silberschlag at the Boston Hebrew College, and was eager to test my skills. I also thought that the project would improve my Hebrew and hone my discipline. I spent an hour a day on the translation, from 8 AM-9 AM, before heading to the office, and then spent a summer writing up the introduction and notes. The volume appeared in 1982 and remains in print.[6] To my surprise and pleasure, the book eventually attracted the attention of the great American historian of religion Jon Butler, who discussed Weinberger, among others, in his article on "God, Gotham and Modernity" in the *Journal of American History.*[7]

Having published two short books of my own plus several edited volumes[8], and many learned articles, I thought that the time had come for me to undertake a large and ambitious project. As a graduate student, I had written on early Christian missions to the Jews of the United States, resulting in one of my best-known articles.[9] In my *Jacksonian Jew*, I likewise included a long chapter on being Jewish in a world of Christians. So I sketched out a full-scale volume on "Jewish-Christian Relations in the United States," and set to work. The American Council of Learned Societies kindly provided me with a research grant to devote a semester to the project, and I assembled a great deal of primary material.[10]

Just as I was preparing to write chapter one, the Jewish Publication Society invited me to produce their centennial history, with a generous advance and a strict 1987 deadline. Nobody had previously examined the amazing, voluminous JPS archive. My father, who had close ties to JPS, was eager for me to take the project on, and the opportunity as a whole seemed too good to pass up. Of course, I knew the dismal fate of most institutional histories—they go unappreciated and unread. My plan, though, was to focus on a big theme, "the Americanization of Jewish Culture." As much as possible, I planned to tell the story of JPS through its books and authors—a galaxy of Jewish writers. So I put aside the earlier project (forever, as it turned out), spent months amid the vast JPS archive, read or at least perused each of the JPS books, and produced a long and I thought interesting manuscript. The project uncovered much that was completely unknown, and taught me a great deal.

The volume also garnered positive reviews.[11] But my hope that it would somehow avoid the fate of other institutional histories went unrealized: the book sold poorly. Later, I drew on the scholarship that underlay *JPS: The Americanization of Jewish Culture* for an article-length history on the Jewish book in America, and for other projects.[12] I have always wondered, though, whether the Jewish-Christian relations book, had I written it, would have made more of an impact on the field.

Hebrew Union College's president, Dr. Alfred Gottschalk, thought that I might have administrative and fundraising skills, so he established The Center for the Study of the American Jewish Experience under my direction. So-called "public history" had come into vogue at that time, and the thought was that the new center might produce externally funded projects. My own dream was to create a documentary history of American Jewish history, but only an experimental volume appeared entitled *Jews and the American Revolution*.[13] I also received a grant to create a "state of the field" study of American synagogue history, which I completed with Sandy Korros.[14] The Center's most substantial project, however, turned out to be a history of the Jews of Cincinnati. Local history, even more than institutional history, has a reputation for being boring and parochial, but I had learned my lesson. I decided to produce a book that Cincinnati Jews would enjoy reading and owning. With the able assistance of Nancy Klein, who knew Cincinnati's Jews much better than I did, and with input from a skillful designer, we produced a beautifully designed volume, rich in illustrations and primary sources, with a scholarly introduction by me that focused on the distinctive nature of the city's Jewish community ("a sort of paradise for the Hebrews"). The book was much better received than most local histories, and every copy sold.[15]

Most of my students in Cincinnati were Reform rabbis in training. American Jewish history formed part of their required curriculum, which covered all of Jewish history in a year, and I also taught courses in Jewish leadership, the contemporary American Jewish community, American Jewish literature, and more. Like Dr. Marcus, I came to envisage my position in broad terms, embracing American Jewry past as well as present. I also followed his lead and included the Jews of the Caribbean as part of my purview. While many of my contemporaries narrowed their focus to the twentieth century and later to the post-war era, I continue to enjoy ranging widely across time and space.

I also had the great good fortune, beginning at a young age in Cincinnati, to co-direct and then direct doctoral dissertations— 36 of them, to date. I consider them my *lamed-vovniks*—thirty-six righteous ones. Nothing gives me greater satisfaction than the success and productivity of my doctoral students, many of whom remain active scholars. They have enriched and extended the field immeasurably.[16]

In 1990, Brandeis University invited me back to Boston to fill its new Joseph H. & Belle R. Braun Chair. I was 35 at the time, and NEJS was at something of a low ebb—its most famous senior faculty had retired, several other faculty members had departed, and morale had plummeted. President Evelyn Handler (who personally recruited me) as well as the then provost and several senior NEJS faculty members promised that, if I came to Brandeis, we could create an academic center for training students in American Jewish history and we could also rebuild NEJS. The decision to leave HUC Cincinnati, with its great library and archive as well as marvelous colleagues and friends, was a difficult one, but the opportunity to build the program at Brandeis was a once-in-a-lifetime opportunity and I seized it. Ruth and I also looked forward to the opportunity to raise and educate our children in the Boston area (our son, Aaron, was two when we moved; Leah came later), and we hoped that Ruth could find an academic job in the community, which she later did, at Boston College. I have been at Brandeis ever since—twenty-seven years and counting.

The years at Brandeis entailed new administrative duties. I served as department chair for much of the 1990s, and devoted long hours to rebuilding the Department of Near Eastern & Judaic Studies (NEJS). I am particularly proud that the first two women faculty members of NEJS won appointments during my chairmanship. The wonder is that this took so long to achieve!

To ensure that I remained an active scholar notwithstanding the many arduous duties that devolved upon me at Brandeis,

I accepted a series of editing projects. I edited a book series at Wayne State University Press (with Moses Rischin) and at Brandeis University Press/University Press of New England (with Sylvia B. Fishman). I planned and coedited a history of the Jews of Boston (with Ellen Smith)—a sumptuously produced, lavishly illustrated volume, sponsored by the Combined Jewish Philanthropies, that appeared in two editions, adorns thousands of Boston-area homes, and serves as a model of how local history can uphold the highest scholarly standards and still reach a mass audience.[17] I also edited a volume entitled *Minority Faiths and the American Protestant Mainstream*[18], another entitled *Religion and State in the American Jewish Experience* (with David Dalin),[19] and a third entitled *Women and American Judaism: Historical Perspectives* (with Pamela S. Nadell).[20] All three looked to broaden the field of American Jewish history in different ways, and aimed to reach scholars and students. None of them, however, transformed the field the way I hoped that a book of mine someday would.

I also produced a considerable number of scholarly articles during these years, including several historiographic articles on the literature of the field[21]; an oft-reprinted article on the history of the Jewish press in the United States (eventually expanded into the article on "The American Jewish Press" in the *Oxford Handbook of Religion and the American News Media)*[22]; an article on the history of American Jewish education[23]; and another article on "Jewish Prayers for the United States Government."[24] For the 50th anniversary of Louis Brandeis's death, which Brandeis University commemorated, I spent an entire summer reading through primary and secondary sources to produce what became the standard work on Brandeis's "Jewish legacy."[25] I also wrote several articles on American Zionism for books inspired by my distinguished colleague, Jehuda Reinharz.[26]

The most important scholarly work that I accomplished after coming to Brandeis, however, was to begin writing my new history of American Judaism. Sydney Ahlstrom, back when I was a graduate student, had encouraged me to undertake this task, and the more I studied the subject, the more persuaded I became that a new history was urgently needed. There were, of course, many histories of American Jews by the 1990s, but no broadly conceived religious history of America's Jews in the Ahlstrom tradition; most of the work on American Judaism had been produced by sociologists like Nathan Glazer and Marshall Sklare. My goal, which I took upon myself when I turned forty, was to fill this lacuna, by writing a book that would appeal to three audiences: American Jews, students of American religion, and Israelis who had no understanding of what makes American Judaism so different from Judaism in Israel and Europe. I knew that my book would need to combine mastery of the secondary literature with a good deal of primary research, and I knew that it would take many years to complete. In the meanwhile, I worked on pieces of the project: colonial Judaism[27], what I called the "Late-Nineteenth Century American Jewish Awakening" (a publication that attracted a great deal of attention because of its relevance to the 1990s),[28] and a centennial history of the *American Jewish Year Book,* with my student, Jonathan J. Golden, which I knew would be an important resource for the twentieth-century part of my book.[29] By the late 1990s, I had completed two chapters of the proposed history, and was ready to market the book to publishers. Harvard University Press turned the project down, but three other publishers, including Yale University Press, loved it. Yale was my alma mater and also had published Sydney Ahlstrom, so I signed a contract with them.

Just at this time, the National Museum of American Jewish History in Philadelphia decided to undertake what they initially described as a "modest project" to expand the museum and create a new core exhibition covering the full span of American Jewish history. I thought it would be interesting to think about the history of America's Jews for a three dimensional museum narrative even as I was writing a two-dimensional book, so I signed on as a consultant and later as chief historian. In time, the "modest project" turned into a large new museum opposite the Liberty Bell, with freedom as its central theme. The opportunity to help shape the world's only museum entirely devoted to American Jewish history taught me a great deal about historical exhibitions. It also permitted me to share some of my understanding of American Jewish history with a large museum-going public.[30]

In the spring of 1999, while working with the museum and also working on chapter three of my book-in- progress and finishing up the history of the *Year Book*, disaster struck. "It occasionally feels like food gets stuck on the way down to my stomach," I complained to my doctor, Nahum Vishniavsky. He replied that it was "probably nothing, just a sign that you should chew your food better," but then he added what turned out to be a lifesaving caveat: "always wise to check just to make sure." So he scheduled an x-ray. The x-ray revealed a growth. The growth turned out to be cancerous. And the cancer turned out to be esophageal cancer—stage three.

"We treat this cancer very aggressively," the renowned surgeon Dr. Michael Jaklitsch warned. "Chemotherapy, radiation and then a full esophagectomy. It's a tough cancer to beat." The chances of surviving esophageal cancer, in 1999, were about one in five. But with two children below the age of twelve what choice did I have except to fight hard? Moreover, as I read up on the cancer, I realized that I was not a typical EC patient, for 90 percent were smokers and drinkers, while I was neither. At forty-four, I was also much younger than most victims, and I had the good fortune to live in a city with some of the best medical care in the world. So, with a lot of support from Ruth and our children, I made it through. Lying in Brigham and Women's hospital, feeling weaker than I ever had in my life, my greatest single professional regret was not having completed my history of American Judaism. So, assuming I survived, I vowed to take on no new assignments until that book was done. I also adjusted my research strategy so as to make more rapid progress. From now on, chapters would have to be based on a combination of primary and secondary research. Having been reminded of my mortality, I wanted to make sure that the book I had been thinking about for so long would actually see the light of day.

Early in 2000, when Yale Press gently inquired as to my progress, I realized that if I worked hard I could finish the manuscript in time for the planned commemoration of the 350th anniversary of American Jewish life in 2004. My editor reminded me that I would need to submit the book in 2003 in order to meet that target, and I promised to do my best. Fortunately, I had a sabbatical due in

2001-2, and the family planned to spend the year in Jerusalem. Only by going far away, I knew, would I be able to focus on the book full time. In addition, Ruth and I wanted our children to come to know and appreciate Israel. A year of schooling, we thought, would make that possible. Of course, we could not have predicted how tumultuous the year would be. The second intifada brought fear to Jerusalem and the attacks of September 11 likewise brought fear to our family in the United States. But we all had a wonderful year notwithstanding these horrors, and by the time we returned, I had completed five chapters, through World War II.

Lara Heimert, my editor at Yale, praised what she read, and told me that she particularly looked forward to the final chapter. "Lots of people will read that chapter first," she smilingly warned, "if they like how you treat the era they personally remember, they will like the rest of the book as well." Her words came to me as a revelation, for I never imagined spending much time on the post-World War II era. Previous histories, after all, had dispensed with that era in a quick "conclusion." Given how much had changed in American Jewish life since 1945, however, I realized that Lara was absolutely right. So began a frantic year of work as I sought to make sense of the post-war years. By most accounts, the resulting chapter, entitled "Renewal," was the most innovative in the book; it remains the one most often cited and assigned. After finally completing it, I spent a few months editing and polishing the manuscript, and hand-delivered it to Yale University Press exactly on deadline. Two great historians of American religion, Martin Marty and Mark Noll, read the book for the press and raved about it. The press became enthusiastic.

The only question that remained was how to entitle the large manuscript. I proposed "Ever-Dying People: A History of American Judaism," believing that would point to an important theme of the book: the recurring fear, beginning in the seventeenth century, that Judaism in America could not survive, that Jews would inevitably intermarry and assimilate out of existence. Yale Press quickly vetoed that idea, insisting that a downbeat title would drive readers away. Other proposed titles—perhaps twenty of them—fared no better. In the end, Lara suggested the elegant and comprehensive title by which the book soon became known: *American Judaism: A History*. The experience taught me an important lesson: in book titles, as in so many other aspects of writing and living, less is more.[31]

As work on *American Judaism* wound down, planning for the 350th anniversary of American Jewish life geared up. Attorney Robert Rifkind, chair of Celebrate 350, one of the two organizations devoted to the anniversary, invited me to serve as its chief historian. Then, he and Carolyn Hessel, Executive Director of the Jewish Book Council, hatched a plan for me to travel around the country to talk about the 350th anniversary and to sell copies of *American Judaism* at the same time. Brandeis agreed to release me for a semester, and Yale produced copies of my book a lot sooner than originally expected. So off I traveled—sometimes, like a presidential candidate, to multiple destinations in a single day.

Tiring as it was, the speaking tour taught me much about diverse American Jewish communities. In Richmond, Virginia, for example, a huge crowd gathered and the mayor read out a proclamation in honor of the anniversary. Richmond takes enormous pride in its Jewish history, reaching back to the American Revolution, and many a non-Jew celebrates that history as well. In Greensboro, North Carolina, by contrast, I encountered a more challenging crowd. "How could you have written a whole book on American Judaism without saying even one word about Greensboro," one local patriot inquired. Fortunately, a satisfying answer popped into my head just in the nick of time. "Greensboro," I said, "is such a fascinating and unique Jewish community that it deserves a whole history to itself!" Cheers greeted this response and many books were sold.

American Judaism received far more reviews, and also better ones, than any book I had previously written. It also won a series of six awards including, to my astonishment, the prestigious Everett Jewish Book of the Year Award from the Jewish Book Council. Thousands of copies of the book sold, even more when the book appeared in paperback, and it continues to be taught in colleges, high schools and adult Jewish education programs across the United States. Most important of all, the book is assigned in Orthodox, Conservative and Reform seminaries, an indication that they found my presentation fair-minded and accurate. The different Jewish seminaries no longer teach from the same Bible commentary or Talmud edition, so the fact that they all teach *American Judaism* is particularly gratifying. I also was thrilled when, with the help of generous donors, the volume appeared in a Hebrew translation, published by Mercaz Shazar. Israelis, in my experience, understand distressingly little about American Judaism. Now, thanks to *Hayahadut BeAmerika*, they can study the subject in their own language. *American Judaism* even appeared in a Chinese language edition (minus a photograph of Rabbi Zalman Schachter-Shalomi meeting the Dalai Lama that was censored out). While only a few thousand copies were published in Chinese, not the tens of millions that I had fantasized about, the numbers sufficed for Ruth and me to be invited to tour China, where I spoke at various universities.

The challenge after publishing a book like *American Judaism* is what comes next? The success of the book, coupled with the excitement surrounding the 350th anniversary of American Jewish life proved deeply satisfying. But at the age of fifty, I hardly wanted to sit back and rest on my laurels. Nor, given the somewhat fragile state of my health, did I want to take on arduous administrative posts, though several were suggested to me. Instead, as so often before when I was between major books, I turned to smaller projects. With my former student (and now colleague), Jonathan B. Krasner, I produced a two-volume Jewish history textbook for young people.[32] I also coedited a volume of essays honoring the anniversary of the American Jewish Archives[33] and another volume in memory of Leah Levitz Fishbane, who died tragically of a brain tumor in the midst of her highly promising dissertation research.[34] None of these books, I knew, approached the significance of *American Judaism,* but they kept my scholarship active.

I also wrote a series of diverse scholarly articles that explored new dimensions of American Jewish life. One entitled "How Matzah Became Square: Manischewitz and the Development of Machine-Made Matzah in the United States," contributed to a burgeoning literature that seeks to study religion within the context of American capitalism.[35] Three other articles introduced new sources to the field: one discussed items dealing with the "lived religion" of nineteenth-century American Jews found in the collection of Arnold Kaplan, recently donated to the University of Pennsylvania[36]; a second analyzed a newly discovered early nineteenth-century *shtar halitzah* (writ of release from levirate marriage) donated to the American Jewish Archives[37]; and the third made use of the newly opened papers of the National Federation of Temple Sisterhoods to shed light on its committee on religion.[38] Yet another article, continuing my interest in the history of American Jewish education, compared nineteenth-century Jewish and Protestant Sunday School texts, demonstrating how they reflected both cultural borrowing and cultural resistance.[39] Somewhat to my own surprise, I also contributed an article to the *Journal of the Society for American Music,* based on an article I wrote for a conference at Harvard University on "Leonard Bernstein and the Boston Jewish Community of his Youth."[40] The research overturned previous work on Bernstein's early influences and inspired in part both a recent doctoral dissertation and a forthcoming museum exhibit. I also wrote pieces on Lewis Feuer's work in American Jewish history,[41] on a transnational controversy involving a proposed monument for Judah Touro,[42] and on the new Russian-speaking Jewish community in the United States—the latter, a monograph praised by no less than Natan Sharansky.[43] Many of these articles began as "invited papers" for different conferences or volumes and might be considered "interventions" in fields distant from my own. For me, however, they represented welcome opportunities to study new materials and to open up aspects of American Jewish history that had not previously been explored.

In 2008, Lara Heimert persuaded me to try my hand at non-academic writing. She had moved from Yale Press to Basic Books and recruited me to write the Jewish volume in the "Letters to a Young" series that she edited; my assignment was the volume "Letters to a Young Jew." The challenge of writing in a popular idiom for a wide audience attracted me—so did the handsome advance that she proffered. So I devised a plan to write "letters" for each of the Jewish holidays that would simultaneously introduce young readers to the Jewish calendar and to central issues in American Jewish life. My daughter, Leah, who was about the age of the book's target readership, kindly agreed to let me address the letters to her, and she also read and commented on every chapter—a thrill for me as a parent. The whole project bounded ahead faster than any academic book I had ever worked on; it moved from conception to publication in less than a year. But though the result won considerable praise, was a finalist for a National Jewish Book Award, and became for a time a popular bat mitzvah present, it never properly found its niche. Nor did it satisfy me the way my American Jewish history books did. I learned my lesson and have not accepted any more such offers.[44]

Instead, I immersed myself in the literature on Jews and the Civil War. The 150th anniversary of the Civil War, beginning in 2011, promised to focus new communal attention on the war, a subject few American Jewish historians had addressed since the pioneering work of Bertram W. Korn more than fifty years earlier. I sensed that there was much new to be said, especially since American writing on the war had changed dramatically in the interval. I also hoped that the anniversary would provide another opportunity to produce innovative scholarship that would be timely and could appeal to a larger audience.

My former graduate student, Adam Mendelsohn, shared my interest in the Civil War and together we produced a collection of articles about the war, along with an introduction and bibliography.[45] We discussed the literature on "Jews and the Civil War," and set forth an agenda of what still needed to be written. One section of our book focused on General Ulysses S. Grant's notorious General Orders No. 11 that barred "Jews as a class" from his warzone, a subject that I had likewise addressed in *American Judaism*. Rereading the scholarly literature, I realized that it left many questions unanswered, particularly with regard to Grant's subsequent warm relations with Jews during his presidency and afterward. The whole subject, I thought, had been ill-treated, and was almost completely overlooked by Grant scholars and general Civil War historians.

As I began thinking about a book on Grant and the Jews, Jonathan Rosen, a friend, former neighbor, dazzling writer, and the brilliant editor of the Nextbook volumes at Schocken Books contacted me to see if I might contribute to his series, featuring short, smart books on Jewish subjects. He at once grasped the potential of the Grant story and offered me a contract. We decided to publish the book just in advance of the 150th anniversary of Grant's order expelling the Jews, in December 2012. Once again, a sabbatical made it possible for me to focus on the book and once again Ruth and I spent our sabbatical in Jerusalem, where I served as senior fellow at the Mandel Institute. My subject, I fear, mystified colleagues in Israel where Grant is barely known. Nor did any library in Israel contain the necessary 31 volumes of the Ulysses S. Grant Papers or the 128 books that comprise the *Official Records of the War of the Rebellion*. But that hardly mattered, for all had become available online. Indeed, the Grant project brought home to me how much the world had changed since my graduate student days. Increasingly, primary sources of all sorts were becoming accessible everywhere in the world thanks to the internet.

When General Grant Expelled the Jews became the first of my books to be reviewed in the *New York Times* and the first to attract a wide-range of readers outside the Jewish community. I even won an invitation to Paducah, Kentucky, one of the cities from which Jews were expelled, where a standing-room only crowd greeted me. Most importantly, scholars of the Civil War and of Ulysses S. Grant praised the book. Since its appearance, all new biographies of Grant have taken account of my findings.[46]

During one of my public lectures about Grant, in New York City, a man approached and asked if he might talk to me about his private collection of documents. I have learned from experience always to accede to such requests. Time and again, they have introduced me to individuals far from the public eye whose private holdings contain invaluable historical gems. So it was in this case. Benjamin Shapell turned out to have the world's largest private collection of materials concerning Abraham Lincoln and the Jews, and also to know more about that subject than anyone I had ever met. From one meeting, I understood that his materials needed to be better known and that the subject of Abraham Lincoln and the Jews, which I had imagined to be narrow and parochial, was actually far more significant than most people assumed. Ben Shapell generously offered me a commission to write a book based on his materials, and I countered with a more ambitious project: a full-scale history of Lincoln's relations with Jews based on all extant materials. He agreed, a contract was drawn up, and Carolyn Hessel once again lent her wide-ranging talents to the project, recommending it to St. Martin's and bringing Thea Wieseltier in as publicist. The goal was to produce a lavish book in time for the 150th anniversary of the assassination of Abraham Lincoln in April, 2015.

Publishing something new about Abraham Lincoln—the subject of more books than anyone in the whole history of the United States—is no easy task. The deadline too proved daunting: research and writing had to be completed within two years. Fortunately, Ben had assembled a fabulous staff and all of us quickly became deeply committed to this project. I did not have a sabbatical this time, but I did spend one semester as a visiting professor at Harvard, and that afforded me additional time to devote to the book. In April, 2014, ahead of planned surgery to correct a hernia at the site of my esophagectomy, I sent off a draft of the manuscript to Ben and the team.

The surgery proved uneventful, except that while walking the floor during my recovery I fainted. "Probably dehydration," everyone thought, and I was soon released. Had they performed more medical tests, I would have been spared a great deal of trouble.

On May 16, we all traveled to Yale for my daughter's graduation. While not back at full strength, by any means, I desperately wanted to be part of this big family celebration. We planned a relaxing weekend. On Saturday, following services and lunch, we were ambling back to our hotel when I suddenly felt weak and told Ruth that I was not "doing well." That's the last thing I remember from that momentous day. I learned from others that I suffered cardiac arrest and collapsed in the middle of the street. Fortunately, a Yale cardiologist named Dr. Grant Bailey, who happened on the scene, jumped out of his car, performed CPR, and saved my life. An army of dedicated doctors and nurses at Yale-New Haven Hospital and then at Brigham and Women's Hospital in Boston subsequently treated me. On June 5, I was successfully stented. By mid-June, I was working from my hospital bed on the copyedited manuscript of *Lincoln and the Jews*. On July 1, I finally made it home. In September, I was back teaching.

Incredibly, *Lincoln and the Jews: A History* appeared on schedule. It won awards from the Civil War Roundtable and the Lincoln Group of New York, became a finalist for several other awards, and was translated into Hebrew and published in Israel.[47] Lincoln scholar Harold Holzer praised the book as "the definitive study of a long-neglected aspect of Civil War history and Lincoln biography." Thousands of people heard me lecture about "Lincoln and the Jews" in New York, Boston, Washington DC and Los Angeles, and an exhibit based upon the book attracted tens of thousands of visitors. Brandeis University also promoted me to a University Professorship, the school's highest academic honor (there have been fewer than ten in Brandeis's whole history).

Looking ahead, I have a long list of projects that I would like to complete. First, I have promised Yale University Press to produce a new edition of *American Judaism* that brings the story down to the present. A surprising amount has happened since I submitted my original manuscript in 2003—the success of the women's movement and the gay rights movement, the 2008 economic downturn, the decline of the Conservative Movement, the American religious recession, and so forth that all require attention in a substantial new chapter. Second, in 2016-17, I have been invited to Jerusalem to participate in a year-long seminar at the Israel Institute of Advanced Studies devoted to Women and Gender Studies. I have already done lots of work on women and American Judaism, but my goal at the seminar is to work on a completely new subject— the life and writings of a little-known nineteenth-century American Jewish woman writer named Cora Wilburn, about whom I have collected material for several years. Third, I have various books that I would like to finish: one dealing with the cycles of religious awakening in American Jewish life, a second dealing with seating in religious spaces and what it can teach us, a third examining Jews and American Presidential elections from Thomas Jefferson to the present; and a fourth (perhaps two books) that would bring together my most significant articles.

In closing, let me say how grateful I am to Brandeis University, Yale University, Hebrew Union College-Jewish Institute of Religion, the American Jewish Archives, the American Jewish Historical Society and, of course, to my family and to colleagues around the world, for making possible my contributions to the field of American Jewish History. Notwithstanding my continuing health challenges, I pray to continue to be able to make scholarly contributions to the field for many years to come.

Notes

1   Zola, Gary P. "Sarna, Jonathan Daniel," In *Encyclopaedia Judaica*, 2nd ed. (Detroit: Macmillan Reference USA, 2007), ed. Michael Berenbaum and Fred Skolnik, vol. 18, 58-59. Offered online by *Gale Virtual Reference Library*, http://libraries.state.ma.us/login?gwurl=http://go.galegroup.com. resources.library.brandeis.edu/ps/i.do?p=GVRL&sw=w&u=mlin_m_ brandeis&v=2.1&it=r&id=GALE%7CCX2587517544&asid=74c082d5d5 99690e436669b5cbc8b71b, accessed June 1, 2017

2   "Jewish Immigrants to North America: The Canadian Experience (1870-1900)," *The Jewish Journal of Sociology* 18 (June 1976): 31-41; see also "The Canadian Connections of an American Jew," *Canadian Jewish Historical Society Journal* 3 (Fall 1979): 117-129, and "The Value of Canadian Jewish History to the American Jewish Historian and Vice-Versa," *Canadian Jewish Historical Society Journal* 5 (Spring 1981): 17-22.

3   See also my necrology for Rabbi Chiel, "Arthur A. Chiel," *American Jewish History* 73 (March 1984): 324-26.

4   *Jacksonian Jew: The Two Worlds of Mordecai Noah*, (New York: Holmes & Meier, 1981); *Mordecai Manuel Noah: Jacksonian Politician and American Jewish Communal Leader—A Biographical Study*, PhD Thesis, Yale University, 1979 (available from University Microfilms).

5   My most important articles from this period include: Jonathan D. Sarna, "The Freethinker, the Jews, and the Missionaries: George Houston and the Mystery of *Israel Vindicated*," *AJS Review* 5 (1980): 101-114; idem, "The Myth of No Return: Jewish Return Migration to Eastern Europe, 1881-1914," *American Jewish History* 71 (December 1981): 256-68; idem, "Anti-Semitism and American History," *Commentary* 71 (March 1981): 42-47; idem, "The American Jewish Response to Nineteenth-Century Christian Missions," *Journal of American History* 68 (June 1981): 35-

51; idem, "The Great American Jewish Awakening," *Midstream* 28 (October 1982): 30-34; idem, "The 'Mythical Jew' and the 'Jew Next Door' in Nineteenth-Century America," in *Anti-Semitism in American History*, ed. David Gerber (University of Illinois Press, 1986), 57-78; idem, "The Debate Over Mixed Seating in the American Synagogue," in *The American Synagogue*, ed. Jack Wertheimer (New York: Cambridge University Press, 1987), 363-394; and Jonathan D. Sarna and Nahum M. Sarna, "Jewish Bible Scholarship and Translations in the United States," in *The Bible and Bibles in America*, ed. E. S. Frerichs (Society of Biblical Literature and Scholars Press, 1988), 83-116.

6   Jonathan D. Sarna, trans. and ed., *People Walk on Their Heads: Moses Weinberger's Jews and Judaism in New York* (New York: Holmes & Meier, 1982).

7   Jon Butler, "God, Gotham and Modernity," *Journal of American History* 103 (2016): 19-33.

8   Jonathan D. Sarna, *The American Jewish Experience: A Reader* (New York: Holmes & Meier, 1986), 2nd ed., 1997; Jonathan d. Sarna, Benny Kraut and Samuel Joseph, eds., *Jews and the Founding of the Republic* (New York: Markus Wiener, 1985).

9   Jonathan D. Sarna, "The American Jewish Response to Nineteenth-Century Christian Missions," *Journal of American History* 68 (June 1981): 35-51.

10 Articles based on this project include Jonathan D. Sarna, "American Christian Opposition to Missions to the Jews (1816-1900)," *Journal of Ecumenical Studies* 23:2 (Spring 1986): 225-238; idem, "The Impact of Nineteenth-Century Christian Missions on American Jews," in *Jewish Apostacy in the Modern World*, ed. T. Endelman (New York: Holmes & Meier, 1987), 232-254; idem, "Jewish-Christian Hostility in the United States: Some Perceptions From a Jewish Point of View," in *Uncivil Religion*, ed. R.D. Bellah and F.E. Greenspahn, (New York: Crossroad Press, 1987), 5-22; and idem, "Is Judaism Compatible with American Civil Religion? The Problem of Christmas and the 'National Faith'," in *Religion and the Life of the Nation*, ed. Rowland A Sherrill (Urbana, Ill: University of Illinois Press, 1990), 154-173.

11 Jonathan D. Sarna, *JPS: The Americanization of Jewish Culture* (Philadelphia: Jewish Publication Society, 1989).

12 Jonathan D. Sarna, "Two Ambitious Goals: Jewish Publishing in the United States," *A History of the Book in America. Volume 4. Print in Motion: The Expansion of Publishing and Reading in the United States 1880-1940*, ed.

Carl F. Kaestle and Janice A. Radway (Chapel Hill: University of North Carolina Press, 2009), 376-391; idem, "Two Traditions of Seminary Scholarship," in *Tradition Renewed: A History of the Jewish Theological Seminary*, ed. Jack Wertheimer (New York: Jewish Theological Seminary, 1997), 54-80.

13 Jonathan d. Sarna, Benny Kraut and Samuel Joseph, eds., *Jews and the Founding of the Republic* (New York: Markus Wiener, 1985).

14 Jonathan D. Sarna and Alexandra S. Korros, *American Synagogue History: A Bibliography and State-of-the-Field Survey* (New York: Markus Wiener, 1988).

15 Jonathan D. Sarna and Nancy H. Klein, *The Jews of Cincinnati* (Cincinnati: Center for the Study of the American Jewish Experience, 1989); see also Jonathan D. Sarna and Henry D. Shapiro, eds., *Ethnic Diversity and Civic Identity: Patterns of Conflict and Cohesion in Cincinnati Since 1820* (Urbana: University of Illinois Press, 1992.)

16 I have directed or co-directed doctoral dissertations by: Jonathon Ament, Aviva Ben Ur, Michael Cohen, Beth Cousins, Philip Cohen, Joshua Cypess, Debora Skolnick Einhorn, Zev Eleff, Eric Fleisch, Jonathan Golden ,Karla Goldman, Rachel Gordan, Jeffrey Haus, Daniel Judson, David Kaufman, Seth Korelitz, Jonathan Krasner, Adam Mendelsohn, Andrea Most, Lincoln Mullen, Mina Muraoka, Kerry Olitzky, Jason Olson, Amaryah Orenstein, Benjamin Phillips, Shari Rabin, Mark Raider, Rona Sheramy, Ofer Shiff, Emily Sigalow,, Holly Snyder, Lance Sussman, Meredith Woocher, Gary P. Zola, and Joellyn Wallen Zollman.

17 Jonathan D. Sarna and Ellen Smith, *The Jews of Boston*, (Boston: Combined Jewish Philanthropies / Northeastern University Press, 1995); 2nd ed., New Haven: Yale University Press, 2005.

18 Jonathan Sarna, ed., *Minority Faiths and the American Protestant Mainstream* (Urbana: University of Illinois Press, 1997).

19 Jonathan Sarna and David Dalin, *Religion and State in the American Jewish Experience* (Notre Dame: University of Notre Dame Press, 1997).

20 Jonathan D. Sarna and Pamela S. Nadell, eds., *Women and American Judaism: Historical Perspectives* (Waltham, MA: Brandeis University Press / University Press of New England, 2001).

21 Jonathan D. Sarna, "American Jewish History," *Modern Judaism* 10 (1990): 343-365; idem, "Reading Jewish Books: The American Jewish Experience," in *The Schocken Guide to Books*, ed. B. Holtz (New York:

Schocken, 1992), 108-127; idem, "Recent Scholarship in American Jewish History," *Jewish Studies* 33 (1993): 11-32 [in Hebrew].

22 "The American Jewish Press," in *The Oxford Handbook of Religion and the American News Media,* ed. Diane Winston (New York: Oxford University Press, 2012), 537-550; an earlier version appeared as "The History of the Jewish Press in North America," *The North American Jewish Press,* 1994 Alexander Brin Forum (Waltham: Brandeis University, 1995), 2-7, and was reprinted in several Jewish newspapers.

23 Jonathan D. Sarna, "American Jewish Education in Historical Perspective,"_*Journal of Jewish Education* 64:1-2 (Winter-Spring, 1998): 8-21.

24 Jonathan D. Sarna, "Jewish Prayers for the United States Government: A Study in the Liturgy of Politics and the Politics of Liturgy," *Moral Problems in American History: Essays in Honor of David Brion Davis* (Ithaca: Cornell University Press, 1998), 200-221; reprinted in slightly different form *in Liturgy in the Life of the Synagogue: Studies in the History of Jewish Prayer,* ed. Ruth Langer and Steven Fine (Warsaw, IN: Eisenbrauns, 2005), 205-224; see also Jonathan D. Sarna, "A Forgotten Nineteenth-Century Prayer for the U. S. Government: Its Meaning, Significance and Surprising Author," in *Hesed Ve-Emet: Studies in Honor of Ernest S. Frerichs,* eds. J. Magness and S. Gitin (Athens, GA: Scholars Press, 1998), 431-440 and "Praying for Governments We Dislike?," *The Lehrhaus,* http://www.thelehrhaus.com/commentary-short-articles/2017/1/2/praying-for-governments-we-dislike.

25 Jonathan D. Sarna, "The Greatest Jew in the World Since Jesus Christ: The Jewish Legacy of Louis D. Brandeis," *American Jewish History* 81 (1994): 346-364; see also Jonathan D. Sarna, "Two Jewish Lawyers Named Louis," *American Jewish History* 94 (March-June 2008): 1-19; and my review of the *The Family Letters of Louis D. Brandeis,* ed. Melvin I. Urofsky and David W. Levy, *Modern Judaism* 25 (February 2005): 99-101.

26 Jonathan D. Sarna, "Converts to Zionism in American Reform Judaism," *Zionism and Religion,* eds. S. Almog, Jehuda Reinharz and Anita Shapira (Hanover, NH: UPNE, 1998), 188-203; Hebrew ed., Merkaz Shazar, 1994, 223-243; Jonathan D. Sarna, "America's Most Memorable Zionist Leaders," in *The Individual in History: Essays in Honor of Jehuda Reinharz,* ed. ChaeRan Y. Freeze et al. (Waltham: Brandeis University Press, 2015), 129-142.

27 Jonathan D. Sarna, "Colonial Judaism," in David L. Barquist, *Myer Myers: Jewish Silversmith in Colonial New York,* with essays by Jon Butler

and Jonathan D. Sarna (New Haven: Yale University Art Gallery in Association with Yale University Press, 2001), 8-23; see also Jonathan D. Sarna, "Port Jews in the Atlantic: Further Thoughts," *Jewish History* 20 (2006): 213-219; idem, "The Mystical World of Colonial American Jews," *Mediating Modernity: Essays in Honor of Michael A. Meyer,* ed. Lauren B. Strauss and Michael Brenner (Detroit: Wayne State University Press, 2008), 185-19; and idem, "Colonial Judaism," *The Cambridge History of Religions in America. Volume I: Pre-Columbian Times to 1790,* ed. Stephen J. Stein (New York: Cambridge University Press, 2012), 392-409.

28 Jonathan D. Sarna, *A Great Awakening: The Transformation That Shaped Twentieth-Century American Judaism and its Implications for Today* (New York: Council for Initiatives in Jewish Education, 1995); reprinted in slightly different form as idem, "The Late-Nineteenth Century American Jewish Awakening," in *Religious Diversity and American Religious History: Studies in Traditions and Cultures,* ed. Walter H. Conser Jr. and Sumner B. Twiss (University of Georgia Press, 1997), 1-25.

29 Jonathan D. Sarna, "The Twentieth Century through American Jewish Eyes: A History of the *American Jewish Year Book,* 1899-1999," *American Jewish Year Book* 100 (2000), 3-103.

30 Jonathan D. Sarna, *"Freedom,"* Dreams of Freedom (Philadelphia: National Museum of American Jewish History, 2011), xiii-xix.

31 Jonathan D. Sarna, *American Judaism: A History* (New Haven: Yale University Press, 2004); Hebrew ed., Mercaz Shazar, 2005; Chinese ed., 2009.

32 Jonathan D. Sarna and Jonathan B.Krasner, *The History of the Jewish People: A Story of Tradition and Change,* 2 vols. (New York: Behrman House, 2006-7).

33 Jonathan D. Sarna, Pamela S. Nadell, and Lance J. Sussman, eds., *New Essays in American Jewish History* (New York & Cincinnati: Ktav/AJA, 2010.)

34 Jonathan D. Sarna and Eitan Fishbane, eds., *Jewish Renaissance and Revival in America* (Waltham, MA: Brandeis University Press / University Press of New England, 2011).

35 Jonathan D. Sarna, "How Matzah Became Square: Manischewitz and the Development of Machine-Made Matzah in the United States," in *Chosen Capital: The Jewish Encounter with American Capitalism,* ed. Rebecca Kobrin (New Brunswick: Rutgers University Press, 2012), 272-288; earlier versions were published as the Victor J. Selmanowitz Lecture by Touro College in 2005 and as idem, "Manischewitz Matzah and the

Rabbis of the Holy Land: A Study in the Interrelationship of Business, Charity and Faith," *Gesher* 140 (Winter 1999): 41-49 (in Hebrew). See also Jonathan D. Sarna, introduction to *Manischewitz: The Matzo Family*, by Laura Manischewitz Alpern (New York: Ktav, 2008), ix-xiv.

36 Jonathan D. Sarna, "Marking Time: Notes from the Arnold & Deanne Kaplan Collection of Early American Judaica on How Nineteenth-Century American Jews Lived Their Religion," in *Constellations of Atlantic Jewish History 1555-1890,* ed. Arthur Kiron (Philadelphia: University of Pennsylvania Libraries, 2014), 49-62.

37 Jonathan D. Sarna and Dvorah E. Weisberg, "A Writ of Release from Levirate Marriage *(Shtar Halitzah)* in 1807 Charleston," *American Jewish Archives* 53:1 (2011): 38-55.

38 Jonathan D. Sarna, "'To Quicken the Religious Consciousness of Israel: The NFTS National Committee on Religion, 1913-1933," in *Sisterhood: A Centennial History of Women of Reform Judaism,* ed Carole B. Balin et al. (Cincinnati: Hebrew Union College Press, 2013), 49-71.

39 Jonathan D. Sarna, "'God Loves an Infant's Praise': Cultural Borrowing and Cultural Resistance in Two Nineteenth-Century American Jewish Sunday-School Texts," *Interreligious Dialogue and Cultural Change,* ed. Catherine Cornille and Stephanie Corigliano (Eugene, OR: Cascade Books, 2012), 59-77; *Jewish History* 27:1 (2013): 73-89.

40 Jonathan D. Sarna, "Leonard Bernstein and the Boston Jewish Community of His Youth: The Influence of Solomon Braslavsky, Herman Rubenovitz, and Congregation Mishkan Tefila," *Journal of the Society for American Music* 3 (2009): 35-46.

41 Jonathan D. Sarna, "Lewis Feuer and the Study of American Jewish History," *Society* 50 (2013): 352-355.

42 Jonathan D. Sarna, "The Touro Monument Controversy: Aniconism vs. Anti-Idolatry in a Mid-Nineteenth Century American Jewish Religious Dispute," in *Between Jewish Tradition and Modernity, Rethinking an Old Opposition: Essays in Honor of David Ellenson,* ed. Michael A. Meyer and David N. Myers (Detroit: Wayne State University Press, 2014), 80-95.

43 Jonathan D. Sarna, "America's Russian-Speaking Jews Come of Age," in *Toward a Comprehensive Policy Planning for Russian-Speaking Jews in North America* (Jerusalem: Jewish People Policy Institute, 2013), 1-27.

44 Jonathan D. Sarna, *A Time to Every Purpose: Letters to a Young Jew* (New York: Basic Books / Perseus, 2008).

45 Jonathan D. Sarna and Adam Mendelsohn, *Jews and the Civil War: A Reader* (New York: NYU Press, 2010).

46 Jonathan D. Sarna, *When General Grant Expelled the Jews* (New York: Schocken / Nextbook, 2012).

47 Jonathan D. Sarna, *Lincoln and the Jews: A History*, with Benjamin Shapell (New York: Thomas Dunne Books / St. Martin's Press, 2015); Hebrew edition, Dvir Press, 2016.

FROM KREMENETS TO NEW YORK:
MY PERSONAL JOURNEY AS A HISTORIAN

Shuly Rubin Schwartz

Aron Shimon Shpall: Hebrew, Russian, and Yiddish writer; high school principal, devoted Zionist and Hebraist. When I contemplate just what set in motion my love of Jewish history, my thoughts go directly to this individual—my maternal great-grandfather—though he died long before I was born. How fortunate I was to have grown up in a family that proudly bore his imprint. His was the first Kremenets home in which Hebrew was the language spoken.[1] Thanks to Shpall's Eliezer-ben-Yehudah-like single-mindedness, his children achieved fluency in Hebrew and when they started families in the United States, they reared their children to speak a fluent, Bible-infused Hebrew. Thanks to my mother's consistent use of Hebrew when speaking to her children, Hebrew was my mother tongue too. My father was a Conservative rabbi and together my parents created a home in suburban Long Island filled with Jewish observance, learning, and culture. My richly Jewish upbringing was enhanced by a yeshiva education anchored in Hebrew, Bible, prayer, and the laws of Jewish observance, with a smattering of Israel studies, Prophets, and a comprehensive secular studies curriculum.

Then, in the summer of 1967, I went to Israel for the first time. This long-dreamed-of, three-week family trip took place a little over a month after the Six-Day War. We traveled all over the country, included newly accessible areas of Hebron, Bethlehem, and the Old City of Jerusalem. I was entranced by archeological ruins, and for the first time, Jewish history resonated with me. I began making tentative associations between the stories I learned in school and the lived experience of the Jewish people in time and space.

That fall, I entered public high school where I studied world history in a much more intensive way, and I continued my Jewish education at the Jewish Theological Seminary's rigorous Hebrew high school, Prozdor. There I was exposed for the first time to the formal study of Jewish history. I'm embarrassed to say that it was only then that I had the "Aha" moment, connecting Jewish history and world history; for example, that the Roman history that I was learning in high school was the context for the Judean ruins that I had seen in Israel and the Second Temple history that I was exploring in Prozdor. Thrilled to connect disparate aspects of my learning, I was eager for more.

Despite this happy revelation, I did not then conclude that I ought to pursue a career as a historian. Entering Barnard College, I expected to major in math—first semester Calculus quickly disabused me of that notion—but in choosing spring courses in my first year, I decided to enroll in the second half of the American history survey. With hindsight in my favor, I could claim that it was my as-yet-unarticulated passion for history that led me to take this pivotal class. But, having served as an undergraduate dean for twenty-five years, I understand that my likely motivation at the time had more to do with the desirable time slot of the class and the fact that my best friend had loved the first semester class and would be taking the second. That experience cemented my love for history, and I enthusiastically chose American history as my major.

During the spring of my sophomore year, I took courses in American religion and American ethnic minorities, and, with the approval of my professors, I wrote a joint research paper exploring my family history. My cousin—Aaron Shimon Citron, z"l (named for our Shpall ancestor) who had completed his PhD in Near Eastern Studies at New York University—had recently shared with me a genealogy scroll as well as several letters and other documents written in gorgeously poetic Hebrew by my great-grandfather. Citron must have recognized my potential as a scholar before I did, and I'm deeply indebted to him for that. Reading through this priceless cache of documents, I was enthralled. I began by translating from Hebrew to English the scroll and select documents. My paper included the translations and contextualized them within the broader eastern European Jewish immigrant experience of the period; the role of Zionism in nourishing many emigrants' hopes and spirits; and the impact of Jewish connections, values, and traditions on the course of their lives. Thanks to these personal primary sources, I was able to anchor the generic immigration story of millions of eastern European Jews in the specificity of one family's experience. Both professors encouraged me to continue to mine this material beyond the semester.

The fall of my junior year, Naomi W. Cohen served as visiting professor at Columbia University, and I loved her survey course in American Jewish history. She assigned what I later learned was one of her favorite exercises, i.e., writing a paper on an American Jewish community based on a close reading of its local Jewish newspaper over several years. When my great-grandfather came to the United States in the 1920s, he had settled in New Orleans—a community I knew little about—so I chose to extend my research into the family history by learning all that I could about the Jewish community in New Orleans from its *Jewish Ledger*. It was then that I discovered that Aron's son and my late great uncle, Leo Shpall, a Jewish educator, had also been an American Jewish historian who had authored countless monographs, including *The Jews in Louisiana*. The following semester, I was fortunate to study modern Jewish history at Columbia University with another master historian Ismar Schorsch. One of his assignments proved to have a lasting impact on me as well: Choose two books and write a comparative book review. The catch—the review had to be ten pages or less. He sternly warned us that he would not read page eleven. I chose to compare Moshe Davis's *The Emergence of Conservative Judaism* and Marshall Sklare's *Conservative Judaism*. Through this assignment, I commenced a life-long exploration of the evolution of American Judaism, and especially of Conservative Judaism. From Schorsch, I also learned the importance of writing lucidly, succinctly, and purposefully. Though I was too intimidated to contribute to the conversation in either of these large classes, I knew I was in the presence of giants and soaked up their every word. Little did

I realize that each would become a crucial mentor to me during my doctoral training and beyond.

For my senior thesis, I turned my focus to the more recent past. I had been an avid reader of American Jewish literature in high school and was fascinated and puzzled by the storm that some cherished writings had provoked among American Jews. For my paper, I decided to study this phenomenon through the lens of Philip Roth, the most controversial of the writers. I wanted to explore the variety of ways in which the American Jewish community had reacted to his writings and try to understand why his works hit such a raw nerve among so many American Jews. My thesis adviser, Basil Rauch, was an eminent historian known especially for his expertise on Franklin D. Roosevelt and his presidency. Though hardly versed in American Jewish history, he heartily supported my topic choice and offered crucial guidance throughout the process.

During the course of conducting research—combing the American Jewish press for articles and reviews of Roth's stories and books; conducting interviews and surveys with American rabbis and reading their sermons—Rauch suggested I contact Roth himself. Much to my surprise, he responded right away, and I had the opportunity to interview Roth in his gorgeous east-side, book-lined Manhattan apartment. I was intimidated by his brilliance while my grandmother was frantic at the thought of me being alone with him during the interview! But the most fascinating reaction was Roth's: he was a bit put off by the focus of my interview. As a history student, I didn't query the sources of his immense literary prowess; rather I probed the more unsettling question of his experiences with and reactions to an American Jewish community that lashed out at him so ruthlessly. Though I never revisited this topic in subsequent research, Roth's brilliant stories and book excerpts have been staples on my syllabi, for his works continue to provide unique and poignant insights into the challenges of crafting a meaningful Jewish identity in mid-century America.

Impacted by feminist thinking during my college years, I nevertheless also remained influenced by traditional gender expectations. The latter prompted me to earn a secondary school social studies teaching license while at Barnard, although I was quite certain that I would never use it. Unsure of what my career path would be, I decided to continue studying what I loved. Having focused on American history as an undergraduate, I chose to immerse myself at the graduate level in the study of Jewish history, to understand more deeply the ways in which the American Jewish experience related to and evolved from it.

I enrolled in the MA program at JTS where I studied the full range of Jewish history. Since so many JTS faculty specialized in the rabbinic period, I experienced much good-natured enticement to shift my focus to the the earlier time period. Professor Max Kadushin, z"l, Visiting Professor of Ethics and Rabbinic Thought and my neighbor in Morningside Gardens, would cajole me when we'd cross paths on our way to or from JTS: "My father was a peddler, your grandfather was a peddler. That's all there is to American Jewish history. Come study rabbinics." A few years later, Shaye J.D. Cohen, who taught at JTS and served as dean of its Graduate School before assuming positions at Brown and then Harvard University, half-jokingly teased me that the ancient period was so much "easier" to study because, unlike modernity, antiquity studies relied on a finite number of extant texts.

But my commitment to American Jewish history held firm. Thankfully Henry Feingold taught at JTS as an adjunct during those years and served as my MA thesis adviser. Interested in the history of American Jewish education and considering a career in the field, I chose to write the history of the founding of Camp Ramah, the Conservative movement's camping arm. No archives existed at the time, but I was given free rein to roam around the JTS attic where I found valuable records from the period. I also visited local Ramah offices, salvaging material on the early history of individual camps that had been left untouched in file drawers for decades. Since many of the founders were still alive, I conducted several oral interviews and incorporated them into the thesis. Feingold proved to be an invaluable mentor, schooling me painstakingly in the art of elegant academic writing.

Not content to stop after the MA, and by this point fully convinced that I wanted to train as a historian and not as a Jewish educator, I continued on at JTS for the PhD. In addition to having the opportunity to work closely on the doctoral level with Schorsch who was now on the JTS faculty, I was fortunate, thanks to the Columbia University consortium, to continue my study of American history and was especially influenced by Robert Handy at Union Theological Seminary and Lawrence Cremin at Teacher's College.

With three years remaining until my late husband would be ordained from JTS, I was determined to finish my coursework and pass my orals while we were living around the corner. With Schorsch as my adviser I was in good hands, for not only was I able to achieve this goal, but he also strongly urged me to audit a course with Naomi Cohen at the CUNY Graduate Center during my final year, lest I leave New York City without having developed a strong and achievable dissertation topic. Drawn to intellectual history at the time and eager to write on a topic that would enable me to utilize my training in the full range of Jewish history, I chose, with Cohen's enthusiastic encouragement, to write on the transference of Wissenschaft scholarship to America, a topic I knew was dear to the heart of my adviser, and therefore one that would also allow me to most benefit from his expertise. Also, having receiving many unsolicited comments on my MA thesis from Camp Ramah pioneers insisting that I had not given them sufficient due, I was eager to write about an earlier period with no living witnesses to testify to the history as they understood it.

It was a long haul after this, as I was isolated in suburbia with young children and no peers with whom to discuss my research. I spent the first year immersing myself in the twelve volumes of the *Jewish Encyclopedia*—an encyclopedia that scholars will recall has no index. While I learned a great deal about all sorts of topics in Jewish studies from this disciplined exercise, I feared that the dissertation would never be completed.

A few crucial touch points kept me going. First, I had remembered seeing Paula Hyman, z"l, the second reader of my dissertation, in deep and animated conversation with Schorsch in the JTS cafeteria when she was so pregnant she could barely reach the table. That image stuck with me, allowing me to believe in the possibility of a woman balancing motherhood and scholarship.

Second, each time I gave birth, Schorsch sent me a congratulatory note that ended with the same handwritten brief addendum: "Mazal tov—but keep working." At first blush, the comment put me off. Was he pressuring me to keep working even with a newborn? But I grew to treasure those notes, for I came to understand that he preserved my intellectual aspirations even when I had to suspend them. Finally, JTS awarded me a summer stipend for dissertation research at the American Jewish Archives. This uninterrupted time in Cincinnati with its plethora of archival gems and the company of other scholars—I met Jonathan Sarna, Michael Meyer, Pam Nadell, and others that summer—catapulted my research and laid the foundation for life-long trusted colleagues, mentors and friends.

A hands-off adviser, Schorsch had confidence that I would—at my own pace—eventually complete the dissertation. He annotated my drafts minimally, but every query and edit mattered. The marginal note "Really?" about an assertion I had made would send me back to the archives for three months to bolster my claim. His vast erudition coupled by his genuine humility, deep love of scholarship, curiosity, and attentive mentorship provided me with invaluable and enduring lessons for my life and my career. I've been so fortunate to have benefitted from his guidance and friendship over the decades.

I earned the PhD in 1987. My husband and four children proudly witnessed this milestone, but the joy of achievement was dimmed by the slim prospect of full-time employment. I decided to focus my energies on revising my dissertation for publication and *The Emergence of Jewish Scholarship: The Publication of the Jewish Encyclopedia* appeared in 1991. At this point, I hit rock bottom. Though I applied for a few academic positions, I understood that this path would likely prove untenable. My husband was a congregational rabbi and we lived in a parsonage; though his compensation was modest, no assistant professor salary would provide us with comparable financial stability to warrant relocating for my job. Thankfully, through the process of interviewing and as a result of many rewarding adult teaching opportunities, I gradually came to understand that a full-time academic position would likely not fully satisfy my career goals. As someone who cared deeply about Jewish communal life, I hoped to have an impact on the Jewish future beyond the class-room and the written word, though how I would do that remained initially unclear.

A few months later, I received a call from a JTS colleague asking if I would consider the position of Assistant Dean of List College, JTS's undergraduate school. I had neither administrative experience nor any notion that I might aspire to or succeed in the role, but I knew that this opportunity would enable me to work in a setting where I might advance my career. I eagerly accepted the role. Within two years, I had joined the faculty and assumed the position of dean. I had quickly realized that I not only had some administrative talents but that I enjoyed impacting students' experiences on a macro level in addition to teaching in the classroom.

During this period, I also began offering courses that incorporated the relatively new field of Jewish Women's Studies, something lacking at JTS at the time. My teaching began to fuel my scholarly interests, and I shifted from a focus on intellectual history to a desire to uncover the history of women whose experiences had been invisible. Teaching students in all five of JTS's schools also reignited my interest in the history of American Judaism, and I wrote several articles on Conservative Judaism and JTS's history. These interests converged in my study of rebbetzins, a topic that also brought me back to my mother and our family's history. I grew up observing my mother and her closest friends serve with passion and dedication as rebbetzins on Long Island, but every academic study I had ever read focused on the important role of rabbis in the post-war expansion of American Judaism with nary a word about their wives. Determined to examine the role of the rabbi's wife as Jewish religious leader, I began exploring the topic, despite well intentioned warnings that I'd find insufficient material. Thankfully, at this point in my career, I had colleagues both at JTS and throughout the academy with whom I could consult regularly. Hasia Diner, Dianne Ashton and others provided the critically important encouragement and astute feedback over numerous meals, coffees, and emails that fueled my evolving project. Though I initially expected to write one article on post-war rebbetzins, I soon realized that the story was a much larger one, one with popular as well as scholarly appeal. Time off for research was difficult to come by as a dean, but thankfully, my mentor—and by this point JTS Chancellor—Schorsch continued to guard my scholarly as well as my academic leadership advancement. Granting me two sabbatical semesters in four years, he enabled me to complete *The Rabbi's Wife* and earn tenure.

In recent years, my co-teaching experiences with Union Theological Seminary professors, Rosemary Keller, of blessed memory, and Mary Boys have enabled me to enrich my insights into American Jewish history still further through the comparative lens. In some ways these experiences have brought me back full circle to my youthful revelation about the Romans. What continually excites me about the field is the unique way in which the American Jewish community remains nourished not only by the full span of the Jewish historical experience but also by its constant interaction with the surrounding American cultural landscape, in both predictable and utterly unpredictable ways.

Over the last decade, my administrative role has expanded to include the deanship of the Gershon Kekst Graduate School, providing me with an opportunity to rethink the role of graduate education in Jewish studies in the twenty-first century. At the same time, my lengthy tenure as dean of List College has given me the privilege not only of working with talented college-age Jews and providing them with the opportunities to gain knowledge and tools to develop their adult selves but also enriching the American Jewish community through the profound impact that List alumni are having as influential lay and professional Jewish leaders in a variety of settings.

The personal always fuels and impacts what drives our work. In my experience, this has proven particularly true. Though I published but one article on Shpall, I still have a cache of letters from him that await translation—a future retirement project perhaps? Either way, I think of Shpall often with much gratitude and with the hope that my own somewhat unconventional career trajectory has enriched the field of American Jewish history as much as it has enhanced my own life.

NOTES

1 Yehuda Kenif, "'Tarbut' School," in *Pinkas Kremenets: sefer zikaron ha-'orekh*, ed. Abraham Samuel Stein (Tel Aviv, Israel, 1954), 137, http://www.jewishgen.org/yizkor/kremenets/kre131.html#Page137, accessed 2 July 2017.

Finding My Place in "the Great Tradition"

Gerald Sorin

"When I saw the old men and old books, and saw the dusty gilt brocade on the prayer shawls, I felt that I was being pulled into some mysterious and ancient clan that claimed me as its own simply because I had been born a block away." The words are Alfred Kazin's in *A Walker in the City* (1951), but might well have been mine in 1953 when I approached the *bima* to recite my Torah portion and become a bar mitzvah. Kazin, who like me was born in Brownsville on Sutter Avenue (two blocks away and a quarter-century apart), went on to say, "Whether I agreed with its beliefs or not, I belonged; whether I assented to its rights over me, I belonged; whatever I thought of them, no matter how far I might drift from that place, I belonged. This was understood in the very nature of things; I was a Jew. It did not matter how little I knew or understood of the faith, or that I was reading alien books; I belonged. I had been expected, I was now to take my place in the great tradition."[1]

"Belonged," repeated four times, is of course, the operative word, and despite its irony, implies an embrace (even if a little too tight). When I read Kazin's enduring masterwork at age sixteen or seventeen, I knew that I too belonged in the same way Kazin did. What I couldn't know, of course, was that other, more manifest ways of belonging, and of taking "my place in the great tradition" lay ahead: by the 1980s, the President of a Reconstructionist Synagogue? Not a chance. Director of a Jewish Studies Program at a State University? Highly improbable. Member of the Managing Editorial Board of *American Jewish History*; and winner of two National Jewish Book Awards? No way! This was never part of any dream of mine, but... *Hineni!* ("Here I Am!")

The decision to venture tentatively into the field of American Jewish Studies came nearly ten years after earning a doctorate in American and European history at Columbia University in 1969. The decision turned out to be... well, as I've suggested, life changing. An innocent flirtation, initiated out of what seemed like mere intellectual curiosity, developed into a passionate love affair. The "subject matter" itself, broader and deeper than I'd ever imagined, was influential. More important, as sometimes happens in academia (perhaps not often enough), a great teacher came my way.

I met Deborah Dash Moore in a former Vanderbilt mansion housing the YIVO Institute for Jewish Research on the corner of 86th Street and 5th Avenue in Manhattan, now the elegant Neue Gallerie museum. The YIVO building, though showing its age in the 1970s, was still impressive. But it did not distract me from my studies with Professor Moore. A newly minted PhD, she was hard at work turning her dissertation into her creative and enduring book, *At Home in America* (1981). Nevertheless, and fortunately for me, she brought her full energy and enthusiasm to bear in her seminar on Jewish Immigration to America. Deborah's passion was contagious. I got hooked on the possibilities of American Jewish history, especially when connected, as it was in class, to an international context. I returned immediately the next semester for Professor Moore's course on Jewish labor in the United States. We read, among many other books and articles, Irving Howe's recently published *World of Our Fathers: The Journey of the East European Jews and the Life They Found and Made* (1976), a stunning and beautifully written, if idiosyncratic (lots of labor activists, few, if any, rabbis or entrepreneurs) interpretation of the lives of Jewish immigrants from Eastern Europe. Deep immersion in that monumental book, and multiple readings, led to my writing, many years later, a biography of Howe, which to my wonder and delight won the National Jewish Book Award in History in 2003.

Deborah's courses and my continuing attempts to synthesize American and Jewish history also influenced my decision to do a biography of the prolific writer and Communist Party activist Howard Fast. This book, *Life and Literature in the Left Lane* (2012), also won the National Jewish Book Award in biography in 2013.

Winning a second time helped me believe that maybe the first time was no fluke.

The crossover from American Studies to American Jewish Studies has been a long and extraordinarily satisfying journey, awards aside. But when did the interest in things Jewish really begin? I realize, biographer that I am, that looking back means putting a construction on the messy material that constitutes my life, any life. There are, however, moments and events in my past that seem like seeds which eventually flowered into a more vigorous Jewishness than the kind in which I had been raised.

I knew I was Jewish, of course. My parents, although hardly religious, identified as Jews. And I *think* they believed in God. If asked, it's likely they would have said what Alfred Kazin's parents apparently said: "We believed and we didn't believe." My father came to the US from Minsk when he was 18 months old. My mother, born in America to immigrants from Poland, grew up in Brooklyn, and like my father, lived in Jewish Brownsville for much of the time between 1905 and 1960. And from 1940, the year I was born, to 1951 so did I—which meant that in my formative years I was surrounded by other Jews and Jewish religious and social institutions, including the Hebrew Educational Society (which housed a synagogue as well as a Hebrew school and recreation center) and a YMHA which in addition to the usual facilities of Ys, had small rooms for classes in Yiddishkayt.

In Brownsville, in the 1940s, in less than two square miles there were also dozens of Hebrew and Yiddish schools stretching from Saratoga Avenue east to Sackman Street and from Pitkin Avenue south to Riverdale. In the same area there were eighty-three synagogues, several in impressive buildings, but most in storefronts and basements, ten on Stone Avenue alone—few however with regular attendance. I could be found with other boys on many a Saturday morning on Stone Avenue within yards of a synagogue, but standing in front of the Rio Movie Theater, where for five cents, two children could see a double feature. "I've got three, who's got two"? was the stronger refrain, not the *Aleinu* ("It is our duty to praise"), the closing prayer of Jewish religious services, faintly, but clearly audible to the right of us.

I was also surrounded by Jewish businesses. There were two kosher delis directly across the street from my apartment house at 412 Sutter Avenue, and between them stood what was called the "appetizing store," also glatt kosher, in which I first heard the word "sable"—a delicate flavored smoked fish highly prized by all the Jews I knew. And one block over on Belmont Avenue was the kosher butcher and bakery, and the great open street market, with its barrels of live herring and sour pickles, and its pushcarts and peddlers, who hawked their goods in more than a few languages, but mostly Yiddish.

Three doors from my house, east toward Rockaway Avenue, was a grocery owned by people my parents called "the refugees." I didn't think to ask my mother or father, "Refugees from what?" until I was ten in 1950. Their answers haunt me still. In that grocery, to which I was often sent for milk and bread, I heard a great deal of Yiddish. My parents could understand Yiddish, but could not converse with any fluency in the Old World language. Nonetheless, I picked up a handful of words, most now part of English—*schlep*, *meshugene*, and *chutzpe*, for example. And some phrases not part of English—yet: *gey in drerd arayn* ("go to hell," or "drop dead," loosely translated) and *aroysgevorfene gelt* (thrown out money).

I did not attend a Yiddish school. But my *alte-zayde* (great-grandfather), a socialist and a regular reader of the *Forverts* (*Forward*) tried to teach me Yiddish when I was eight—somehow, I think now, in defiance of the fact that the language had so recently been effectively erased by Hitler. We stopped the lessons when I was eleven because I entered the Hebrew school on Pennsylvania Avenue between Belmont and Sutter Avenues to prepare for my bar mitzvah. I also attended, in the same building, Boys' Congregation services—mostly as what the rabbi-in-training called "a blue-moon member."

My *alte-zayde*, thinking I should learn Yiddish and Hebrew simultaneously, was unhappy about losing his *uhr-eynikle* (great-grandson) as a student. I loved my *zayde* Berche, but, unbeknownst to him, I was mostly unhappy throughout our lessons, and I felt the same during the two years of Hebrew school. I didn't hate either experience, but both deprived me of time for stickball. We Jewish boys were addicted to that game.

I have two powerful and enduring memories of stickball games, which I now understand had something to do with shaping my Jewish identity. At age twelve I was playing the outfield in Thomas Jefferson High School's fenced-in schoolyard when a homerun was hit onto Sheffield Avenue. As I went to retrieve the proverbial "Spaldeen," a rabbi, wearing a radiantly colored tallit which looked like a cape, ran toward me in a panic. He assumed I was a goy—playing ball on Shabbos after all—and pointed to the fire-alarm, urging me to pull the lever—quickly. Guessing that there was a fire in the little *shul*, I, of course, obeyed.

I didn't think much about this at the time, needing to get back to my position in the outfield. But later I thought, why did the rabbi need me to pull that lever? Would he have pulled it if I hadn't been there? My father, whose 86-year-old mother was immersed in Torah and Jewish lore, knew enough about these questions to tell me that Orthodox Jews were forbidden to "work" on the Sabbath. But when he told me that if no one were around to help, the rabbi *would* have pulled the lever himself, because not pulling it might have cost the lives of people in the shul, I was captivated. I wanted to know more. The Children's Library on Stone Avenue, the first public library in the world devoted to children, was not very far away. The librarian asked me if I was smart. When I said, "maybe," she went to fetch, if I am remembering this correctly, Milton Steinberg's classic *Basic Judaism.* Well, I wasn't that smart. Perhaps I learned a tiny bit from the book, but I wondered afterward why it had been in the Children's Library.

Some ten years later my friends and I, Jewish boys all, were playing ball—again on Shabbos—right next to a synagogue building. I had a bat in my hands ready to swing when the strains of, I believe, Psalm 9 (I did not know that at the time!) emanated from the shul. I also did not know that while Psalm 9 is part of nearly every congregation's Friday evening service, it is rare but not out of the question for Saturday morning. Maybe I was just lucky. In any case, I automatically rested the top of my bat on the ground and stood still, and I saw my friend Stu quickly stop whatever it was he was doing. We exchanged smiles which seemed to say, "We're outside the building, and there's something joyful inside, but in truth, something still alien to us."

In high school most of my teachers and fellow students were Jewish, but rarely more than nominally. At Columbia College, however, I had exposure to teachers and students who did not take their Jewishness for granted. The late Joseph Rothschild, a professor of political science, was an inspiration for me, a model teacher and a genuine intellectual. He seemed completely secular, even to the point of telling *risqué* jokes in class (all boys). After a session featuring Marx and Hegel, and some jokes about standing people on their heads, we left Hamilton Hall together. Immediately, Professor Rothschild pulled a skullcap from his jacket pocket, put it on and rushed off to what I now know must have been a *mincha/ maariv* service (combined afternoon and evening prayers).

How hard it must be, I thought at the time, not yet familiar with the teachings of Mordecai Kaplan, to live fully in two different civilizations. Then I got some help. I was fortunate enough to befriend two Orthodox Jewish students, Zvi Gitelman, now Professor Emeritus of Political Science at the University of Michigan, Ann Arbor, and Harold Jacobson, Professor Emeritus of Classics at the University of Illinois, Chicago. In addition to studying hard at Columbia, Zvi and Harold were carrying twelve credits at the Jewish Theological Seminary at Broadway and 122nd Street. Yet somehow, they found the time to play Frisbee, touch football, and in past years, of all things, stickball—but not on Shabbos. Needless to say I was impressed with their energy and academic stamina, and even more by their religious commitment, keen intellect and *joie de vivre*.

There were no such models at Wayne State University in Detroit where I pursued a master's degree in American History with a minor in Europe. I had by now discovered—in addition to personal antisemitism suffered within the academy—that these histories were integral parts of each other and had to be studied in tandem for fullest understanding. I did not yet see that Jewish history would also become connective tissue in that same work, nor that Jewish Studies would have such personal appeal. Several professors, Lee Benson, my mentor, Edward Lurie, and Barry Rothberg were Jewish, but none practicing nor in any visible way identifying. My wife Myra and I were surprised at how lonely we felt in this regard. Yet, back at Columbia in 1963 for my doctoral studies, surrounded by busy Jews, I slipped right back into experiencing my Jewishness as faint background music.

It was only in New Paltz, where I began teaching in 1965 at the State University that I learned that there were ways of being Jewish other than Orthodox practice. Jay Bloom, a colleague in economics, who would along with his wife, Judi Zuckerman Bloom, become our very good friends, taught us mostly by example, but soon also by long and wide-ranging conversation and intellectual arguments about "how to be Jewish." None of the four of us were believers by conventional definition, but I don't think any one of us would be uncomfortable were we characterized as having faith in "something"—something we couldn't name, an alertness, perhaps, to another dimension of being that is not empirically provable— something that promotes the possibility of goodness, and stands in the place of an interventionist deity.

The Blooms were deeply knowledgeable about Judaism and Jewish history. Judi was the daughter of Arthur J. Zuckerman, the author of *Jewish Princedom in Feudal France, 768-900*, and the Director of Hillel at CCNY for many years. She had been raised in a household saturated in things Jewish. Jay, who was president for a time of the Hillel chapter at City College, also knew a good deal about Jewish philosophy even before meeting Judi. He learned lots more as he became her *fiancé* and husband, and Arthur Zuckerman's son-in-law.

Well before this time I had become an avid reader of American Jewish writers, including, of course, Bellow, Malamud, and Roth, a trio once characterized by Bellow, not without some disparagement, as "the Hart, Schaffner, and Marx" of American Jewish letters. These three writers and many others, including Edward Lewis Wallant, Grace Paley, Tillie Olsen, and Joseph Heller, provided my first bridge into the world of the Blooms, and into the joint decision to build a Jewish Study Group of four or five families—to which most of us still belong fifty years later.

At this point in my teaching, I began to notice in the books we used for courses, including "Western Ideas and Institutions," a near absence of Jews. Little by little. I began to use Jewish material in classes and found it more and more appropriate to do so. Indeed, in my modern American history offerings I came to agree with Professor Steven J. Whitfield's observation, in his perceptive book, *In Search of American Jewish Culture*, that twentieth-century American culture and the culture of the sons and daughters of East European Jewish immigrants were inextricably intertwined. For me this meant that my offerings in U.S. history would not only continue to include the contributions, and multiple mutual influences of African-Americans and women and other earlier overlooked groups, but also the important role and impact of Jewish involvement. In doing this, I discovered that I was swimming against the current of Jewish exclusion from the conversation about the new constructs of multi-culturalism. My response? Full steam ahead!

And that's how I found myself in Deborah Dash Moore's courses at YIVO. In her seminar on Jewish Labor I did a "term paper" on Jewish Socialists. The hypothesis that directed my research was stimulated by a student in my class at New Paltz on Post-Civil War America. We were talking about industrialization and the labor movements it spawned, when he asked about the motivations of people who become active in movements for social justice.

The question resonated quite directly with me, I think, because my earlier research on slavery and abolitionism had had virtually the same focus: "What animated abolitionists and led them to take political and even physical risks in pursuit of justice?" In the books I wrote trying to answer to that question, *The New York Abolitionists: A Case Study of Political Radicalism* (1970) and *Abolitionism: A New Perspective* (1972), I argued that many abolitionists, out of a moral vision deeply infused with religious values, had not only called for an end to slavery, but advocated for political and economic equality for freed blacks, a radical position that imagined a very different United States.

The paper I wrote in the seminar reached a comparable, if tentative, conclusion about the Jewish socialists. Even as I leaned over backward to avoid putting the socialists into a procrustean bed, it appeared to me that their activism grew out of a moral vision, similar to that of the abolitionists, a vision shaped by religious values, however secularized. Deborah returned my paper saying, "There's a book in this." Nice to hear, but scary too.

I worried about being seen as an interloper. I had heard that American Jewish Studies and its practitioners were often treated as junior partners within the larger field of Jewish Studies. How much more resistance would there be to my crossing over then, with only a degree in American History? Deborah Dash Moore, who in all probability experienced some of the bias against American Jewish Studies, strongly encouraged me to take the leap. She told me that in the basement archives of YIVO there were file drawers filled with transcripts of interviews, done about twenty years earlier, with Jewish immigrant socialists. In Yiddish.

Would the Yiddish I learned from my *alte-zayde* thirty years earlier serve me now? Well, yes and no. I could tell by reading the transcripts, in most cases, which of them would be relevant for my research. Many dozen. I took copies of the transcripts to my mother-in-law, Faye Cohen, herself an immigrant, who came to New York at age fourteen, from Raciaz, Poland. Together we refined my very rough and incomplete translations. It was a labor of love for both of us and an exercise in deepening personal connection.

I was also excited about the possibility of interviewing surviving activists, something that had been impossible, of course, with the nineteenth-century abolitionists. A dozen former socialists not only talked with me at length, but made me feel welcome in their homes, and by their warmth and openness allowed me to share, if only vicariously, in a variety of intense social and political experiences. Out of all this came *The Prophetic Minority: Immigrant Jewish Socialists, 1880-1920* (1985). Doing that book moved me, after twenty years of teaching American Studies, to reinvigorate a Jewish Studies minor, which was on life-support at SUNY New Paltz. I had enough chutzpah to "appoint" myself Director.

Deborah continued to be influential in my scholarship and in my life. She was teaching at Vassar College in Poughkeepsie, just across the Hudson River, from New Paltz, and our paths crossed more or less regularly. In 1986, Irving Levine, who worked at the American Jewish Committee, had read Deborah's *At Home in America* and approached her about doing a book on the Brownsville Boys Club (BBC), a group of men in their sixties who had remained friends since their teen-age years. She could not take on the project, but recommended me. I was in scholar-author heaven.

A Brownsville boy myself, although younger and never a member of the BBC, I looked forward to interviewing these men who when boys, as young as fourteen, had been kicked out of their schoolyard play area, and organized a club to campaign among storekeepers, landlords, community leaders, and politicians, for space to play basketball. Their project grew well beyond basketball. Seeing what they could accomplish when organized and committed, the boys created an association with the aim of providing a place not only for sports, but as importantly, for social solidarity and education for neighborhood youth, even as the area shifted, in the 1950s and 1960s from Jewish in ethnic composition to African-American. My interviews and research culminated in *The Nurturing Neighborhood: The Brownsville Boys Club and Jewish Community in Urban America* (1990).

My original title was "Street Corner Jews," an allusion to William Foote Whyte's observer-participant study, *Street Corner Society* (1943) and Alfred Kazin's in-your-face *New York Jew* (1978). But some of the "boys," unfamiliar with the scholarly literature and the games we writers sometimes play, felt demeaned by the phrase. I was reluctant to go with *The Nurturing Neighborhood*. But that title did characterize my analysis of working-class Jewish youth whose idealism and moral vision moved them to activism for social good in an urban setting. The book was generally received by critics as a reliable account of neighborhood life, adolescent culture, American ethnicity, and generational change, which demonstrated links between the Old World culture of the parents and the New World culture of their children.

While I was working on *The Nurturing Neighborhood*, the resuscitated SUNY New Paltz Jewish Studies program caught the attention of Louis Resnick, a local philanthropist who wanted, he told the college president, to see even more things "Jewish" at New Paltz. I wrote a proposal which moved Mr Resnick to make a generous gift, enough to endow an ongoing lecture series under my coordination. For twenty-nine years now, the series which is international in its scope, has featured academics, writers, playwrights, and musicians – all of whom have helped me continue my education in Jewish Studies. But it all started with Deborah Dash Moore's seminar and my first two "Jewish" books, *The Prophetic Minority* and *The Nurturing Neighborhood*.

These books garnered a moderate amount of positive attention in the appropriate journals, and I sensed no resistance to my having crossed over. On the contrary, Henry Feingold, a respected senior scholar in American Jewish History, invited me to participate in an ambitious project sponsored by the American Jewish Historical Society: a five-volume history of the Jewish people in America. I was fortunate enough to be asked to write the third volume, *A Time for Building* (1992), covering what Moses Rischin, the doyen of American Jewish History, called the "block-buster period," 1880-1920.

I felt I had arrived. This feeling was reinforced after I wrote an essay for *Reviews in American History* (RAH) sharply critical of Arthur Hertzberg's *The Jews in America. Four Centuries of an Uneasy Encounter: A History* (1989). I was especially tough on his conclusion that "American Jewish history will soon end, and become part of American memory as a whole," and ended by saying that we are still without a satisfactory short and accessible history of American Jewry. Stanley Kutler, the editor of *RAH*, in response to my complaint urged me to write "the missing book."

Perhaps it was *bashert* (destiny) but not too long thereafter Henry Y. K. Lee, the editor of Johns Hopkins University Press, publisher of *The Jewish People in America*, asked me to do a one-volume analytical narrative on Jews in America. That became *Tradition Transformed: The Jewish Experience in America* (1997), part synthesis, part packed with the results of my own research and reading. By the time *Tradition Transformed* was published, I was beginning spade work for a biography of Irving Howe, a man it seemed to me whose political values were at least partly shaped by an ethno-religious cultural milieu. Howe, a democratic socialist, famously identified as a "partial Jew."

Rereading Irving Howe's work was mostly a joy, and an experience in time travel, particularly as I read the many articles he wrote in the 1950s and 60s for *Partisan Review, Commentary, The New York Review of Books* and *Dissent*. But I began to hesitate as I faced the prospect of having to go through the mounds of writing (not yet digitalized) Howe put out as a journalist early in his career working for radical newspapers like *Labor Action*, and *New International*. And because Howe saved none of his correspondence, I would have to track down his letters scattered across the country in twenty-seven different archives. I would also have to reread the twenty-nine books he wrote or edited, and interview his contemporaries (forty men and women, it turned out). At fifty-seven with a full-time teaching load, did I have the stamina to do it?

More important, did I have the imagination, the *saychel* (common sense). the capability of mind, to wrestle with one of the leading American intellectuals of the post-war period? Added to these questions were Mark Twain's admonition that a person's real life is known only to themselves, Freud's warning that whoever turns biographer commits oneself to lies, and more recently, Janet Malcolm's characterization of the biographer as a "professional burglar, breaking into a house, rifling through certain drawers... and triumphantly bearing his loot away."[2] My enthusiasm for the Howe biography was waning. But I attended a conference of the American Jewish Historical Society in 1996 and was turned around. Scholars made me feel welcome—as an equal, and that was revitalizing. More important, I think, were the genuine encouragement and support I received for the Howe project from many colleagues—including and especially, Jeffrey Gurock, Beth Wenger, Jeffrey Shandler, Pam Nadel, Daniel Soyer, and of course Deborah Dash Moore.

Writing the biography turned out to be such an exciting and enriching experience, that soon after I went forward with another, on Howard Fast, one of the most inexhaustible Jewish writers in American history, and for fourteen years, the "face of Communism" in the United States. Fast, less known, and even less read today, despite his *Citizen Tom Paine, My Glorious Brothers*, and *Spartacus*, was nonetheless worth exploring.

Fast, after all, in 1947 and again during the fifties, refused to "name names." He was, after several trials, convicted of Contempt of Congress and served three months in prison. His courage in this regard was not the only thing that made him interesting to me. By the time Fast died in 2002, he had published over 100 books, many with Jewish content, and he was someone whose social justice activism *might* have grown in part out of Jewish values. That turned out to be true. But Fast, who had correspondence with activists (several Jewish) in many different countries, and traveled to the World Peace Conference in Paris in 1949 where he met important Soviet Communists, failed to expose and denounce the antisemitism rampant in the Soviet Union, about which he had intimate and early knowledge. That he chose loyalty to Stalin and to the Party, and betrayed fellow Jews, certainly complicated the question of his Jewish identity. Dealing with that complexity in Fast's politics and writing, as it spun itself out over many years of study, was sometimes perplexing to me, but always stimulating, and in the end a very satisfying experience.

The work on Howard Fast, but even more so on Irving Howe, brought my interest in literature to another level. I took off my biographer-historian hat (not permanently) and began, as a novice literary critic, to write essays and reviews about the work of dozens of American Jewish writers from Abraham Cahan and Anzia Yezierska to Dara Horn and Rebecca Goldstein, from Saul Bellow, Philip Roth, and Cynthia Ozick to Lara Vapnyar, Yelena Akhtiorskaya, Nathan Englander, and Michael Chabon. Having also recognized over the years the transnational character of the Jewish world, I took on writing about European and Israeli writers as well: Kafka, Imre Kertesz, Irene Nemirofsky, Elie Wiesel, Affinity Konar, Howard Jacobson, Meir Shalev, Yael Hedaya, David Grossman, Aharon Appelfeld, and Amos Oz.

It has been a thrill for me to see those essays and reviews published in, among other journals and magazines, *American Jewish History*, *American Jewish Archives*, *Haaretz*—and *The Forward*—today not quite what it looked like sitting folded beside my *alte-zayde* as he tried to teach me Yiddish seventy years ago.

So, I end near where I began. The prize winning novelist Dara Horn said not too long ago about the creative imagination that "It is a group effort." I think that applies as much to good historical research and writing as it does to art and literature. I could not have done my work in Jewish history and biography, had it not been for the early giants in Jewish Studies and American Studies whose shoulders I tried to reach; and as important, had it not been for the energetic, stimulating community of scholars, young and old, who have nurtured my interest in the field of Jewish Studies every step of the way.

Notes

1   Alfred Kazin, *A Walker in the City* (New York: Harcourt, Brace and Company, 1951), p. 45.

2   Janet Malcolm, *The Silent Woman: Sylvia Plath and Ted Hughes* (New York: Vintage, Reprint, 1995), p. 7.

PERIPATETIC JOURNEYS

Beth S. Wenger

People are often surprised to learn that I was not born in New York. After all, my first book focused on New York Jews and my accent is hardly detectable, so few would guess that I am a Southerner. Unlike most Jewish historians who have written about New York, I did not grow up in the urban centers of the Northeast but rather in the suburbs of Atlanta where my parents—both native New Yorkers—joined the growing ranks of postwar Jews relocating to the American South. Although I did not realize it at the time, my approach to New York history as an outsider turned out to be part of a larger pattern that characterized my scholarship. I often worked from the margins in one way or another, and traversed back and forth between several distinct academic, political, and social environments in ways that decisively shaped my development as an American Jewish historian.

When I was growing up, Atlanta had already adopted the slogan "the city too busy to hate." But the progressive spirit of the city could not conceal simmering racial tensions. Although I was too young fully to comprehend their meaning, Atlanta's racial politics informed my understanding of both race and Jewish identity in America. By all appearances, my family lived in a suburban environment but our house stood just a few blocks within the city limits, so I attended Atlanta's public schools until I concluded the fifth grade. I recall vividly watching small groups of African American children arrive each morning on school buses, traveling from neighborhoods where I had never ventured. Atlanta was struggling to achieve integration and in the early 1970s, initiated a limited busing program as part of a compromise attempt to address ongoing inequalities.[1] The predominantly white students at my school, and the minority of Jewish children like me, did not fully appreciate the magnitude or consequences of Atlanta's long struggle for racial equality. In elementary school, we easily befriended our black classmates, but realized at some level that their experiences were different from ours; we spent time together in school but seldom visited each other's homes when classes ended. We could sense the racial barriers that existed and the tensions brewing around us, even if we could not grasp their full import. As a Jewish child in a predominantly Christian environment, I knew that I was different, but these years marked my first realization that difference had complex layers that I could not yet imagine or articulate. By the time I was born, most legal barriers to integration had fallen, but racial discrimination remained potent, and visible reminders of segregation lingered. I recall visiting my mother, who worked as a cardiologist at the city's public hospital, in a building that retained two identical, parallel wings—an architectural remnant of a time when the hospital housed separate black and white facilities. The structure, like so many others in the city, stood as an enduring legacy of segregation and testified to its persistent ripples in Atlanta society.

Being a Jew in the cosmopolitan South meant negotiating a complex matrix of race, religion and ethnic identity. As Jewish children, we learned that *as Jews*, we ought to support civil rights and equality. Implicitly and explicitly, at home, in synagogue, and at Hebrew school, we were taught that a potent black-Jewish alliance not only existed but ought to form a fundamental core of our identities as Jews. Our shared history of oppression and our Jewish "values," we were told, motivated us to champion all movements for equality. The nuances of racial privilege never appeared in these maxims of Jewish identity. Still, even as young children, my Jewish friends took note that our parents usually voted differently from those of our non-Jewish classmates. Our Jewishness defined us as a distinct subculture in Southern society; we belonged fully as far I could tell, but at the same time, we also occupied a particular social, religious, and political position.

I lived in Atlanta until I left for college, and all that time, I retained a primary community in the city's tight-knit Jewish world, attending Hebrew school three days a week at Ahavath Achim synagogue, then the largest Conservative congregation in the city. In those years, the synagogue, the school, and Jewish youth groups constituted a genuine, though perhaps a rather staid, middle-class community. They provided a solid, if not cutting edge, Jewish education, informed by liberal political and religious values.

My intellectual life took the first of many turns when in sixth grade, my parents chose to send me to the newly created Solomon Schechter day school. In the 1970s, Atlanta maintained only one Jewish high school, affiliated with the Orthodox movement. But the declining state of the city's public schools and the growing interest in Jewish day school education sparked the creation of the city's first Conservative day school, originally designed to extend through high school. Lacking a permanent building, the school operated out of Ahavath Achim's synagogue in its early years. The small classes, the spirit of experimentation, and the dedication of mostly young faculty looking to create something new enlivened the school; for me, it represented a dramatic change from public school and offered a highly stimulating intellectual environment in both Jewish and secular subjects that sparked a deeper interest in Jewish life. But it did not last. The community could not sustain the school through the twelfth grade and went forward (successfully) by limiting the program to the elementary and middle school levels. I could have remained at Solomon Schechter for one additional year, but I would have had to relocate yet again. Instead, after one year in a Jewish day school, and on the cusp of entering the seventh grade, I joined my older sisters at the Westminster Schools, a private, non-denominational Christian school founded in the early 1950s.

The intellectual and social journey—from public school to Jewish day school to Christian preparatory school in a matter of three years—provided an early education in negotiating difference. It turned out to be the first of many times that I made dramatic moves in educational settings. Being a Jewish student in a Christian world altered my worldview, and further defined my Jewish identity. Other Jewish students attended Westminster, largely for the same reasons that I did, in order to gain a quality education. On its campus of one-hundred and eighty acres and more than a dozen buildings, Westminster housed separate girls' and boys' schools; it represented a predominantly white, upper-middle class Southern population, though also admitted a small group of minority students, who I imagine felt even more as outsiders in that setting than I did. Most of all, the school stressed a rigorous academic program and an abiding commitment to educating children in the Christian faith. Westminster had always accepted non-Christian students, but I entered at a moment in the late 1970s when the school began to take a fundamentalist turn. A decade after I graduated, Westminster made national news when it banned the hiring of non-Christian teachers and the appointment of non-Christian trustees— a departure from previous policy but the culmination of a longer ideological direction that guided the institution during my high-school years.[2]

Despite the otherness of being Jewish in a Christian school, I enjoyed the intellectual dimensions of Westminster's religion curriculum. I benefited enormously from studying the New Testament (and indeed, won the New Testament award one year). In many respects, my experiences there provided the best introduction to the nuances of textual interpretation. I listened to Westminster instructors offer their readings of both the Hebrew Bible and the New Testament and then took their conclusions to my Hebrew school teachers who expounded upon and differed vigorously with their analysis of linguistic meanings and intertextual references. I never regarded these interpretive exercises as some kind of search for "truth"; my commitments to Jewish tradition never wavered, but as it turned out, I delighted in the exploration of texts and ideologies. Certainly, there were many times when I felt like an outsider at Westminster, but the dissatisfaction that I often harbored as a student stemmed less from the school's Christian emphasis and more from the competitive academic atmosphere and the focus on test scores and grades. The school certainly provided a high-quality education but not one that fit my own intellectual makeup. I was an uneven high school student, engaged particularly with literature and reading but not always fully committed to every class and assignment, and certainly not yet possessed of any particular passion for history. My primary friendships remained outside of school with friends in Atlanta's B'nai B'rith Youth Organization (BBYO), many of whom also joined me at evening classes at Ahavath Achim synagogue. Youth group activities occupied most of my time, and I spent summers at BBYO's international programs in upstate New York and on its sponsored trip to Israel. My social and intellectual life may have been bifurcated, but it taught me how to navigate as both an insider and an outsider as well as to derive benefits from different kinds of environments. It turned out to be a useful lesson.

After high-school graduation, I eagerly left for college in the Northeast. Although to this day I remain deeply connected to the South, I wanted to explore new places. Wesleyan University in Middletown, Connecticut, offered those possibilities, and it fit my left-leaning social and political outlook. Wesleyan represented the polar opposite of Westminster not only in terms of its progressive politics but also in its educational approach and intellectual freedoms. When I left high school, I would have laughed at anyone who suggested that I might one day become a professional scholar; by my senior year at Westminster, I took every opportunity to escape classes. But everything changed for me at Wesleyan. The atmosphere of a small, liberal arts college suited me, and I became fully engaged as a student perhaps for the first time.

I immersed myself in the academic culture of Wesleyan, exploring all sorts of disciplines, but slowly gravitating toward history. Some semesters, I purposely took complimentary courses in an attempt to engage with a subject from multiple perspectives: one term I would combine a class in African American history together with a course in African American literature; the next I would do the same with women's history and feminist literature. But it was the study of history that quickly captured my fascination more than anything else. The faculty sparked my interest and made me appreciate history as much more than a compilation of names and dates, which was how I had experienced it in high school. I began to read voraciously in all kinds of history, and to appreciate its sources and methods. At Wesleyan, all history majors took a required course on historical theory and historiography, and

I found myself thoroughly engrossed with the intricacies of writing about the past and with the craft and interpretive nuances of the discipline. I became captivated by social, cultural, labor and gender history, but also ventured beyond my comfort zone. I enrolled in Professor Eugene Golub's demanding seminar with the imposing title, "Aspects of Modern Intellectual History: The Critique of Rationalism and the Possibility of a New Consensus." In a carrel in the corner of Olin Library, I plunged into the collected works of Charles Sanders Peirce, the founder of American pragmatism. The research paper that I produced had little relation to any of my later work or interests as an historian, but I felt myself an expert by the time I had finished—at least as much as a college student working on a semester-long paper could be. At the end of the term, Gene Golub asked me what career I intended to purse. I told him that I was contemplating law school; my parents were both physicians and my sisters became ones as well. I considered a career as a lawyer not because I had any particular passion for the law but rather simply because it seemed the only alternative to medicine, which I knew was not my calling. I can still recall vividly sitting in Professor Golub's office, piled high with books and papers, as he told me, "I am sure you would make a fine lawyer, but you might think about following your passion for history." I had never before considered history as a viable profession. Was it possible? Could I actually do that for a living?

Slowly, I began to entertain the notion of becoming an historian and to discover what such a career might require. I knew that I enjoyed the vicarious pleasure of exploring times and places that were not my own as well as the excitement of searching for gems in the archives. When I reflected on what genuinely sparked my interest, it was obvious that almost every paper that I had written in all my history courses had been about Jews (my semester-long foray into the philosophy of Charles Peirce notwithstanding). My curiosity for Jewish history was a constant thread in my college career, but I had simply never considered it a realistic professional choice until the middle of my college years. I began to discuss the possibility with other members of the faculty, particularly Ron Schatz, who sparked my passion for American history, and who offered great encouragement. (I remain in touch with him to this day and in recent years, he has developed his own course in American Jewish history.) I found wholehearted support in Wesleyan's history department, but the university did not have a bonafide Jewish historian at the time, and in fact, Jewish Studies remained a small program on campus. If I were serious about Jewish history, I would have to go elsewhere to be prepared for graduate training.

In my senior year, while still enrolled at Wesleyan, I became a visiting student at the Jewish Theological Seminary (JTS)— a surprising decision to most of those around me, but as someone who had moved academic settings many times before, it made sense to me. I spent the year immersed not only in Jewish history but in Jewish Studies more broadly. There, I sought out Paula Hyman who agreed to supervise my work, although I was only visiting for the year, and she later played a formative role in my career as advisor and mentor. In fact, both Paula and Ron Schatz oversaw my senior thesis that focused on Atlanta's Jewish clubwomen. I had always been interested in women's history, and as I have written elsewhere, I belong to a generation fortunate to inherit a nascent field of gender study, to benefit from existing scholarship, and to take college classes in women's history.[3] As a pioneer in Jewish women's history, Paula took special interest in my project. The senior thesis topic certainly reflected my own background and personal interests; I wanted to explore Southern Jewish history and Jewish women's history, and the research constituted a wonderful immersion in the archives that cemented unequivocally my desire to become a Jewish historian. Although my first published article grew out of that senior thesis, I did not return to writing about Southern history, as other scholarly issues captured my interest in graduate school and beyond. Gender, on the other hand, remained a constant part of my intellectual work and an abiding concern within my scholarship.

By the time I graduated from Wesleyan, I harbored no doubts about my desire to pursue an academic career in Jewish history. I also knew that I wanted to write about American Jewry and to explore a Jewish culture that took root and evolved outside of traditional European centers. American Jewish history had come into its own in 1980s and 1990s. The pioneering generation of scholars, including

Jacob Rader Marcus, Moses Rischin and Arthur Goren, had led the way, but there was a new cadre of historians who had created, for the first time, a genuine academic subfield in American Jewish history. To the frustration of many, including myself, the field struggled for recognition, as many established scholars refused to consider American Jewry a culture worthy of full-fledged academic engagement. But as a student beginning graduate school, I could read the works of Deborah Dash Moore, Jeffrey Gurock, Riv-Ellen Prell, Gerald Sorin, Jonathan Sarna, Hasia Diner, and many others who had lifted the field to academic legitimacy. At the same time, my mentor Paula Hyman, along with scholars like Todd Endelman, Steve Zipperstein, and others, who had anchored their careers in the study of European Jewish history, began to include works about American Jews as part of the corpus of their scholarship. Indeed, many graduate students who studied with me and those who came later, were trained as modern Jewish historians who specialized in the study of American Jews, just as others might focus on French or German Jewry. For our mentors and for us, this represented the ideal approach, and it framed most of our work in American Jewish history, which has always been transnational by its very nature. The study of American Jews seemed to me an exciting and new arena in the 1990s. The field appeared to be crystalizing both thematically and methodologically, and its practitioners constituted a small community of scholars who embraced new scholarship and welcomed graduate students who wanted to participate in its growth.

The decision of where to pursue graduate training was not so simple, and as had been characteristic of my academic career, my life as a graduate student took a winding but ultimately fulfilling road. At the time, many (but not all) leading Jewish historians at universities expressed little interest in training students who wanted to focus on the study of American Jews. At the Jewish Theological Seminary, I had experienced support for my desire to work in the emerging field of American Jewish history. After much deliberation, and a couple of disheartening conversations with other potential advisors in Jewish history programs where I had been accepted, I chose to remain at JTS where I could continue working with Paula Hyman and could benefit from studying with scholars such as Ismar Schorsch and Jack Wertheimer. At the time, I did not weigh the long-term professional consequences of earning a degree from a seminary. Perhaps I was naïve or simply not quite so calculating about charting a future career at the outset of graduate school, but my decision emerged solely from intellectual concerns. At the same time, I remained uneasy about immersing myself in Jewish history alone at an institution populated only by those engaged in the same field. I made the highly unorthodox decision to pursue a Master's Degree in American History at Columbia University while simultaneously enrolling in the doctoral program at JTS. This unusual path made sense to me and allowed me to keep a foot in different intellectual worlds—a position that by that time had become not only comfortable but rewarding for me. A few years into my training, Paula Hyman accepted a position at Yale University, and I decided follow her. By that time, I had benefited from my years at JTS, and felt ready for a new chapter. I left New York with Masters Degrees from the Seminary and Columbia, and completed my PhD at Yale. At the time, I was the only graduate student in Jewish history in Yale's History Department; others working with Paula and David Ruderman enrolled in Religious Studies, where both had joint appointments, and graduate students traveled between the two communities. At Yale, I studied alongside other students in Jewish history while participating in a dissertation writing group with others working in American history. It was the ideal setting for me to finish my graduate career. On paper, my curriculum vitae suggests a well-plotted academic trajectory, though it more accurately reflects a confluence of my intellectual pursuits and fortuitous circumstances.

When it came time to write a dissertation that later became my first book, I was fortunate to follow the burst of scholarship in American Jewish history that began in the 1980s. I decided to write about New York Jews in the Great Depression not because I had a burning desire to write about New York Jewry or because I had a particular interest in economic history.[4] On the contrary, I selected this avenue of research as a direct response to the body of scholarship that had shaped my understanding of American Jewish history.[5] Most of the existing literature at the time had emphasized the successful acculturation of American Jews and the record of achievement in American Jewish communal life. Because the United States offered rapid rights of citizenship and less potent expressions of anti-Semitism, American Jewish history had often been presented as a story of constant success and mobility. Along with fellow historians of my generation and the next, I wanted to complicate the dominant portrayal of American Jewish history as a linear story of adjustment, achievement, and progress. By exploring the 1930s—a time of economic regression, heightened anti-Semitism, and challenges to the confidence that Jews had placed in American life—I found a vehicle to shed light on the doubts and anxieties that accompanied the construction of American Jewish culture. I initially chose New York because more than forty percent of American Jews lived in the city during 1930s, but in the course of my research, this native Southerner forged a lasting fascination with the vibrancy of New York's rich urban culture. The project also left me with an enduring interest in questioning the ways that the narratives of American Jewish history have been told.

Along the way, I became interested in constructions of Jewish memory in the United States. While doing research on my first book, I had come across several accounts of New York Jews visiting the Lower East Side and reflecting upon the "old" immigrant neighborhood. I was not sure precisely where the project might lead, but knew that I wanted to pursue the subject of Jewish cultural memory. I began with an article that explored the ways that later generations of Jews invented the Lower East Side as a site of memory and as a physical space that grounded their collective pasts in the United States. A few years later, together with Jeffrey Shandler and Hasia Diner, I organized a conference on Lower East Side memory that evolved into an anthology.[6] While I ultimately chose not to continue writing about the Lower East Side, I became thoroughly engaged with exploring the dimensions of American Jewish memory. By that time, several works about Jewish historical memory had appeared, including Yosef Yerushalmi's influential *Zakhor*, but few scholars considered the comparatively young Jewish community of the United States capable of creating a full-fledged memory culture of its own.[7] I wanted to explore the ways that Jews had constructed their own narratives of the American Jewish past, and I gradually came to the conclusion that this process constituted more the creation of cultural heritage than the expression of historical memory alone. The sources that ultimately graced the pages of *History Lessons*—popular histories, children's stories, holiday celebrations, and more—were the sorts of self-congratulatory materials that historians had dismissed as mere embellishment and factual distortion.[8] They contained almost unbridled celebration of America's possibilities for Jews and Jews' unwavering loyalty to the United States. My purpose was to take these popular accounts seriously as cultural productions. Decades before the explosion of the heritage "industry" and the ethnic revival of the late twentieth century, American Jews—like other ethnic groups in the United States—had already begun piecing together popular renditions of their past in ways that could be transmitted to future generations. *History Lessons* represented my attempt to chronicle the creation of that complex and multilayered sense of American Jewish history and heritage. Although I am not sure I realized it at the time, I had moved from one project that challenged what I perceived as an overly triumphalist scholarly interpretation of American Jewish life to an attempt to uncover where those celebratory narratives had originated in popular Jewish culture.

Perhaps it was this ongoing engagement with the narratives of American Jewish culture that led me to an active career in public history and steered me to new and unexpected projects and passions. My first foray into this arena came shortly after graduate school when Jeffrey Shandler and I served as co-curators of a museum exhibition at Philadelphia's National Museum of American Jewish History, titled *Encounters With the "Holy Land": Place, Past and Future in American Jewish Culture*.[9] The exhibition and the accompanying catalogue explored the ways that Americans, and particularly American Jews, imagined the "Holy Land." We examined how tourism, advertising, philanthropic campaigns, and the popularization of archaeology came to shape both American and American Jewish conceptions about Palestine in the century before statehood. Several years after the exhibition, I served as consultant to the six-hour PBS documentary *The Jewish Americans*, which aired in 2008, and also authored the companion volume to the series. I embraced the opportunity to create a serious, popular work in American Jewish history that would be both accessible to a wide audience and maintain a sophisticated approach and presentation.[10] I consciously chose not to write a one-volume synopsis of American Jewish history, since two quality works of this kind had been recently published. Instead, I created a collection of first-person accounts of American Jewish life spanning the course of three centuries. I purposely sought out a wide range of voices, including American Jews from all sorts of social, economic and cultural backgrounds, both men and women, the prominent as well as the ordinary. My intention was to create a popular work that offered some synthesis for general readers while also introducing them to primary historical sources. The volume found an audience in educated lay readers and although not specifically intended for this purpose, I have been pleased to learn from colleagues that they use portions of the book in academic courses.

My public history endeavors also include an enduring commitment to Philadelphia's National Museum of American Jewish History, which opened in 2010. I served as one of a four-member team of historians who shaped the Museum's central narratives and oversaw the script of its core exhibition. Working on a museum from its origins through its evolution has been a fascinating journey. While I might not agree with all of the portrayals of American Jewish history presented in the exhibition, participating in that process further shaped my development as an historian. Public history has enriched my historical understanding, brought new perspectives to my teaching and research, and sharpened my writing skills. Over the years, I have found that constructing historical narratives through material objects, with limited space for textual explanation, and writing accessible prose for public audiences have helped me to distill meanings more precisely and work for greater clarity of expression.

****

I write this essay from my office at the University of Pennsylvania, where I arrived almost immediately after completing my degree. I began my career squarely in the middle of the growth of the field of American Jewish history. I had genuine mentors and a body of scholarship readily available; I studied with Paula Hyman, and with Deborah Dash Moore, who served as an outside reader of my dissertation. Yet, I entered the profession when American Jewish history was an established though not fully developed subfield of Jewish history. Not all Jewish historians considered the study of American Jewry on par with other fields in modern Jewish history. The challenges of securing a tenure-track position opened my eyes to the barriers that remained, and I quickly realized that it was more difficult for an Americanist to find a position in Jewish history, and that American historians, even those committed to ethnic history, often had little interest in the study of American Jews. The tide has been turning, albeit very slowly. As the literature has expanded and transnational history has increasingly brought American Jewish experience into broader conversation with other fields, the state of American Jewish history has greatly improved.

I was fortunate to find a long career at the University of Pennsylvania, where I have been able to work comfortably in Jewish and American history, to teach broadly, and to find colleagues in multiple fields. In an ironic departure from my previous educational trajectory, I have spent nearly two decades at Penn. I began my journey by moving from place to place, searching for ways to put the pieces of an intellectual puzzle together. I still enjoy adding new components to my scholarly purview, but as American Jewish history has established a sturdier foundation, I seem to have found the ability to seek new academic pursuits without the need for constant relocation.

Notes

1   Ronald Bayor, *Race and the Shaping of Twentieth-Century Atlanta* (Chapel Hill, NC: University of North Carolina Press, 1996), 197-251. See also Kevin Kruse, *White Flight: Atlanta and the Making of Modern Conservatism* (Princeton, NJ: Princeton University Press, 2005).

2   Peter Applebome, "Atlanta School's Ban on Hiring Non-Christians Opens a Debate," *New York Times*, December 23,1992, accessed June 23, 2017. http://www.nytimes.com/1992/12/23/education/atlanta-school-s-ban-on-hiring-non-christians-opens-a-debate.html.

3   Beth S. Wenger, "Notes from the Second Generation" in Miriam Peskowitz and Laura Levitt eds., *Judaism Since Gender* (New York: Routledge, 1996), 113-119.

4   Wenger, *New York Jews and the Great Depression: Uncertain Promise* (New Haven: Yale University Press, 1996).

5   I was particularly influenced by Deborah Dash Moore's *At Home in America: Second Generation New York Jews* (New York: Columbia University Press, 1981), which offered the first thorough exploration of the urban Jewish communal culture created by the children of immigrants.

6   Beth S. Wenger, "Memory As Identity: The Invention of the Lower East Side," *American Jewish History* 85:1 (March 1997): 3-27; Hasia Diner, Jeffrey Shandler, and Beth S. Wenger, *Remembering the Lower East Side: American Jewish Reflections* (Bloomington: Indiana University Press, 2000).

7   Yosef Hayim Yerushalmi, *Zakhor: Jewish History and Jewish Memory* (Seattle: University of Washington Press, 1982).

8   Beth S. Wenger, *History Lessons: The Creation of American Jewish Heritage* (Princeton: Princeton University Press, 2010).

9   Jeffrey Shandler and Beth S. Wenger, *Encounters With the "Holy Land": Place, Past and Future in American Jewish Culture* (Philadelphia: National Museum of American Jewish History; The Center for Judaic Studies, University of Pennsylvania; and the University of Pennsylvania Library in association with Brandeis University Press, 1997).

10 Beth S. Wenger, *The Jewish Americans: Three Centuries of Jewish Voices in America* (New York: Doubleday Press, 2007).

Stephen J. Whitfield

I belong to the last generation of historians of American Jewry to have emerged *ex nihilo*. Some of us were thus created under conditions that no longer apply, in that we earned our doctorates in graduate programs under mentors who showed little formal scholarly command of the American Jewish past. Until about four decades ago, graduate students found it nearly impossible to study with historians whose own research had directly fathomed the American Jewish experience. That qualifying adverb "nearly" is intended to signal that the rabbinical students at Hebrew Union College enjoyed the good fortune of studying with Jacob Rader Marcus, as did others at the Jewish Theological Seminary of America and at Yeshiva College. Harvard also constituted a slight exception, thanks to Oscar Handlin, who had published a tri-centennial survey of American Jewish history, entitled *Adventure in Freedom*. That 1954 volume lacks footnotes, by the way, though the "Suggestions for Further Reading" at the end add up to four pages. Yet even Handlin, who was one of the great teachers of historians, failed to attract more than one doctoral candidate to explore that adventure: Moses Rischin, the author of *The Promised City: New York's Jews, 1870-1914* (1962).[1]

Otherwise, as Jeffrey S. Gurock has noted in his introduction to this volume, the first books that most leading figures in American Jewish historiography wrote characteristically began as dissertations under the supervision of scholars whose formal qualifications in American Jewish history were limited, or whose interest in the topic was quite ancillary to their expertise. Others, like myself, moved more laterally into this field, which failed to police its borders with any severity and thus welcomed historians who maintained an interest in other topics. In the decade in which I earned a doctorate with a biography of a radical economist, Scott Nearing, two of the enduring works in the field of American Jewish history stemmed from authors who were not even trained as historians—Eli N. Evans's *The Provincials: A Personal History of Jews in the South* (1973) and Irving Howe's magisterial *World of Our Fathers* (1976).

The successor generation is less likely than mine to examine any historical problems outside the field, either because of the relentless pressures of specialization, or because the incentives for versatility have become weaker. Professionalization can entail indispensable virtues (from pinpoint accuracy of research to high standards of evaluation), but can sometime come at the cost of breadth. Younger historians are far less likely to have begun their careers in any field other than the American Jewish past, and may be even less driven to stretch themselves into a different field. But because the formal boundaries of American Jewish historiography have been so porous, because it has been so inclusive, I feel privileged to have gone rogue. I have been given the chance to reconcile the challenges of scholarship with the immediacy of personal concerns. Thus I have sensed no impediment in satisfying my curiosity about the evolution of American Jewish life; I have not needed to brandish credentials entitling me to do so. (The consequent danger is duly noted: dilettantism.) To put a twist on the legend of the *lamed-vovniks*, count me among the last of the just plain Americanists who have ventured into Jewish history as a sideline, and who have turned a sort of hobby into an abiding fascination.

My own path to the scrutiny of that past was a bit more sinuous than others' because I did not even start in American history—much less in Jewish history. From late adolescence through my twenties, the books that left me most awestruck, the works that somehow pulled me most powerfully into the frisson of an academic career, fell under the rubric of European intellectual history. Case in point: Jacques Barzun's *Darwin, Marx, Wagner: Critique of a Heritage* (1941, 1958). I read it in the twelfth grade, which was far too soon. The pretensions of precocity certainly exceeded my capacity to appreciate Barzun's interpretation of the mid-nineteenth century revolution, which asserted how fully humanity belongs to the animal kingdom, how drenched the annals of the past have been in injustice, and yet how spectacular creativity in the arts might redeem us from lives otherwise reduced to tedium or in toil. Barzun does not mention—nor did I notice the coincidence until decades later—that two-thirds of his titans happen to have perpetrated a couple of the most notorious antisemitic tracts of that century. But the combination of dazzling erudition and cultural engagement that *Darwin, Marx, Wagner* demonstrated sparked my realization that to be educated meant acquiring a facility with ideas.

Exposure to specifically Jewish ideas was limited. My parents belonged to a Reform synagogue in Jacksonville, Florida; and we sometimes (though not regularly) attended services on Friday evening. I was enough of a nerd to enjoy the horizon-widening two hours every week of religious school, which was usually called "Sunday school." I cannot be blamed for failing to foresee that one of my Hebrew teachers would later become my father-in-law. Perhaps I can be reproached for lacking any genuine piety. But even then I appreciated the influence—both intellectual and moral—that Rabbi Sidney M. Lefkowitz exerted upon me. (That he had conducted the first Jewish worship service on liberated German soil in the fall of 1945 was never mentioned.) In retrospect the limitations of my Jewish education are obvious, but the peripheral role that classical Reform Judaism played in my adolescence then seemed about as natural and as unassailable as the permanence of the racial segregation of the city.

I was enrolled in the same public school for all twelve grades. The hegemony of the majority religion was not obtrusive, but it wasn't exactly absent either. We stood in line to receive our Gideon Bibles, though not every year. I ignored them. Nor did the annual Christmas pageant have any effect upon me. I remember mostly the guffaws from some of the other boys because of the casting of a classmate, who was reputed to be quite sexually active, as the Virgin Mary. I also recall a substitute teacher who once wanted to reassure us that mistakes on our tests need not be treated as costly because, after all, "there was only one perfect man, and he died on the cross." Did I feel uneasy? Maybe a little. Did I feel resentful? No.

Who back then would have summoned the knowledge or would have shown the bravado to invoke the opposition of Jefferson and Madison to anything less than a strict wall of separation between church and state? But somehow, because I was Jewish and also an avid reader, I did know that I was different.

Here special mention should be made of Samuel Proctor. He was the only Jewish adult from Jacksonville I knew of who opened up the possibility of avoiding a career in business. I was aware that he taught history at the University of Florida in Gainesville, which meant that I might therefore imagine an academic career for myself. Sam would eventually co-edit an early anthology on Southern Jewish history, and his brother would become the president of our synagogue. Absorbed in the history of Florida, Sam edited the *Florida Historical Quarterly*, and became something of a pioneer in the practice of oral history. It is fair to say that his own scholarly achievements were rather modest. But Sam was consistently generous and nice to me; and by personifying the possibility of becoming an actual, hard-core historian, he—or rather the *idea* of Sam Proctor—changed my life.

Majoring in history at Tulane, I enrolled in only a couple of courses in American history. None in Jewish studies were offered, though perhaps a fifth of the undergraduates in the early 1960s were Jewish. A senior year spent at the Sorbonne was followed by a master's degree from Yale, where I specialized in European history. The power of Barzun's book would quickly be matched by the experience of reading H. Stuart Hughes's *Consciousness and Society* (1958) and Fritz Stern's *The Politics of Cultural Despair* (1961), as well as the most probing book that I've ever read devoted to a single thinker—Philip Rieff's *Freud: The Mind of the Moralist* (1959, 1961). It is a pleasure to recite these titles. However subtly, such books helped spur me to try my hand at intellectual history. Of my first three books, two are biographical studies of radical intellectuals; and the third examines an idea—Hannah Arendt's analysis of totalitarianism. And when I moved more fully into American Jewish history, the inclination to tackle ideas (or at least the figures who subscribed to those ideas) persisted, leading to articles on the thought of academics like Lewis S. Feuer, Max Lerner and Herbert

Marcuse, among others. I could not treat ideas as disembodied abstractions, but instead as struggles for meaning that particular thinkers wrestled with in concrete institutional or political settings.

But the most important book that I ever read could be categorized as European intellectual history in the broadest sense, for the isms that Hannah Arendt diagnosed (antisemitism, imperialism and totalitarianism) were far more obvious as political forces than as elements in the lineage of ideas. My interest in *The Origins of Totalitarianism* (1951) began at Tulane, and has been recorded elsewhere.[2] By 1980 I finally felt ready to reckon with her account of the Holocaust and its origins; *Into the Dark: Hannah Arendt and Totalitarianism* is one of the very first books ever published on Arendt. The effort to analyze her work required me to reflect on the plight of the Jews (first in Europe), including the refugees, which inspired one of her most brilliant chapters. My own parents were among these refugees, though they themselves enjoyed exceptional luck. In 1936 my father had fled Germany for Romania, where my mother had been born and raised. They managed to find refuge in the United States and reached Houston in 1940, where I was born two years later. *Into the Dark* is dedicated to the memory of a first cousin who had been murdered in Auschwitz, where he had chosen to go to accompany his mother from Theresienstadt. That is probably a biographical clue—should anyone be interested—to account for my shift into a field in which I lacked training, bereft of mentors and of Jewish languages.

It was somewhat accidental that my entrée into American Jewish historiography was regionally inflected. I bounded into it from the periphery. The defunct Southern Jewish Historical Society became a candidate for resuscitation in 1976; and I happened to be present at the creation, in Richmond. The occasion was stellar. There I first met Eli Evans, who delivered with characteristic panache the keynote address. His portrait of the region's co-religionists, *The Provincials*, is written with such verve and perceptiveness that his "personal history" merits recognition as a contribution to Southern letters as well. Also present in fine form was John Shelton Reed, the most talented of contemporary sociologists of the South (and the funniest too). In Richmond I also met another sociologist, then teaching at the University of Virginia: Lewis Feuer, a polymath who became a friend. That someone of his distinction saw fit to attend the founding conference endowed the revived Society with the sort of prestige that impressed me. Buddies of mine showed up in Richmond too: Raymond Arsenault, Richard King and Richard Tedlow. Though their own scholarly contributions to the nascent field of Southern Jewish history did not endure past that memorable conference, the 1979 anthology that came out of the various sessions, *"Turn to the South": Essays on Southern Jewry*, testifies to the involvement of gifted non-specialists. Without much deliberation, and certainly without foresight, I soon found myself becoming a historian of Southern Jewry.

I've savored the meetings of the Society because savants have bonded so easily with the sort of laypeople who prove that stories of Southern hospitality are not apocryphal. (A recent memoir that Alexandra Zapruder published about her grandfather, an immigrant who had been born in Ukraine and would be fated to film the Kennedy assassination, mentions that when he first arrived in Dallas, he was leaving a store when a sales clerk uttered the standard "Y'all come back!" Abraham Zapruder had never heard the phrase before; he therefore dutifully turned around to go back inside the store.)[3] Gatherings of the Southern Jewish Historical Society also showcase pride in family and community. Having rooted themselves for generations in the South, its Jews have constituted a vast and intricate kinship network to which anthropologists (bewitched instead by the Kwakiutl and the Inuit) have devoted insufficient attention. In 2009 in New Orleans, for example, I delivered a paper tracing the history of a family of Tulane friends; and their relatives inevitably showed up in full force. I happened to mention the name of an eminent scholar of jurisprudence, Edmond Cahn (who had earned all of his degrees at Tulane). My lecture was suddenly punctuated by an outburst from a member of the audience, a pillar of the Society, who yelled: "He's mah *uncle!*" So indecorous an interruption rarely occurs, in my experience, at sessions of the American Historical Association.

But I must also admit that I have not been immune to the imperatives of lineage myself. In 2009 *Southern Jewish History* ran the longest article ever to appear in that journal, thanks to the editorial indulgence of Mark K. Bauman. At 111 pages, "Commerce and Community: A Business History of Jacksonville Jewry" validated a remark that a friend from graduate school, the Pulitzer Prize-winning historian David Oshinsky, once made about my work—that my books are too short, my articles too long. He has a point. But "Commerce and Community" did enable me to assemble familiar if dimly remembered faces from the past, and to rearrange them into a context. Bauman thus permitted me to pay tribute to the merchants who had nurtured and strengthened that community. Admittedly, Jacksonville's Jewry could not boast of singular attributes that might pique the curiosity of others (and maybe not even of other Floridians). With a few exceptions, those businessmen did not attract any national or even regional notice of any consequence. But the research that I conducted connected me to my own adolescence, without having to trespass onto the dicey terrain of autobiography. My own father's business career had been modest; my mother had taught very young children and had ended her career in a Jewish kindergarten. But my wife as well as her mother had been born in Jacksonville, and their knowledge of local Jewish history proved to be invaluable.

Though I cannot claim to have elevated the profile of Jacksonville Jewry, the personal meaning invested in such a project had made me doubt if any other research has ever given me greater pleasure. "I don't want to live in the past," J. J. Gittes (Jack Nicholson) remarks in *The Two Jakes* (1990). "I just don't want to lose it." Yet, Jacksonville also gestated, paradoxically enough, my vocation as a Jewish historian. The portrait of the historian as a young man would not be complete without mentioning my first piece of research, written as a senior in high school, on Benjamin Disraeli. The paper was so well documented that the teacher considered its apparatus of footnotes excessive, and lowered the grade to a B. That demeaning and punitive B must have spooked me for the rest of my career, for never again would the magnitude of my research stun readers or reviewers. Preferring to work from published sources, I admit that my passion for archives is banked. Instead of trying to find unexamined documents, I try to come up with insights. Indeed the author of an authoritative overview of Southern Jewish historiography has observed that my writing tends to be "more impressionistic than empirical."[4]

But the choice of Disraeli looks in retrospect quite characteristic of me. As Lord Beaconsfield he worshipped with evident fidelity at the Church of England; and I have subsequently been drawn to profiling Jews who lived well outside the precincts of normative Judaism or of the organized community. A businessman like the New Orleans-based "Banana King," Samuel Zemurray of United Fruit, is illustrative of my choices of subjects. So are two scholars at Columbia University: Franz Boas, the most formidable foe of racism in the annals of American anthropology, and the protean anarchist intellectual-turned Latin Americanist Frank Tannenbaum. Here J. D. Salinger might be included as well. My article on the strange influence of his only novel, "Cherished and Cursed: Toward a Social History of *The Catcher in the Rye*," has itself enjoyed an unusual fate. The piece appeared in 1997 in the *New England Quarterly*, and the article has recorded the second most frequent number of hits on its website in the history of that journal (founded in 1928). "Cherished and Cursed" has also been reprinted in three different anthologies. I cannot account for such interest, though a pattern is apparent; I tend to write about not-very-Jewish Jews. Their ethnic identification is elusive enough to be intriguing, and invites consideration. Their loyalty to Jewish peoplehood may be thin. But enough traces can sometimes be detected, in my opinion, to vindicate their place within a collective destiny. (Even Salinger's mother had converted to Judaism before his bar mitzvah ceremony.)

After intellectual history and after Southern history came the third byway in a circuitous path to the study of American Jewry. My eighth book was the first I ever wrote from scratch on a topic specific to American Jewish history; and yet *In Search of American Jewish Culture* (1999, 2001) also betrays an indebtedness to the training that I acquired in American history itself. The republic has given Jews tantalizing and unmatched opportunities for both self-advancement and self-expression. Like nowhere else in the millennia of the Diaspora, the Jews of the United States have achieved a seemingly frictionless reconciliation of the right to be equal with the freedom to be different. Such circumstances have impelled me to try to trace how they have exercised such options, in projecting the values and images that constitute Jewish culture (especially in its vernacular forms). Something gratifying and agreeable about being Jewish in America has become commonplace for my generation of historians, and I have sought to connect the American ambiance to Jewish creativity. When Billy Crystal was once asked which features of being Jewish were most enjoyable, he replied with another question—"You mean, besides the circumcision?"[5] My inquiry into the movies, the musicals and, yes, the mirth such comedians have generated has been designed to reveal the vitality of the community that has catapulted its artists and performers into the most inescapable culture that any nation on the globe has ever fostered.

My engagement with this topic, as with my association with the Southern Jewish Historical Society, was not merely academic. The question lingers: Will the past that is the object of scholarship be threaded into a vibrant future? By the twenty-first century, the vestigial force of the immigrant generations has receded. We're on our own. Neither the fate of Israel (whose newspapers and novels only a miniscule minority of American Jews can read, and whose politics are as indecipherable as they are troubling), nor the memory of the Holocaust (that dark matter that will forever frustrate the struggle to grasp such horror) can be expected to serve as foundations for a community that must be built and rebuilt on native grounds. The synagogue remains an indispensable institution, but too few Jews can accurately be called "co-religionists." Judaic tradition has proven to be resilient, but the fervor of observance is not widespread. Therefore, if the corrosive impact of assimilation is to be blunted, the remedy lies not only in what we recall, but even more importantly in what we affirm. That means culture, which is to say, how the imagination can be cultivated. How meaning is articulated will determine the perpetuation of Jewish life in the United States, and has governed much of my own recent work in assessing the popular arts.

Such existential concerns do not alone explain the dominant role that American Jewish history has come to play in my research

agenda. The absurd austerity of the twenty-minute panel presentations that conferences of the American Studies Association and the
Organization of American Historians offer is frustrating. Contrast
the more grandiloquent oratorical opportunities provided within
the Jewish community, with its insatiable programming needs.
They are far more pleasant to satisfy, and so I made projects related
to Jews more of a priority. To serve as a scholar-in-residence (SIR) in
a synagogue compels me to come up with fresh and pertinent topics
in American Jewish history, pushing me into themes that I might
not otherwise have considered, and with the enticement of travel
to cities that I might otherwise not have visited. The challenge of
addressing audiences outside of the classroom, so that a premium
is placed on lucidity and concision, also helped make me communicate more effectively within the classroom. (So, to SIR with love!)

But the single most important factor in becoming an American
Jewish historian is the accident of getting a job at Brandeis
University—and it *was* an accident. At the annual meeting of the
American Historical Association, held late in 1971 in Washington,
D. C., I was chatting with a friend in the corridor of the convention
hotel when a door from a meeting room suddenly opened.
A familiar figure emerged, an assistant professor whom I'd seen on
the Brandeis campus, where I was finishing my dissertation. Jacob
(Jerry) Cohen told me that he was in Washington to recruit possible
candidates for a position in the new Department of American
Studies (born a year and a half earlier). He encouraged me to
submit my candidacy. That spring, before the Department could
reach a decision, its chairperson, Lawrence H. Fuchs, alerted me
to the three reservations that he and his colleagues harbored about
me. They preferred to hire someone with a doctorate in American
Studies; mine was about to be granted in history. For the sake of
diversity, they preferred that their new colleague come from an
institution other than Brandeis. For the sake of even more diversity,
the Department preferred that the successful candidate be female.
Gender was the only one of the three conditions that I might have
been able to correct; but though I badly needed the job... I somehow
managed to secure it. I had never taken a course in American Studies
before having to teach it.

Though I have offered courses in American Jewish history at the Hebrew University of Jerusalem and at the Ludwig-Maximilians-Universität in Munich, I never taught the subject at Brandeis. With Jonathan Sarna serving in the Department of Near Eastern and Judaic Studies, American Jewish history is handled spectacularly well. But whatever the curricular cards that I was dealt, the institution has mattered. The setting in which I would spend nearly all of my professional life was bound to affect my interest in Jewish experience and identity, and getting to know scholars of Judaism and of Jewry proved decisive in reorienting my research. To be sure the encounters were not always intellectual. Early in my first semester, in 1972, I confessed to Nahum Glatzer of my nervousness in entering the classroom. He assured me that butterflies still fluttered in his stomach when every new academic term began. If this venerable and learned champion of the legacy of Franz Rosenzweig, if the successor to Martin Buber at the University of Frankfurt in 1932 could not expel his anxiety, then I could grant myself something closer to *shpilkes*.

No liberal arts institution could excel Brandeis in enabling me to discover the value of the Jewish experience. I got to know not only Sarna's predecessor in teaching American Jewish history, Leon Jick (like Jacob Rader Marcus, a Reform rabbi), but also Ben Halpern, a historian (and champion) of Zionism who introduced one of the first university courses anywhere on the Holocaust; and Marshall Sklare, the pre-eminent sociologist of American Jewry. When I met Leonard (Laibel) Fein, he was moving away from an academic career (in Jewish communal and political studies) and into founding (with Elie Wiesel) a monthly magazine called *Moment*. It would be hard to exaggerate Laibel's effect upon me. The insights that he offered into Jewish life in the United States were illuminating, often grounded in keen knowledge of the key participants. His sparks of both wisdom and wit seemed effortless. Though no one who is intimately familiar with communal operations can avoid a dose of cynicism, Laibel never lost his idealism, his devotion to principles of integrity or his humane curiosity. He immersed himself in general culture (especially serious music and literature), and his unwaveringly liberal political instincts were never parochial. Until joining the faculty at Brandeis, I had never thought much about connecting my sensibility as a Jew to my place in higher education. But the example of such colleagues showed that it was not only possible but honorable to meet the highest demands of critical scholarship without forfeiting a dedication to the plenitude of Jewish life.

But no one on the faculty influenced me more than Lawrence H. Fuchs. Though trained in the methods of political science, he made himself into an Americanist. Though fascinated by the varieties of ethnicity, he showed tenacity and imagination in promoting the particular welfare of the American Jewish Historical Society. His resourcefulness in helping to keep it financially stable may not be discernible in the records of the Society, but I know that it consumed much of Larry's inexhaustible energy. He even facilitated the change by which the slightly cumbersome name of the journal, the *American Jewish Historical Quarterly*, became the streamlined *American Jewish History*. Larry not only studied ethnic groups; he helped make them even more integral to American politics. After all he had helped to ghost-write Senator John F. Kennedy's pamphlet, *A Nation of Immigrants* (1959), which the Anti-Defamation League published, and contributed to Presidential speeches for him thereafter. In 1957 Larry's article on "Presidential Politics in Boston" came within a whisker of earning credit for having put the term "WASP" — in a non-entomological sense — into circulation.[6] For well over three decades of conversations, Larry illumined for me how Jews in particular had historically fit into the mosaic of American pluralism.

One of his own mentors was David Riesman, with whom Larry engaged in a lively correspondence. In one exchange in 1985, the Harvard sociologist condemned particularism and especially what he took to be Jewish ethnocentricity (as well as Zionism); Larry rebutted by asserting that Jewish allegiances were hardly fated to clash with democratic ideals. In his letter, with copies sent to the sociologist Robert Bellah and myself, Larry claimed "never [to have] found that love of one's ethnic ancestry was incompatible with humane values, including an appreciation and a respect for others, in my own life or in those of close friends and associates."[7] He then offered evidence and elaboration. In succinctness and cogency, this letter may have topped anything that Larry ever put in print, even though his prize-winning book on *The American Kaleidoscope* (1990) persuasively framed the expressions of ethnic and religious diversity within what he called "the civic culture." He took full cognizance of the claims of minorities—including those of color who held the most powerful grievances against the polity. But he also valued the authority of the political and legal institutions that ensure a reasonably irenic resolution of differences.

The genealogy of this conception of the social order can be traced to Horace M. Kallen's "cultural pluralism"; and in 1998 I was grateful to Ronald Bayor for giving me an opportunity to retrace that lineage by inaugurating a series for Transaction Books on classics in social science. The extensive introduction that I provided to Kallen's *Culture and Democracy in the United States* (1924) was based in part on his papers in the American Jewish Archives. They enhanced my admiration for Kallen, despite the genetic determinism that mars his version of how the one and the many should be blended. Though Kallen does not quite suffer from scholarly neglect, perhaps no thinker in American Jewish history remains more deserving of a full-scale intellectual biography. That is not anomalous. Perhaps that is another way of saying that, in the museum of American Jewish antiquities and artifacts, it is not yet closing time.

Notes

1   "Students of Oscar Handlin," in *Uprooted Americans: Essays to Honor Oscar Handlin*, ed. Richard L. Bushman, Neil Harris et al. (Boston: Little Brown, 1979), 366.

2   "Hannah Arendt's *The Origins of Totalitarianism*," Classics Series for website blog of the Society for U. S. Intellectual History (January 3, 2016), http://s-usih.org/2016/01/stephen-j-whitfield-on-hannah-arendts-the-origins-of-totalitarianism-1951.html.

3   Alexandra Zapruder, *Twenty-Six Seconds: A Personal History of the Zapruder Film* (New York: Twelve, 2016), 68.

4   Mark K. Bauman, "A Century of Southern Jewish Historiography," *American Jewish Archives Journal* 59:1-2 (2007): 22-23.

5   Cindy Sher, "What Does Billy Crystal Love About Being Jewish?" *Forward*, March 8, 2017, http://forward.com/culture/365412.

6   Lawrence H. Fuchs, "Presidential Politics in Boston: The Irish Response to Stevenson," *New England Quarterly* 30 (December 1957): 435.

7   Lawrence H. Fuchs to David Riesman, May 31, 1985, in Box 24, Publications (Miscellaneous), 1983-85, Lawrence H. Fuchs Papers, Archives and Special Collections, Brandeis University.

On Rabbis, Doctors,
& the American Jewish Experience

Gary Phillip Zola

There are many versions of the familiar quip, "When rabbis became doctors, Judaism became sick." The origin of this barb is obscure, though many say it may have been inspired by a parable that Solomon Judah Rapoport employed in תוכחת מגולה, his 1845 open letter to Reform rabbis gathered in Frankfurt am Main to discuss the reformation of Jewish practice. Later, in 1957, Milton Himmelfarb, the highly regarded director of information and research services for the American Jewish Committee, gave the remark new popularity when he published a review essay on a volume titled *Great Ages and Ideas of the Jewish People*, edited by Leo W. Schwarz. Himmelfarb used the phrase to explain why his American Jewish contemporaries were enthralled by Jewish history.

According to Himmelfarb, one reason American Jews found Jewish history appealing had to do with the fact that modern Jewish historiography and historicism arose in nineteenth-century Germany in order to advance the popular causes of emancipation and enlightenment. The historical enterprise, he theorized, boosted democratic values and represented the ideals of modernity. Yet, Himmelfarb contended there was a second explanation for the "popularity of Jewish history." American Jews could relate to history, he believed, because of their "equivocal relation" to Judaism and Jewish tradition. Most American Jews were no longer capable of studying biblical or talmudic texts as primary sources, Himmelfarb explained. History, on the other hand, was an easily accessible and comprehensible course of study for the highly assimilated Jews of America. Himmelfarb concluded his analysis with an arresting sockdolager: American Jews exchanged "worship of the Lord who chose Israel... [for] a worship of [their] ancestors, the people of Israel..."

My own interest in American Jewish history lends credence to Himmelfarb's hypothesis. In reflecting back on the path that brought me to my current professional circumstances, it would be fair to assert that the study of Jewish history served as a curative for a secularized upbringing that had clearly fostered an "equivocal relation" to Judaism and the Jewish tradition.

Two questions are presented to me with some regularity: (a) What made you decide to become a rabbi? and (b) Which title do you prefer, "Rabbi" or "Doctor?" It occurs to me that the answers to these two queries stem from a central theme in my career—the relationship between Jewish history and Jewish identity. This essay offers me an opportunity to reflect on how and why the study of Jewish history—particularly American Jewish history—became the touchstone of my American rabbinate.

My interest in history began long before I had any sort of Jewish identity. Reading biographies was a favorite childhood pastime. To be sure, I had no interest in reading *Jewish* biography (with the possible exception of Ehrich Weiss, much better known as Harry Houdini). My interests led me to read about the lives of American presidents, inventors, artists, and military generals. By the time I entered high school, subjects such as algebra, chemistry, and biology had become tortuous undertakings, but my classes in the humanities—especially history—never seemed to be a chore.

An awareness of my Jewish identity revealed itself in a memorable encounter. One day, perhaps taking note of my fiery red hair, my first grade teacher, Mrs. Small, asked me if I was a Catholic. "Yes," I replied innocently. Later that same afternoon, I asked my mother if I was a Catholic. Once I explained how this question arose, she scolded me in no uncertain terms: "Don't *ever* say you are Catholic," she admonished. "Remember, you are *Jewish*!"

My mother's emphatic reaction made an indelible impression on my young mind: I was *Jewish*... whatever that meant.

It is quite possible that the secular nature of our home was due to my father's unmistakably ambivalent attitude toward his own father, Sam Zola (*né* Shmuel Zlotkopf). My grandfather was a sixteen-year-old Belarusian Jewish immigrant who arrived in the US in 1904 from Tykocin, a small town in northeastern Poland. Evidently, he was an unrepentant greenhorn who eked out a humble living as a tailor and spoke English poorly, with a thick Yiddish accent. This made my father run as far as he could in the opposite direction. There was no Jewish practice in my own household: no mezuzah, no holiday celebrations, and definitely no blue Jewish National Fund container in the kitchen. Jewish self-discovery came upon me unexpectedly, and primarily from two types of teachers: rabbis and doctors.

Rabbis

One day, my father returned home from work and informed my mother that Mr. Jacob Cohen (viz., the founder and owner of Continental Coffee Company where my father worked for the entirety of his career) had asked him if I had already begun studying to become a bar mitzvah. My father interpreted Mr. Cohen's query as being more than a suggestion, and shortly thereafter our family joined a synagogue—the Reform synagogue where Mr. Cohen and his family belonged! To the best of my recollection, I had never set foot in a synagogue until the fifth grade, the year I began attending religious school at the temple.

My first day as a student in religious school was memorable. Most of the children in my grade were experienced temple-goers, but the entire landscape was foreign to me. During Sabbath worship services on that first day, Rabbi Victor H. Weissberg, the congregation's rabbi, removed a large scroll from a cabinet on the stage and began to speak about it. Innocently, I leaned over to the boy sitting next to me and asked what was written in that scroll. He stared at me as if I were an alien creature. "You don't know what *that* is?" he asked with incredulity. "That is the Torah! It is the *holiest* thing in all of Judaism!" I recall having absolutely no idea what the word "holy" meant either, but I wisely refrained from posing another embarrassing question.

Rabbi Weissberg was a truly impressive and unique figure. Articulate, dynamic, charismatic—it seemed to my young and impressionable mind as if he was a never-ending font of knowledge—both secular and Jewish. To my astonishment, Rabbi Weissberg appeared to know more about the secular world than my public school teachers! He spoke of history often, and this was alluring. Temple members could be overheard praising the rabbi for the breadth of his learning. And the rabbi enjoyed spending time with the congregation's young people—myself included—encouraging us to learn more about our Jewish heritage. He loved his calling, and he urged me and many others to consider the possibility of studying for the rabbinate.

The year I became a bar mitzvah, the rabbi sent home a letter notifying my parents that the temple would provide us with a $200 scholarship if I chose to attend the Reform Movement's summer camp, Union Institute, located in Oconomowoc, Wisconsin. The previous summer, my parents had sent me to Camp Chi, a large and beautiful JCC camp, which I enjoyed. Upon hearing that my parents wanted me to attend a place called "Union Institute," I complained bitterly: "I do not want to go to a different camp. I want to go to Camp Chi!" Much to my dismay, the temple's $200 offer won the day with my father. "One camp is as good as the next," he solemnly declared, and I was sent that summer to Oconomowoc. My father was wrong, however, when he told me that one camp was as good as the next. My life changed entirely once I began to attend Union Institute.[1]

There were many reasons why Union Institute enthralled me, but one in particular was the ubiquitous presence of the camp's rabbinic faculty. At Union Institute, youthful rabbis such as Hillel Gamoran, Lawrence Mahrer, Mark Shapiro, Fred Schwartz, Don Splansky, and Leo Wolkow became friendly mentors as well as inspiring teachers. They taught us about our Jewish heritage as they interacted with us in our daily activities. It happened that many of the rabbis serving in the Chicagoland congregations at that time were members of "Generation Exodus," German-Jewish refugees who, after having fled from Hitler's inferno, settled in the US and proceeded to transform the American Jewish community.[2] The camp's contingent of the rabbinic "Generation Exodus" was a star-studded cast: Ernst Lorge, W. Gunther Plaut, Karl Richter, Frank Rosenthal, Herman Schaalman, Manfred Swarsensky, and Karl Weiner. Scholars have already noted that "the influence of this generation of [immigrant] rabbis in the United States and Canada was considerable."[3] These men had been steeled by adversity, and they inspired me as well as a host of fellow campers and students with their erudition, their determination, and their ethical compass.

Doctors

I matriculated to the University of Michigan in the fall of 1970, where I was required to enroll in a year-long survey course in American history, taught by Professor Harold C. Livesay. Livesay, who specialized in the history of American business and labor relations, was a wonderful, accessible, and affirming teacher who exuded a love for his profession. He urged me to major in history and, ultimately, I took his advice. The following semester I enrolled in an elective course that he taught even though I was not keenly interested in the history of American business; I had learned that if the teacher was effective, the subject matter did not matter all that much. Professor Livesay stimulated class participation, and encouraged his students to interpret, to analyze, and to offer their opinions. We were neophytes, but Professor Livesay engaged us in the historical enterprise. Before long, I abandoned my fleeting dalliance with the idea of majoring in political science and declared myself a history major.

The Department of History at the University of Michigan was brimming with remarkable scholars who were concomitantly inspiring teachers. I studied Russian history with William G. Rosenberg. Gerald F. Linderman taught intriguing courses that focused on the history of America at war. Professor Sidney Fine may well have been the first historian to overwhelm me with his erudition and his pedagogy. Fine's lectures were *sui generis*. He spoke from a carefully prepared text, but he delivered his lectures with humor and verve. He regularly exemplified his points with citations from primary source documents—a technique that was new to me. Fine's lectures were masterworks.

Among the offerings in Michigan's Department of History, I discovered a new field of study: Jewish history. In the early 1970s, the idea of earning college credit for studying something Jewish struck me as a novelty. There was a new, young professor named Jehuda Reinharz teaching a two-semester sequence on modern Jewish history. Reinharz's courses in modern Jewish history brought together for the first time two personal interests: the study of history and a growing appreciation for my late-blooming Jewish identity.

Rabbis and Doctors

The road to rabbinical school at the Hebrew Union College (HUC) was circuitous and riddled with potholes. My father was not enthusiastic about my idea of entering the rabbinate. Such a step would be, from his point of view, a regrettable return to the "world of his father" and a senseless rejection of the limitless professional opportunities available to me as my American birthright. My father urged me to consider any reasonable career option—law school, medical school, business school—anything *except* the rabbinate. None of these options seemed very appealing at the time, so, after completing my undergraduate diploma at Michigan, I went to work for a year.

In the fall of 1975 I enrolled in Northwestern University's one-year MA program in Education. Although the MA curriculum was lock-step, it was possible to squeeze in an elective or two. I eagerly enrolled in a course on the history of American education. In contrast to my experience as an undergraduate at the University of Michigan, graduate history students at Northwestern were expected to submit a term project based on original research using primary source data. The instructor recommended that we consider making use of the university's archives. The school's young archivist, Patrick Quinn, had an infectious appreciation of the primary source materials preserved in the archive's metal cabinets. Upon hearing of my rabbinical interests, Quinn suggested that I consider writing a term paper on a new collection that had only recently been accessioned: the papers of Professor Charles W. Pearson (1846–1905), a Methodist minister who had served for many years as a professor of English literature at Northwestern. In January 1902, Pearson had published an essay in the local press wherein he posited that some elements of the Bible were fictitious. A flurry of negative publicity ensued, followed by calls for Pearson's resignation. Ultimately, the school's president sided with the fundamentalist inquisitors, and Pearson was compelled to resign his faculty post. After studying the archival sources as well as the original news accounts, Pearson's "inquisition" became the topic of my term project. It was the very first time I tried my hand at reconstructing a historical event based (almost) entirely on primary source documents. The experience was transformational.

After completing my MA at Northwestern, I decided to begin the rabbinical curriculum at Hebrew Union College (HUC). I was still somewhat ambivalent about entering the rabbinate, but I began with the belief that my studies would lead me either to remain a rabbinical student or would convince me that I should pursue an alternative path, which my father would have unquestionably preferred. HUC required all rabbinical students to spend their first year studying Hebrew at its Jerusalem campus, and the prospect of living in Jerusalem was alluring for me and my new wife. The "Year-In-Israel" curriculum focused almost exclusively on a wide range of Hebrew proficiencies, including biblical grammar and vocabulary, Rabbinic Hebrew, contemporary Hebrew writings, and spoken Hebrew. Fortuitously, Michael A. Meyer, Professor of Modern Jewish history at HUC's Cincinnati campus, was in Jerusalem for his sabbatical that same year. He volunteered to teach the first-year students a course on Reform Jewish history, which provided me with a very appealing preview of what was awaiting me when I continued my studies at HUC's historic Cincinnati campus.

In Cincinnati, all second-year rabbinical students enrolled in a year-long course in Jewish history, from the biblical era up to the modern period. The final ten weeks of that course were devoted to the study of American Jewish history, and were taught by the famous scholar and founder of the American Jewish Archives (AJA), Jacob Rader Marcus (1896–1995). Prior to my arrival on the Cincinnati campus, I had never heard of Marcus, nor had I read even one of his books. Over the course of that second year, the sessions we were to have with Marcus received quite an impressive buildup from students, faculty, and alumni. "You are going to *love* studying with Marcus," we were repeatedly told. "Dr. Marcus knows everything about American Jewish history," fellow students reported. "He is the 'Dean of American Jewish Historians.'" Even students with little interest in American Jewish history looked forward to studying with "The Doctor."

It is difficult to describe the disquietude that overtook me when I first set eyes on the famous professor, an eighty-three-year-old man standing in front of the class, dressed handsomely in a black three-piece vested suit. He seemed to be a throwback to a bygone era. Would this distinguished, elderly gentleman really have anything interesting or relevant to teach us?

The first words he spoke that day seemed to confirm my worst fears. "It is a longstanding rule at the Hebrew Union College for instructors to call the roll on the first day of class," he began, "and I shall not breach this tradition." Not since grammar school had one of my teachers called roll! Was Marcus really going to call roll for graduate rabbinical students? Then, unexpectedly, Marcus proceeded to dazzle and delight us. After calling each of our family names, one-by-one from A to Z, he spontaneously anatomized every name for the class's edification, followed by a breathtakingly learned and panoramic historical excursion into some historical subject matter relating to the student's name. Marcus's opening performance was a *tour de force*—an impressive display of his remarkable mental agility, his comprehensive grasp of Jewish history, his computer-like ability to retrieve and present data in an instant and, of course, his wonderfully winning personality. My colleagues and I instantly realized we were in the presence of a scholar who had mastered not only *his* field—but every period in Jewish history from the biblical narrative forward. After only a few sessions, I decided I wanted to learn more from this extraordinary teacher.[4]

Having first encountered Marcus when he was eighty-three years old, it was an unanticipated privilege to study with him for the last *seventeen* years of his life. He died just months before his hundredth birthday, and remained vibrant in mind and body until his ninety-seventh year. I had ample opportunity to spend time with Marcus—both in and out of the classroom. Every spring, for instance, Marcus taught a course titled "Topical Documents in American Jewish History." I took that same course two or three times. The course title never changed, but each semester the class examined an entirely new set of documents. It was fascinating to listen to Marcus hold forth on the lessons one could glean from a primary source document. Once he learned that I was interested in Hebrew, Marcus introduced me to the world of American Hebraica. Rabbinical graduates of HUC should be capable of reading American Hebraica, he opined, as this would allow them to contribute to the field by making these documents accessible to an English-speaking audience. I wrote my master's thesis (known at HUC as a "rabbinical" or "ordination" thesis) under his direction— translating and annotating Zvi Hirsch Masliansky's fascinating memoirs, זכרונות.[5]

Marcus was always generous with his time and eager to share his learning. He worked from his home, and he enjoyed having students meet with him there. He would host lunches and snacks, and spend many hours offering advice (and gossiping, too—one of his favorite diversions). One of his oft-repeated slogans was "students always come first." As this Dean of American Jewish Historians aged, his interest in securing the future of the field he had nurtured seemed to intensify. He particularly worried about the future of the American Jewish Archives, and strategized over how he could safeguard the long-term future of his beloved AJA once he had gone from here to eternity. In the last years of his life he frequently paraphrased the words of the talmudic sage Eliezer ben Hyrcanus, who famously compared his arms to the staves of the Torah scroll while proclaiming: "Much Torah have I studied, and much have I taught."[6]

Particularly in the classroom—though also evident in his writings—Marcus emphasized five overarching ideas that characterized his perspective on the history of Jewish life in America. All of these ideas find their geneses in his rabbinical sensibilities. First, Marcus asserted that the American Jewish experience has been consistently influenced by the total historical experience of the Jewish people. To fully understand the American Jewish past, he insisted, the historian must bear in mind that this community is but another link in the long chain of Jewish history which traces its beginnings to the stories in Bible. Second, he asserted that studying the American Jewish past illuminates our understanding of contemporary issues in American Jewish life. Armed with a sophisticated knowledge of the past, he insisted, "a perceptive community can then plan socially and, if successful, assert itself as the subject, not merely the object, of history."[7] Third, Marcus believed that American Jewish history possessed inspirational value that could reinforce Jewish identity. He wrote and taught history with the conviction that when American Jews study their past the likelihood increases that they will become "proud exponents of the best in our Jewish heritage."[8] Fourth, Marcus believed that American Jewish history was, at its core, the study of how the lives of individual Jews interrelated with their own ethno-religious community in America. In the preface to his four-volume magnum opus, *United States Jewry*, Marcus confessed: "I am committed to the thesis that the story of the Jew in this land lies not in the vertical eminence of the few but in the horizontal spread of the many."[9] Finally, Marcus repeatedly gave voice to his religiously based conviction that the Jewish historical experience is immortal. "Jews glory in their survival," Marcus wrote, "they refuse to disappear."[10] Here, Marcus followed in the footsteps of the Jewish historians he studied in his youth—Nachman Krochmal (1785–1840), Isaac Marcus Jost (1793–1860), Heinrich Graetz (1817–1891), and Simon Dubnow (1860–1941)—all of whom believed in the immortality of the Jewish people. Marcus taught his rabbinical students that although civilizations and nations may rise and fall, Jews, if they cling to their ethical legacy, would always endure. "Our prophetic exhortations are the last and best hope of humanity," he preached. "If we raise but a handful of disciples who treasure our ideals we will survive. We are an *am olom*, an eternal people . . . ."[11]

Marcus's personality and his scholarship were seasoned with this distinctive religious perspective. A secular historian would not have written about the American Jewish past as Marcus did, and this ideology spoke to my own professional and intellectual interests. His distinctive approach to the American Jewish experience was an alloy composed of two cardinal elements: Marcus the rabbi and Marcus the critical scholar. This amalgam appealed to me. He convinced me that there actually was a higher purpose and transcendent meaning to the work of the American Jewish historian.

After receiving ordination in 1982, I accepted an offer from HUC to serve as the school's National Dean of Admissions. One of the perquisites of this post was the opportunity it afforded me to continue working with Marcus and, at the same time, to pursue a doctorate through HUC's School of Graduate Studies. Marcus always encouraged my interests but, when I told him I wanted to work on a PhD, he recommended that I speak to the school's newly appointed assistant professor in American Jewish history, Jonathan D. Sarna, who had recently received his PhD from Yale. Marcus, who had brought Sarna to Cincinnati in 1979 to serve as a post-graduate fellow at the American Jewish Archives, quickly recognized Sarna's extraordinary scholarly abilities; "he's a *wunderkind*," he once told me. During his year as an AJA fellow, Sarna explored the AJA's every nook and cranny. By the end of his fellowship year, Sarna had familiarized himself with the school's extraordinary riches, and proved himself to be a remarkably gifted scholar, teacher, and writer. Marcus was eager to have Sarna join the school's faculty.

Like Marcus, Jonathan Sarna is by nature an extremely generous and supportive colleague. One day, not long after I had begun working at HUC, he approached me to say that he had just finished reading a term paper I had written on the career of Rabbi Max Heller of New Orleans, the first HUC graduate to publicly identify as a political Zionist. Marcus put every term paper he received into the AJA, so Sarna must have come across it one day while he was burrowing through the AJA's catalogue. "Your paper on Heller is excellent," Sarna effused buoyantly. "You should publish it!" These few words proved to be a watershed experience in my life. The idea that this "wunderkind" thought my term paper was worthy of publication motivated me to pursue a goal that I had never before even considered. His encouragement—not to mention the many hours he spent helping me to revise the essay from beginning to end—eventuated in the appearance of my first publication.

In the years that followed, Sarna never failed to display the three vitally important qualities that have made him an effective mentor both to me and to dozens of students and colleagues. First, he selflessly alerted me to source materials and secondary readings that I might well have overlooked without his attentive interest. Second, he willingly vetted almost every essay, article, and volume I wrote—sparing me from humiliating errors and excessive blather. Finally, Sarna's general scholarly predilection has always inclined toward encouraging all those who earnestly aspired to contribute to the field. Just as Marcus's ideology inspired me, so, too, was I inspired by Sarna's generous and encouraging disposition.

All told, it is fair to say that Jacob Rader Marcus was the teacher who ignited my passion for the study of the American Jewish experience. He inspired me with his ideological perspective and his distinctive rationale as to why the enterprise of American Jewish history mattered. Yet it was Jonathan Sarna who encouraged me—by offering guidance, support and training—to think of myself as an American Jewish historian. These two individuals influenced me profoundly, and the lessons they taught serve as a lodestar that guides me still.

The American Jewish Experience

The field of American Jewish history has developed significantly since my days as a graduate rabbinical and doctoral student at HUC in the late 1970s and 1980s. In retrospect, it seems correct to say that my career began not long after the advent of a new historiographical phase that began in the 1970s, when a generation of young American Jewish historians had appeared on the scene.

These young scholars—today's "senior scholars"—unquestionably transformed the study of the American Jewish experience. I and many of my contemporaries were influenced by these scholars' initiatives. The half-dozen men and women who, in the 1970s, picked up the historical mantle from Marcus's generation were all trained in American universities. They were all fluent in Hebrew. Even as graduate students they were already conducting original research in some facet of the American Jewish experience. By the early 1980s, these newly minted scholars of the American Jewish experience had become faculty members at one university or another. In a decade's time, they had produced a cornucopia of new articles, monographs, and book-length studies that ventured into previously unexplored scholarly territory.

Since these men and women had received their academic training at leading American universities, and under the tutelage of Americanists or specialists in modern Jewish history, they made use of the historiographical trends that emerged in the 1960s and 1970s, such as women's and gender history, social histories employing demographic and quantitative techniques, regional studies, and a new focus in urban history. Soon these scholars began producing disciples of their own and, as the 1990s approached, the number of graduate students preparing to become specialists in American Jewish history markedly increased. Some of these scholars were appointed to professorships in American Jewish history—a truly remarkable development when one considers that up until the early 1980s, HUC's Jacob Rader Marcus was the *only* scholar in the US who officially bore the title "Professor of American Jewish History."

At the time I assumed the directorship of the AJA in 1998, it was easy to see that it was poised to serve the needs of this rapidly expanding cadre of American Jewish scholars. Expanding and enhancing The Marcus Center's "Fellowship Program" became a top priority. Within a few years, the AJA was annually hosting eighteen or twenty researchers—graduate students as well as senior scholars—for a month of study.

No doubt it was Marcus's *wissenschaftlich* training at the University of Berlin in the early 1920s that kept him indefatigably committed to the task of finding and preserving historical data.

He famously admonished: "the fact scrubbed clean is more eternal than perfumed or rouged words."[12] As a pioneering scholar tilling a relatively unplowed field of research, Marcus realized that the field's future depended upon the preservation of "the *stoff*" of history, namely the primary source material. This impulse to preserve drove him to establish the American Jewish Archives in 1947. In directing the AJA over the past two decades, I have stayed the course that the founder charted seventy years ago.

Over the past three decades, however, a series of noteworthy developments have radically transformed the way we preserve, study, and write American Jewish history. The advent of new technologies has given rise to a new world of research possibilities, and it did not take me very long to recognize that the historical enterprise must embrace change. My own students are always amazed when, for example, I tell them that when I was working on my rabbinical thesis in 1981, I took notes on index cards and wrote my thesis on a typewriter. Five years later, in 1986, I already owned a "portable" computer, which enabled me to collect and organize my research data and, of course, "type" my dissertation.

In some respects, the dawning of the digital age may have been the impetus for efforts to expand and enhance archival resources and collections pertaining to the history of American Jewry. The excitement over the technological revolution and the un-hemmed opportunities that were rapidly unfolding made it possible for me to find philanthropists who were willing to provide the AJA with new physical resources that would enable the institution to take advantage of this new world. This surge of interest resulted in the erection of a new four-story archival repository in 2000 that was attached directly to the AJA's remodeled historic home in the Bernheim Library Building. This expansion attracted new and important collections to the AJA, and it was possible to launch a serious program of electronic archival preservation. A few years later, in 2005, The Marcus Center dedicated yet another wing—the Edwin A. Malloy Educational Building, containing space for new exhibits, conferences, and a state-of-the-art distance learning center—which gave The Marcus Center the ability to keep pace with the changing academic environment.

It is important to note that similar changes took place at the AJA's sister institutions. In 2000, the American Jewish Historical Society (AJHS) moved into a new Center for Jewish History located in New York City. The Center provided the AJHS with greatly expanded academic and programmatic resources. The National Museum of American Jewish History (NMAJH) dedicated a magnificent new facility located on Independence Mall in Philadelphia in 2010, attracting national attention to the historically significant role American Jews have played in the shaping of the American nation.

Yet even while these important institutional expansions and enhancements have taken place, some countervailing trends have caused me to consider new and important questions about the future of the past. Over the past twenty years, a number of significant archival collections have been given over to secular universities where they are now catalogued as "special collections."[13] The long-term implication of donating established archival collections to large secular universities for preservation is difficult to assess. On the one hand, it is surely hoped that these large secular institutions will always have the fiscal wherewithal they need to provide our precious archival legacies with the long-term financial support they so desperately require. Ideally, secular academies also will be able to integrate these Jewish archival holdings into a broader scholarly context so that American Jewish history increasingly finds its way into the hands of scholars who write about American history, transnational history, religious history, as well as many other disciplines in the humanities.

On the other hand, one cannot help but wonder how this new trend might impinge upon the study of American Jewish history in the years ahead. Will the university librarians who have assumed responsibility for these Jewish "special collections" actively pursue new archival acquisitions so that their collections grow and flourish? Will they see themselves as advocates for the use and promotion of these "special collections"? Will scholars have more, or less, access to these primary source data that will have been firmly integrated into large and diverse university library systems? Will special fellowship funds be available in these university settings so graduate students and junior scholars who depend upon these grants will be able to examine these important holdings in some great depth? Will these secular institutions be able to provide visiting researchers with knowledgeable archival support, and will they invest time and effort in showing how these "special collections" benefit the work of American Jewish historians? The answers to these and many related questions will become evident in the coming decades, when we discover just how this new trend has affected the ongoing work of the American Jewish historian.

****

In 1874, the Hebrew writer Aaron Judah Horowitz published a volume comparing and contrasting Jewish life in Romania with Jewish conditions in the US.[14] After offering his readers a largely sympathetic description of American Jewry, Horowitz, making reference to Jewish clergy in the US, writes: "rabbis and doctors are very plentiful in America." With regard to my own small place among those who are presently striving to preserve the heritage of American Jewry, there is little doubt that much credit is due to the ongoing and symbiotic contributions that have come from a bountiful array of inspiring and talented American rabbis and doctors.

"The truth is..." Vice President Joe Biden declared in a speech given in 2013, "Jewish heritage, Jewish culture, Jewish values are such an essential part of who we are that it's fair to say that Jewish heritage is American heritage..." This is a valid statement, and it provides a meaningful and sobering rationale for the study of the American Jewish experience. Yet my own personal experience may well serve as a reminder that the historical enterprise possesses the ability to renew and even resuscitate Jewish identity. Inspiriting and learned teachers—rabbis and doctors alike—continue to play a pivotally important role in reaching the coming generations of American Jews who, with their help, will yet be taught to "glory in their survival... and refuse to disappear."[15]

NOTES

1   Michael M. Lorge and Gary Phillip Zola, *A Place of Our Own: The Rise of Reform Jewish Camping—Essays Honoring the Fiftieth Anniversary of Olin-Sang-Ruby Union Institute in Oconomowoc, Wisconsin* (Tuscaloosa: University of Alabama Press, 2006).

2   Walter Laqueur, *Generation Exodus: The Fate of Young Jewish Refugees from Nazi Germany* (Hanover, NH: Brandeis University Press, 2001).

3   Ibid., 285.

4   Marcus referred to the students who studied with him, or with whom he had established a personal relationship, as "his boys." The pioneering women rabbinical students who studied with Marcus in his elderly years did not seem to mind when, out of habit, he inadvertently addressed them with this same endearment.

5   Zevi Hirsch Masliansky, *Kitve Maslianski*, 3 vols. (New York: Hebrew Publishing Company, 1929). See also, Gary Phillip Zola, "The People's Preacher: A Study of the Life and Writings of Zvi Hirsch Masliansky (1856–1943)," rabbinical thesis (Hebrew Union College-Jewish Institute of Religion, 1982).

6   Sanhedrin 68a.

7   Michael A. Meyer, ed., *Ideas of Jewish History* (New York: Behrman House, Inc., 1974), xi; Jacob Rader Marcus, *United States Jewry, 1776–1985*, vol. 1 (Detroit: Wayne State University Press, 1989), 20–21.

8   Jacob Rader Marcus, "America: The Spiritual Center of Jewry," in *The Dynamics of American Jewish History: Jacob Rader Marcus's Essays on American Jewry*, ed. Gary Phillip Zola (Waltham, MA: Brandeis University Press, 2004), 37–42; also, ibid., "Three Hundred Years in America," 116–126.

9   Marcus, *United States Jewry*, vol. 1, 15–16.

10 Jacob Rader Marcus, *The American Jew, 1585–1990: A History* (Brooklyn, NY: Carlson Publishing, 1995), 383.

11 Jacob Rader Marcus, "Testament," in *Dynamics*, 146–151.

12 Herbert C. Zafren and Abraham J. Peck, comps., *The Writings of Jacob Rader Marcus: A Bibliographic Record* (Cincinnati: American Jewish Archives, 1978), front matter.

13 In the 1990s, the Jewish Historical Society of South Carolina placed its historic holdings in the "Jewish Heritage Collection" located in the

College of Charleston's Addlestone Library. The Philadelphia Jewish Archives Center, founded in 1972, donated its valuable holdings to Temple University Libraries' Special Collections Research Center in 2009. In 2010, the Judah L. Magnes Museum located in the East Bay near San Francisco became the Judah L. Magnes Foundation, which gave its diverse collection of Judaica and its archives—much of which documents the history of Jewish life in the American West—to the University of California in Berkeley. The Jewish Museum of Florida transferred ownership of its two Art Deco buildings (formerly synagogue buildings) as well as its historical collections, endowments, and other assets to Florida International University in 2012.

14 Aaron Judah Loeb Horowitz (1847–1926), רומניה ואמריקה (Berlin, 1874).

15 For Biden quote, see Jennifer Epstein, "Jewish Heritage is American Heritage," *Politico*, May 21, 2013, http://www.politico.com/blogs/politico44/2013/05/biden-jewish-heritage-isamerican-heritage-164525, accessed July 15, 2017. For final quote, see Marcus, *The American Jew*, 383.

Index

A
Adelphi University, 38
Adler, Cyrus, 10, 21
African Americans, 22, 29-30, 37-38,
    53-54, 63-64, 70-71, 86-88, 116-
    117, 126, 205
Agnew, Theodore, 54
Agnon, S. Y., 137
Ahad Ha'Am, 80
Ahavath Achim synagogue, 59, 214
Ahlstrom, Sydney, 163, 170, 171
*A Religious History of the American
    People*, 163
Akhtiorskaya, Yelena, 210
Amalgamated Clothing Workers'
    Union of America, 105
America-Holy Land Studies, 100
American Academy for Jewish
    Research, 10
American exceptionalism, 75
American Historical Association
    (AHA), 10, 11, 235
American Jewish Archives (AJA), 42,
    43, 45, 58, 165, 194, 247, 250,
    252, 253
American Jewish Archives Journal, 10,
    60, 62, 210
American Jewish Historical Quarterly,
    55, 237
American Jewish Historical Society
    (AJHS), 10–12, 17, 58, 124, 162,
    254
American Jewish History, 10, 49, 57, 60,
    62, 198, 210, 237

American Jewish Year Book, 135, 171
American Philosophical Society, 45
American pragmatism, 217
American Studies Association, 235
Amherst, MA, 36
Ankori, Zvi, 82, 84, 87
anthropology, 147, 149–151
anti-lachrymose theory, 84
anti-semitism, 11, 26, 39, 108, 126,
    203, 221
anti-war protest, 52
Antler, Joyce, 21
*Jewish Radical Feminism: Voices from the
    Women's Liberation Generation*, 32
*The Journey Home: How Jewish Women
    Shaped Modern America*, 31
*You Never Call; You Never Write! A
    History of the Jewish Mother*, 31
Arbeter Orden, 105
Arendt, Hannah, 229, 230
The Origins of Totalitarianism, 230
Arsenault, Raymond, 231
Ashmore, Harry, 53
Ashton, Dianne, 22, 32, 195
*Four Centuries of Jewish Women's
    Spirituality*, 45-46
Hanukkah, in America, 46–49
*Rebecca Gratz: Women and Judaism in
    Antebellum America*, 45
Askowith, Dora, 142
Athol, MA, 36
Atlanta, 212–214
Atlanta Constitution, 53
Atlanta History Bulletin, 55